MAKE YOURS IN STOCKS AND BONDS AT LITTLE RISK

A BUY-SELL SYSTEM THAT MAKES THE DIFFERENCE

A. W. Bigus

HAMPOL Publishing Co., Boston, Mass.

Library of Congress Catalog Card Number: 82-82931

Although credit for quoted individual experts is made in the reference section of this book, general acknowledgement is given for quoting from the following sources:

Reprinted by permission of *Barron's National Business and Financial Weekly*, © Dow Jones & Company, Inc., 1969, 1972, 1973. All Rights Reserved.

Reprinted by permission of *The Wall Street Journal*, © Dow Jones & Company, Inc., 1972, 1973, 1975, 1976, 1977, 1979, 1980. All Rights Reserved.

ISBN: 0-9609330-1-8

Printed in the United States of America

HAMPOL Publishing Co., Box 36, 47 Harvard Ave.,
Boston, Mass. 02134

To make it,
you must first be sure
not to lose.

CONTENTS

PART THREE
PORTFOLIO MANAGEMENT

PREFACE

Can we continue our economic growth at our accustomed long-term average of 3.5% a year real rate indefinitely?

At this real rate of increase the gross national product (GNP) will have grown 31.2 times the present one in 100 years. And in the next 500 years it will have grown 30 million times.

Another calculation shows that as we extract and use 10.3 $\times 10^9$ tons of the ten most used minerals at an increase of 3.5% a year for 700 years, the total weight of these will exceed the weight of the earth.

Such gains seem improbable.

And as we keep in mind that the economy must expand by 3% a year to make room for additional workforce because of productivity improvements and increasing population, we can expect that the economy will not be able to provide for the usual improved standard of living for the population over the decades ahead, and that Western civilization (or business civilization as we know it) will gradually become extinct long before these centuries come up—probably within a hundred years.

But we have economic, social, and political problems closer to our lifetimes that will interfere with near-term economic growth and productivity improvements, which, in turn, will impede corporate profit growth and common stock price growth over the next several decades.

For example, right now there are more people collecting from the government than there are producing taxpayers.

And the rate of annual increase in social welfare payments is greater than the rate of GNP growth. By the year 2000 over half of the productive workers' effort will be spent on such programs. By the year 2017, the productive effort will equal social welfare payments, according to one computation. (Who will work for zero?)

Regarding social welfare programs, those now collecting Social Security payments are collecting 5 to 7 times what they would be collecting if the payments were based on what the recipients put into the system. And note that by the year 2050 the payments for Social Security will be $4 trillion more than will be collected to pay for the program.

And the HUD program for rent subsidies has saddled future taxpayers with $250 billion beginning in 1980. If the 40% of all families now eligible for this subsidy program take advantage of it, the future taxpayers' burden will approach $1 trillion.

The tax money extracted from the productive section of the population, businesses and those who work for them, to pay for these and other social welfare programs results in increased consumption and less saving, which will inhibit increases in capital investment and improvements in productivity.

Then note that corporate debt as a percentage of total capital is considerably higher now than it was in 1929. And household debt as a percentage of disposable income is disturbingly higher now than it was several decades ago. We have financed much of our past growth on debt. Continued growth through further increases in the debt ratio now seems doubtful.

We import over 90% of our mica, manganese, cobalt, graphite, chromium, and lesser rates of other minerals, making us vulnerable to interruption in economic growth should sales of these to us be cut off.

Then, business is experiencing excessive regulation that stifles productivity growth. And the news media are not sympathetic to business; much of the time they are antagonistic to it.

A trend toward an every-man-for-himself attitude prevails today as opposed to a once observable community spirit several decades ago.

And the U.S. is no longer calling the shots in international affairs as it once did.

But, except for those impediments to very long term growth, we can correct those problems that will interfere with economic growth over the next several years: excessive taxes, excessive government spending, excessive government regulation, inflation, and defense.

If the short-term investment climate improves, the investor may expect a rising stock market for the next several years.

Nevertheless, the investor had best play it conservatively from here on, making those gains at little risk.

Probably more important to the investor is that the security evaluation system described in this book does not depend on a boom or a slump to work. It works any time.

The investor with a few thousand or several hundred million dollars to invest should improve his net worth using this worry-free system.

A. W. Bigus
Brookline, Massachusetts
1982

ACKNOWLEDGEMENTS

I want to thank the courteous librarians at the Brookline Main Library and the Kirstein Memorial Library of the Boston Public Library for their help in supplying much of the data I needed for this project.

Theodore E. Andrews, Leonard M. Heine, Jr., Annette Joseph, John F. O'Connell, Justin O'Neil, Harry Palais, and Jacob E. Smart after reading the manuscript made many constructive comments for which I am grateful.

Particularly I want to thank Philip Donham and Joseph Barth for the extensive effort each put into analyzing the original manuscript which led to its substantial revision.

INTRODUCTION

Investors have tried to make it in many different ways in the stock market: buy-hold, forecasting, new companies, growth companies, technical action, and luck. But, according to three studies, 85% of investors who play the market lose, confirming Paul A. Samuelson's observation that "a factual examination of the great fortunes of the past shows a strong element of luck in many of them." Since luck is an unplanned event, it is not considered in our security evaluation system.

Adding to the problem of investing, economic, social, and political factors point toward a slowing of economic growth in the U.S. over the long pull.

Consequently, the buy-hold policy of investing in common stocks, which requires a rising market for success, may not, from here on, be as profitable as it had been from 1941 to 1965.

The investment policy outlined here consists primarily in buying on market dips and selling on the rises—but not by forecasting the dips and rises.

We place great stress on evaluating the balance sheet of a company. If it doesn't fit our conservative criteria, we pass up the company. if it does meet these standards, we buy it at a predetermined price, then sell it at a computed investment value (selling price).

In our overall investment policy we place greater stress on not losing than on making a pile next year. If the investor misses one market rise, his money will be available for the next one, while he parks his funds in cash type items.

The 25-year retrospective study ending in 1974 by the

author, "Managing Portfolios with Graham & Dodd," using a conservative security evaluation system, showed a 60-times improvement in the 25-year period vs. an 8-times improvement, dividends reinvested, for the Dow Jones industrial average.

That result encouraged the development of this conservative system that includes small companies, which is outlined in this book.

Part One covers investing methods probably not appropriate for the general investor. Part Two constitutes the principal portion of the book, security analysis: balance sheet analysis and determining investment value (I.V.) and buy price. Part Three shows our conservative method of managing a portfolio; some money always out of the market but ready to be invested if the subsequent discounts are big enough. And finally, Part Four covers other aspects of investing important to the investor.

The reader will find the back-up for the system and our story on the decline of Western (business) civilization, in the appendixes. References for the quotations can be found in the reference section.

The investor using this system of security analysis would have eliminated from consideration four prominent companies that later went into bankruptcy proceedings: Braniff International Corporation, W. T. Grant Co., Wickes Companies, Inc., and Penn Central Transportation Co. Their balance sheets did not meet our criteria.

Using this system he would have avoided investing in some of the phenomenal growth companies while also neglecting the new companies, the vast majority of which generated losses for investors.

From his reading effort here, the investor will discover that it is not that easy to make it in the stock market, and that a conservative program based on analyzing fundamentals will not only preserve his capital but add to it over the decades ahead, if the market continues to fluctuate as it has over the past century.

PART ONE

HOW *NOT* TO PLAY THE MARKET

WHICH METHOD DO YOU USE?

I
STOCK MARKET PERFORMANCE SINCE 1870

Let's explore some of the methods investors have used in trying to make it in the stock market.

BUY-HOLD POLICY

"Buy good stocks and hold them," said Doug Conrod, a Boston investor for over half a century who had a successful career in the stock market.

But note the stock market performance over many periods of the past century (prices only) using Cowles P-1 index, all stocks, and the Dow Jones industrial average.

end 1870–June 1932	(61½ years)	=	− 0.03%/yr.
end 1870–end 1937	(67 years)	=	1.3%/yr.
end 1896–Sept. 1929	(33 years)	=	6.2%/yr.
end 1941–end 1965	(24 years)	=	9.5%/yr.
high 1929–end 1976	(47 years)	=	2.1%/yr.
high 1929–low 1932	(3 years)	=	−89.%
end 1965–end 1975	(10 years)	=	−12.%
high 1973–low 1974	(1 year)	=	−45.%
end 1975–end 1981	(6 years)	=	2.7%

Performance varies considerably from adverse to superior for the buy-hold policy over long and short investment periods.

Such a buy-hold plan would have worked well for the 24-year period, 1941–1965, and the 33-year period, 1896–1929.

But in the 1896–1929 period, if the investor had continued to hold after 1929, he would have waited 25 additional years for prices to reach those of 1929, reducing his gain to 4.3% per year.

Then note the 67½-year period from the end of 1870 to June 1932, when stock prices declined 0.03% per year. To wait that long and experience such poor results would have been most disappointing to the investor. In another example, if the investor had bought at the high of 1929, he would have had to wait 8 years with dividends reinvested merely to break even.

But, obviously, the buy-hold strategy was a profitable one for *some* periods over the past century. Nevertheless, we have not been able to pick such periods except in retrospect and do not expect to be able to pick them in the future.

Playing the downs and ups in the market according to a conservatively prescribed investment plan will do more for the investor than will a buy-hold plan over the long pull in spite of the interesting stories one hears regularly.

FULLY INVESTED POLICY

Along with the buy-hold plan many investors place all of their money in common stocks and keep it there.

We don't subscribe to this policy either, since conservatism dictates that the investor keep funds aside to take advantage of continuing inordinate market declines.

There have been 25 major market declines over the past century of which 8 were 40% or more, the greatest being the 89% drop during the Depression.

The portfolio management system discussed in Part Three is designed around taking advantage of continuing market drops, including one of 90%.

ANOTHER 1929?

Paul Samuelson's analysis indicates that we "are unlikely to experience old-fashioned, prolonged depression again." And the Citibank economists stress that "a catastrophe of the 1930s type is not likely to recur," while John K. Galbraith observes that "no one, wise or unwise, knew or now knows when depressions are due or overdue."

Notice that none of these economists is willing to state categorically that we will not have another depression. But when we review some of the differences between the 1930s and the present, the investor will see easily why there is little likelihood of another severe, prolonged economic downturn:

1. Today bank customers have their deposits insured up to $100,000 by various agencies, such as the Federal Deposit Insurance Corporation (FDIC). Depositors are reasonably assured of the safety of their deposits no matter what happens to the bank; consequently, we don't see people lined up outside a bank to withdraw their money because of a rumor of bank failure.

That was not the case in the early 1930s, when there was no FDIC, when depositors en masse, making withdrawals, caused bank failures, further reduced economic confidence, and spurred on the Depression.

2. Wealth distribution is less lopsided now. These days the worker has the opportunity to make a comfortable living, but that was not true in the 1930s.

3. The government take in taxes is 36% of the produced wealth. It then distributes some in the form of Social Security benefits, unemployment compensation, and welfare payments, all of which keep people sheltered and eating whatever the economic condition.

In 1929 all taxes amounted to 7% of the gross national product and whatever dole payments existed at that time were meager. (Nevertheless, a continued increase in distribution payments could cause us another type of economic problem from which it may be hard to recover.)

4. Many economists understand the role of fiscal and monetary policy better today than in the 1930s, when the money supply fell and the government tried hard to balance the budget. However, in spite of a structure in the economy today that militates against a depression, we could still have one. Here's one possibility.

If a large number of the population thought, for any reason, that bad economic times were around the corner and held back on spending, retail sales would contract, then manufacturing would decrease, causing lay-offs, emphasizing the correctness of people's thinking, who would cut back further on spending, etc., causing a depression.

When we recall that two-thirds of the gross national product is made up of consumer spending and that the economic system is based on confidence, we might begin to visualize the *possibility* of a severe economic dip even though the probability may be slim.

Even though government fiscal policy would ease the economic pain of those laid off through our dole system, monetary policy, through its attempts to increase the money supply, may have little effect if industry, operating below capacity, declined to borrow for investment.

The investor would notice a decrease in profits along with an almost certain and probably drastic decrease in stock prices.

The investment policy described in Part Three is designed to take advantage of the possibility of a severe plunge in stock prices through a funds distribution system.

II
INFLATION AND THE STOCK MARKET

STOCK PRICES VS. INFLATION—LONG-TERM

Heard and preserved for posterity in many publications is the injunction: Play the market because of inflation. The implication being that the market will rise and make up for purchasing power losses.

Reviewing some long-term data, we find that industrial stock prices in the U.S. over the past 110 years, from 1870 to 1980, rose at a compounded rate of 3.6% per year while the wholesale price index (WPI) rose 1.6% per year for a real gain to the stockholder of 2.0% per year.

In Britain from 1867 to 1970, 103 years, stock prices were up 1.6% faster than the WPI, while in France from 1856 to 1970, 114 years, stock prices declined 0.1% faster than the WPI.

Phillip Cagan of Columbia University studied stock price movement and consumer prices for a 30-year period to 1969, including World War II, for 2 dozen countries. He found that stocks provided a hedge against inflation for long periods except mainly for hyperinflation and war devastation, but that it took 15 years to regain purchasing power. Consequently, "stocks if broadly selected [have passed] the test as an inflation hedge only for long-term holdings."

Another of Cagan's studies including 5 to 10 countries for 6-year, 20-year, and 50-year periods, from about 1860 to

1939, showed that stock prices for some countries for some of the periods did not keep up with inflation. But with dividends included, all of the periods, except for the 6-year World War I period, would have produced real gains.

It appears, then, that for long-term holdings stocks have been an inflation hedge in the past for buy-hold plans.

But let's study several shorter periods of U.S. stock market prices and compare these to the wholesale price index.

STOCK PRICES VS. INFLATION—SHORT-TERM

Note from Table II-1, Market Rises vs. WPI (Appendix II-Chapter II), that the stock market *rose* 365% in one 8-year period (1921–1929) when wholesale prices *declined* 3.7% per year, while in another instance the market *rose* 129% in a 4-year period (1942–1946) when wholesale prices *rose* 6.6% per year.

We are looking for a correlation between stock price movement and inflation, so we note that of the 26 market rises in the 110-year period we had

9 rises during deflationary periods,
3 rises during modest inflationary periods of 1% or less, and
14 rises during inflationary periods of over 1%.

Obviously, for short periods, stock market prices rose during inflation, stable, and deflationary periods. Consequently, these data dispute the view that inflation is good for the stock market 100% of the time for short market cycles.

Let's examine stock market *declines* and wholesale prices compiled in Table II-2, Market Drops vs. Wholesale Price Index (Appendix II-Chapter II).

Of the 25 market declines that occurred since 1873, we had

8 declines during deflationary periods,
1 decline during a neutral period,

5 declines during WPI rises of 2% per year or less, and
11 declines during WPI rises of over 2% per year.

As we would expect, the data for market declines for short periods are similar to those of market rises, in that market declines have occurred during inflationary, stable, and deflationary periods. But the picture is quite different when we compare stock prices, dividends reinvested, with the wholesale price index.

STOCK PRICES INCLUDING DIVIDENDS VS. WPI—SHORT-TERM

From Table II-3 (Appendix II-Chapter II) we note that for the 110-year period there were but two 10-year periods when industrial stock prices, dividends reinvested, performed worse than the inflation rate, 1910–1920 and 1970–1980, or worse than the yield on high-grade bonds, 1930–1940 and 1970–1980.

Then, trying out 20-year periods, we found that stock prices with dividends reinvested rose faster than the WPI.

Evidently, the longer the investment period the greater was the chance of the investor beating the inflation rate and, therefore, of making real stock market gains in the past.

Nevertheless, when stock prices rise during an inflationary period, they rise in spite of inflation, rather than *because* of it. Therefore, price should be the predominant criterion for buying rather than economic factors such as inflation.

III

FORECASTING

EARNINGS, MARKET LEVEL, ECONOMY, AND INTEREST RATES

What are the possibilities of an investor making extraordinary gains from forecasting correctly either corporate earnings, general stock market level, economic activity, or interest rates? Let's explore each of these.

FORECASTING CORPORATE EARNINGS

In scanning a graph of corporate earnings and stock prices one will note the high correlation between the two.

A study by Victor Niederhoffer and Patrick J. Regan showed that "unmistakably, the most important factor separating the best from the worst-performing stocks was profitability."

In his *An Introduction to Risk and Return from Common Stocks,* Richard A. Brealey cited a study of 48 stocks selected at random from those reviewed by The *Value Line Investment Survey* for each of 14 years, 1950 to 1963. The 8 stocks with the subsequently greatest percentage increase in earnings returned 30.4% per year to the investor, in contrast to those 8 stocks that had the smallest gain in earnings, which produced an annual return of only 1%.

Even aggregate profits and stock averages show a similar relationship, according to a study by Jack W. Cox.

For example, profits rose 156% from the first quarter of

1958 through the second quarter of 1959. And the Standard & Poor's 500 index rose 145% from the last quarter of 1957 to the second quarter of 1959. From 1961 to 1966 profits rose 208% while stock prices rose 190% from 1960 to 1968.

Apparently, if the investor could predict earnings either for individual companies or in the aggregate from past data, his investment worries would be over.

But another study by Brealey shows that correlations are usually low and frequently negative between past earnings trends as a predictor of subsequent earnings.

Therefore, James H. Lorie and Mary T. Hamilton, who have analyzed the top studies on stock market activity, conclude that the "extrapolation of recent rates of change in corporate earnings is not likely to be useful."

FORECASTING STOCK MARKET LEVEL

Then Benjamin King showed that 50% of the fluctuation of stock prices was due to general stock market movement. Consequently, the investor would benefit from finding a system that predicts the direction of the market level.

Here are some of the better known market forecasting systems.

Dow Theory

In 1933 Alfred Cowles III studied 90 recommendations from 1904 to 1929, made according to the "Dow Theory." He found that only 50% were correct, a result similar to that of betting on the toss of a coin, a basis for buying and selling that would yield uncertain portfolio results.

Short-Interest Ratio (Short interest for the month divided by the mean daily volume for the same period.)

H. A. Krow in his *Stock Market Behavior* concludes from a study of the short-interest ratio as a market indicator that "on the whole, it can be postulated that a very high short-interest ratio (2.00) is quite bullish, while a very low short-interest ratio (.80) is mildly bearish."

But recently these signals did not work well for the investor. In 1973 the Dow Jones industrial average (DJIA) hit a high of 1051.70, but the short-interest ratio ranged from 1.09 to .97 in that period, low but not low enough for a sell signal if one adopted 0.80 as the signal for unloading. The DJIA dropped 45%, the largest drop since World War II.

Then in October and December 1974 the DJIA hit a low of 577, but the short-interest ratio in this period ranged from 1.34 to 1.62, not high enough for a buy signal. Yet the DJIA rose to 880 by July of 1975, over 50%.

Obviously, this indicator is not consistently reliable either.

Money Supply

Beryl Sprinkel in his *Money and Markets* shows the connection between money supply and market action. He found that "an investor who based his market decisions over the past 52 years [ending in 1971] upon expanding and contracting monetary growth would have participated in all bull markets. He would have avoided most bear markets [except those of 1939–40, 1962, and 1966] but in recent years, only if he recognized the shortening lead of monetary growth over bear markets." Even so, he emphasizes that "choosing peaks and troughs of the monetary growth rate, even in hindsight, is sometimes difficult."

Michael S. Rozeff, in a study, found *no lag* between money supply and stock prices and that there "were some indications that *the market* anticipates future money-supply changes with some accuracy" (emphasis added).

Summing up, A. F. Ehrbar in *Fortune* concludes in a commentary that "money growth and stock prices are hard to convert into trading profits."

Stock Market Price History

Will a study of stock market price history show the investor the way to improved profits?

A rough calculation shows that stock prices for industrials

have increased at 3.6% per year compounded for 110 years, from 1870 to 1980.

In between those years the rates of return varied widely, considering prices only, at compounded rates:

1870–1937 (67 yrs) = 1.3%/yr. Cowles P-1 index, all stocks
1937–1965 (28 yrs) = 7.7%/yr. DJIA
1965–1981 (16 yrs) = −0.6%/yr. DJIA

But for shorter periods the fluctuations were considerably greater and vary in time from top to bottom and bottom to top, as note in Tables II-1 and II-2 (Appendix II-Chapter II).

There is no historical pattern of stock price movement that will help the investor predict subsequent price movement.

There are many other systems devised by analysts purported to be used for predicting market level, but none appear to give consistently accurate signals, which leads Lorie and Hamilton to observe that "the visible record of professionally managed portfolios indicates that many play the timing game and that few, if any, win it."

ECONOMIC FORECASTING AND THE STOCK MARKET

So, let us explore the potential in economic forecasting and stock market profits.

Ezra Solomon in a study covering 1874 through 1955 found that "the real growth in stock values has proceeded at about two-thirds of the rate of the real growth in gross national product."

But Lorie and Hamilton's extension of Solomon's data to the end of 1969 forecasted a 35% increase for the Standard & Poor's 425 price index while "the actual increase was about 98%." (The difference is explained by the higher P/E ratios "in recent years than during most of the period between 1874 and 1955.")

Forecasting the economy itself is a formidable task, as Susan R. Roesch points out in the Federal Reserve Bank of St. Louis *Review:* "Few, if any, economic analysts foresaw the 5% decline in real output which occurred during 1974. Few predictions in late 1973 indicated a 12% increase in prices or over a 7% unemployment rate by year's end," or that interest rates would move higher in 1974.

Even the Commerce Department, a group having access to more economic data than any private group, made a devastating error in underreporting the buildup in inventory in 1973 and early 1974. Timely knowledge of this buildup might have alerted business to slowing down its inventory accumulation, possibly softening the wide swing in business activity from 1973 to 1975.

And "in 1978 and 1979 most economists were warning of imminent recession . . . that stubbornly refused to show up as consumers continued to spend in the face of soaring inflation. The majority of business forecasters late in 1979 were calling for a moderate recession . . ." in 1980, which turned out to be more severe.

Apparently the nature of economic forecasting is such that even experienced economists are not able to predict accurately on a consistent basis.

And that fact makes it even harder to predict the tops and bottoms of the stock market from business tops and bottoms since the market tops and bottoms occur several months before another base point, which itself cannot be predicted.

Here are two more examples emphasizing the hazards in predicting from history.

Note from Figure III-1 that deflation followed 4 of the 5 wars. An investment policy based on a prediction that a deep recession or a depression would follow the end of World War II, along with a deep stock market drop, would have shown relatively poor results.

FIGURE III–1

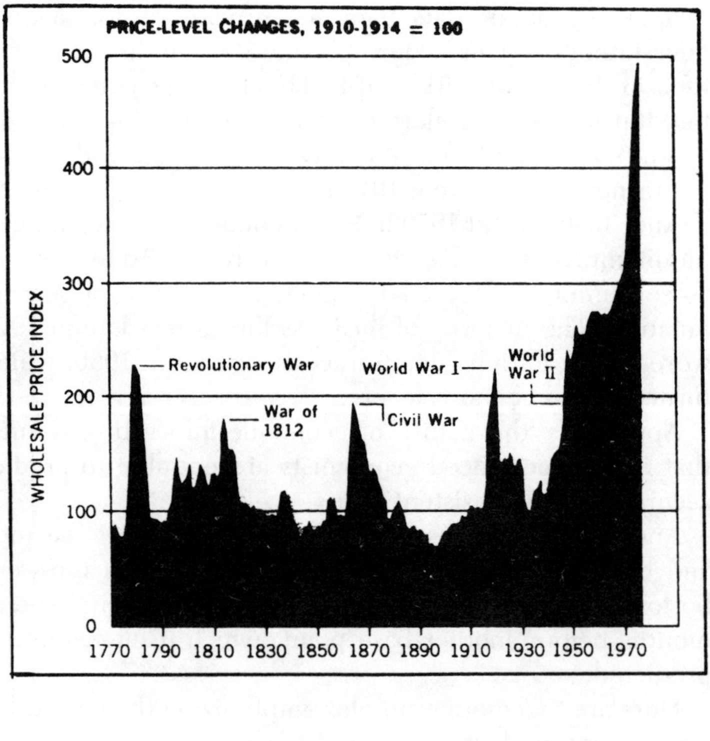

From: *Economics*, 10th ed., by Paul A. Samuelson. Copyright © 1976 McGraw-Hill, Inc. Used with the permission of McGraw-Hill Book Company, p. 271.

FORECASTING INTEREST RATES

Predicting corporate earnings, market action, or economic activity is obviously hard to do but predicting interest rates is probably even harder.

The trick is to unravel the impact on interest rates of a federal budget deficit funded or not funded by the Federal Reserve Board's monetary policies, the outlook for inflation, whether industry and households will borrow to the hilt or save and pay off old debts, how much foreign money will enter or leave the U.S., and whether or not a recession is coming and when.

Forecasting any of these elements is risky, let alone all of them then weighting each for a single money-making forecast.

As for forecasting from history, note this series of interest rate highs for high-grade bonds over a 95-year period:

	YIELDS	
1968	6.61%	(In between
1920	6.06	the yields
1873	6.20	were lower.)

It might have been very tempting for an investor perusing this 95-year series of interest rate fluctuations to buy long-term bonds, probably on margin, in the expectation that the direction of interest rates would be down after 1968. But by 1970 they rose to 8%, and higher by 1981, causing losses for long-term bond holders.

Well, then, how about practicing up to gain a knack for accurate forecasting?

Walter B. Wriston, chairman of the First National City Bank Corporation, offered that "we have always been wrong when we guessed which direction interest rates were going to take over time."

And Benjamin Graham decided that it is completely impossible to predict interest rates.

Apparently, forecasting the direction of interest rates from historical data or from any other basis is a losing game.

So, making money in the stock market or in bonds through forecasting has been unprofitable and promises future frustration for those investors who continue to try to make it this way.

IV
NEW COMPANIES AND GROWTH COMPANIES

NEW COMPANIES

As a sobering experience, study the following list of securities offered to the public in the late 1960s.

TABLE IV–1

	HIGH PRICE IN 1968 OR 1969 AFTER OFFERING	LOW AFTER OFFERING	DECLINE HIGH TO LOW
California Medical Centers	$17½	$3 (1969)	83%
Data Products Corp.	28⅞	1⅞ (1974)	94
Four Seasons Nursing Centers	90¾	0	100
Media Home Enterprises	39½	2¼ (1973)	94
Nationwide Industries	35½	1 (1969)	97
Performance Systems	23	0	100
Professional Health Services	20	1 (1969)	95
United Convalescent Hospitals	32	2⅜ (1972)	93
Universal Airlines Company	26	2½ (1970)	90
Viatron Computer Systems Corp	62½	¾ (1970)	99

There are many other issues that produced similar results. New-company stocks at the time were popular, were sold to investors during a period when people expected new issues to make money for them.

Any time a large enough group thinks this way, it will

push up prices far beyond reasonable levels. But nothing goes up forever. So the very same group, the buyers, now sell en masse, taking losses on the way down, wiping out the final holders.

This cycle repeats every so often. It has been going on for the past several hundred years. People acting as a mob forget what has happened in the past, or fail to learn from it, or lose their common sense, but visualize those tremendous potential gains and plunge in.

Because so few of the new issues succeed and it is so hard to pick the potential, long-term money maker, the investor's best bet, overall, is to stay out of all of them.

We suspect that the buyers of stocks of new companies usually end up in the 85% bracket of market players who lose.

GROWTH COMPANIES

Next, see Table IV-2 for examples of why investors try to find and invest in growth companies:

TABLE IV–2

	HIGH		GAIN	
IBM	1949 Low to 1973	(24 yrs)	113 times,	11,300%
Polaroid	1950 Low to 1972	(22 yrs)	812 times,	81,200
Tampax	1938 Low to 1972	(34 yrs)	1960 times,	196,000
Xerox	1960 Low to 1972	(12 yrs)	95 times,	9,500

Can you spot companies like these 10, 20, or 30 years in advance of their growth?

We can't.

And buying growth companies later in the game produced adverse results (see Table IV-3).

Nevertheless, with a potential increase of 100 to 2000 times for a growth company, a small original investment could grow to $1 million or more.

The big trick, though, is to find these in the initial stage

TABLE IV–3

	1960–1976 HIGH	CLOSE PRICE 1976
Avon	140	49½
Du Pont (after GM Distribution)	261	135⅛
(before GM Distribution)	293¾	
East Kodak	151¾	86
G.E.	75⅞	55⅜
IBM	365¼	279⅛
Litton	94½	14⅞
MMM	91⅝	56⅝
Polaroid	149½	38⅞
Tampax	136	36½
Xerox	171⅞	58½

of growth out of the many that are purported to be growth companies.

Philip A. Fisher outlines his system in *Common Stocks and Uncommon Profits*. His method is time-consuming but worthwhile if the investor does find, as a result, a true long-term growth company.

But this search for a growth company is not for the ordinary investor, since any analyst will have difficulty judging which technical innovation will take off.

How many in 1948 predicted that IBM or Polaroid would take off?

Many stocks come into fashion because they are in what appear to be growth industries: aluminum in the 1950s, then airlines, mobile homes, and computer leasing, for example. The common stocks of some of these industries made impressive gains, but then the trick was in banking these gains. We don't have problems like that.

According to our manner of evaluating securities (Part Two), the investor would pay no attention to fashions and growth labels of the day, since it is easier to lose than to make on securities such as those listed in this chapter. He would buy them, though, if they had a sound balance sheet, a 10–15 year earnings history, sold at a bargain price, but would sell them once their prices rose to investment value. He would miss out on any sustained price rise.

He would also miss out on any prominent price drops, which is more important to the conservative investor.

V

OTHER INVESTING SYSTEMS

Investors use many other systems in playing the stock market. Let's discuss some of them.

TECHNICAL ANALYSIS

The basis for this system is that supply and demand determine price. Good start.

The investor plots price changes and volume on a graph and from these data deduces future price action, investing if his deduction indicates a further price increase in that stock.

He has many chart patterns to test his geometric discerning competence:

1. Head-and-Shoulders
2. Multiple or Complex Head-and-Shoulders
3. Rounding Turns
4. Symmetrical Triangle
5. Right-Angle Triangle
6. Rectangle
7. Double and Triple Tops and Bottoms

However, R. D. Edwards and John Magee indicate that "false moves are one of the most difficult phenomena with which the technical analyst has to cope" and that "you will not see very many formations [on the charts] as perfect and symmetrical as our ideal picture." Continuing, "it is not the chart itself but its interpretation that is important," pointing up that "chart analysis is neither easy nor fool proof."

Therefore, to interpret these charts intuitive "skills" must come into play, which is why two experienced chartists, exploring the same chart, may reach opposite conclusions on the price trend, prompting Paul Samuelson to conclude that those who study technical indicators have "holes in their shoes."

One chart reader recalls that when he first looked at charts there were not too many others looking and that what he saw on the charts then reflected what was going on in the market. But by 1965 chart reading had become so popular that he found it more difficult to be certain of what strength on the chart meant any more.

And from our viewpoint, buying something because the price has gone up or selling it because the price has gone down seems to be the opposite of what a true conservative investment policy is about.

TAPE WATCHING

1. Gerald M. Loeb, the most important prominent tape watcher, obtained his initial and principal investment leads from the tape (price and volume). He then analyzed the company. If the company was in adequate financial shape, he'd buy a small amount of the stock of that company. If the price continued to increase, he'd buy larger amounts.

If the stock price dropped on his initial purchase, he would sell it. He took losses quickly and kept a cash reserve.

Loeb agreed that it takes a flair to play the market in this way. Being able to judge whether the market in general is on the way up or down and selecting the stock to play would certainly require some intuitive sense, a "sense" that cannot be taught to anyone.

Prices do not go straight up and down, although the general trend may be one way or the other. Buying a stock, selling for a 10% loss, say, then on the way up buying again, but selling for another 10% loss could deplete a bank account.

The investor lacking the intuitive sense for this activity should not spend the tuition cost to confirm that he doesn't have it.

2. J. E. Granville bases his investment leads on volume action of the stock, in the view that the initial, larger than normal purchases of stocks do not move the price substantially, and that only after this insider buying and after the basis for the rise (increased earnings) become apparent will the buying increase along with the price. His analyses show him that volume action is a prior indicator of price action, which in turn is the indicator of a subsequent, further price rise, frequently. But in down markets, virtually all market prices go down, even those for companies that report increased earnings. And Granville missed it altogether for the 1973–1974 market decline, a 45% drop, recommending that his clients hang on throughout that 20-month or so decline.

3. Nicolas Darvas, in explaining his system, pointed out that he has been a mental chartist "making decisions more on feeling than on cool, technical data." And, as for Thiokol Chemical Corp., on which he made $862,000, he "really 'felt' this stock." Then on setting up his overall method of when to buy and to sell he realized "there was bound to be a lot of guesswork in the operation."

With so much feeling and guesswork, Darvas' system is for Darvas only. There is no way to pass on to anyone else a feel or intuitive sense for anything.

INSIDER TRADING

The Securities and Exchange Commission issues a weekly report on buying and selling by specialists and member firms and a monthly report on corporate insider trading activity, both of which are available to the public.

Heavy insider selling may indicate that a stock's price is headed down.

Richard A. Brealey quotes several studies which show that insiders who bought or sold their companies' stocks judged correctly the price direction over a 6-month period, two-thirds of the time.

Another study extended over two separate, consecutive 3-year periods, from 1957 to 1964, showed that insiders of 30 companies who bought or sold their company's stock, correctly interpreted the direction of price movement from 22 to 93% of the time. The median for each of these 3-year periods showed that 55% of the guesses on direction of price movement were correct.

A monthly report by Perry Wysong, discussed by *Fortune* in two articles, lists 20 companies that have several insiders buying their company's stock. For 30 twelve-month periods his list outperformed the DJAI, usually by a wide margin. Four of these periods were wholly or partly in the market decline of 1966 and did not outperform the New York Stock Exchange composite index. Wysong's buys performed better in up markets according to the two-and-a-half-year study. When the market declines, so do Wysong's insiders' stocks.

Another study by Portland State College, also discussed in *Fortune*, showed that "one year is the most advantageous holding period."

What we like here is that there is a buy and sell signal in this system.

But the conservative investor should almost never buy without first making a balance sheet analysis and then determining buy price.

If any one on Wysong's list meet these criteria, buy the stock, but attempt to extract more from the transaction by hanging on beyond the computed sell price signal, then sell the stock when its price drops 10% below its high.

For example, if a company on the list meets the balance

sheet criteria, and has an investment value of 30 and a buy price of 20, as usual, buy at 20 but not necessarily sell when the price rises to 30, expecting a further climb. If the stock registers a high of 40 then declines to 36, or 10%, sell it at that point. (Chapters VII and VIII show how to analyze a common stock.)

BROKERS' RECOMMENDATIONS

Investors frequently take the easy way out and look for and act on brokers' suggestions.

But recall those buy recommendations from respected brokerage houses for Levitz Furniture Corp., New Process Company, Topper Corp., Sterling Homex, and Equity Funding Corp. They all recorded lower prices later, some going bankrupt.

What are the reasons for the bad advice?

1. Brokerage houses make their money from commissions on buys and sales. Without this activity many would be out of business. When the market is high, with few or no bargains available, the broker will find it difficult to recommend that the investor stay out of the market.
2. Being directors of some companies, brokerage house officers might find it hard to issue an adverse report on those companies.
3. Some analysts make a career out of studying and reporting on an industry. In order to retain access to continued information the analysts may feel that they have to dampen adverse criticism of a company in their industry in order to retain it as a source of future information.
4. A brokerage house that underwrites a stock will have trouble issuing an adverse report on the underwritten company.

Brokerage houses issue sound and bad advice. The general investor will have trouble making the distinction, but he should always be wary of taking advice from the seller.

More important, though, is that the investor should be

familiar with security analysis so that he may be better able to dissect a brokerage house recommendation.

ADVISORY INVESTMENT SERVICES

Although the investor must be wary of brokers' advice, how about taking it from one of the many advisory services?

Here are some facts on advisory services:

Alfred Cowles in a study found that "24 financial publications engaged in forecasting the stock market during the 4½ years from January 1, 1928, to June 1, 1932, failed as a group . . . to achieve a result as good as the average of all purely random performances."

Then in another study Cowles noted that of the 6904 forecasts recorded during a fifteen-and-a-half-year period, ending in July 1943, four-and-one-third times as many were *bullish* than bearish in a period when 53% of the period was *bearish* with a market that ended at two-thirds the level of the start of the study.

"The records of 11 leading financial periodicals and services since 1927, over periods varying from 10 to 15½ years, fail to disclose evidence of ability to predict successfully the future course of the stock market."

A similar study by W. X. Sheinman for a later period showed that "in January 1966, shortly before the market began a 265-point decline, the experts were bullish by better than 10 to 1—52% bulls to 5% bears."

Similarly, for several more market cycles into 1969 the forecasters were predominantly on the opposite side of what actually happened: If the majority were bullish, the market declined; if bearish, the market rose.

The market forecasters today apparently do no better than those of the 1920s and 1930s.

But Roger Babson thought that ". . . almost every investor would be better off to have the advice of some honest investment service."

The investor should doubt that the recommendations of even the honest advisory services on what to buy or where the market is headed will be any better than they have been.

To round out our commentary on advice to students of the market, listen to what some "names" said just before the 1929 crash:

Melvin A. Traylor, president, First National Bank of Chicago, Oct. 1927:
"There are grounds for belief that there has been a change for the better in certain aspects of the business cycle . . . [and] that the two phrases 'recession' and 'depression' may be rendered less disastrous in the future . . ."

Myron E. Forbes, president, Pierce Arrow Motor Car Co., on Jan. 1, 1928:
"There will be no interruption of our prosperity."

Herbert Hoover on July 27, 1928:
"The outlook of the world today is for the greatest era of commercial expansion in history."

Andrew W. Mellon, Secretary of the Treasury, Sept. 1928:
"There is no cause for worry. The high tide of prosperity will continue."

Irving T. Bush, president, Bush Terminal Co., Nov. 15, 1928:
"We are only at the beginning of a period that will go down in history as the golden age."

President Calvin Coolidge on Dec. 4, 1928:
"No Congress of the United States ever assembled on surveying the state of the Union, has met with a more pleasing prospect than that which appears at the present time."

Col. Leonard P. Ayers, vice president, Cleveland Trust Company on Aug. 15, 1929:
"This is truly a new era in which formerly well-

established standards of value for securities no longer retain their old significance."

Roger W. Babson on Sept. 5, 1929:

"Sooner or later a crash is coming which will take in the leading stocks and cause a decline of from 60 to 80 points on the Dow-Jones barometer."

(But the actual decline was for 340 points on the Dow Jones industrial average, or 89%, far more serious than he predicted.)

Charles E. Mitchell, chairman, National City Bank on Sept. 20, 1929:

"There is nothing to worry about in the financial situation in the United States."

Irving Fisher on Oct. 16, 1929:

"Stock prices have reached what looks like a permanently high plateau."

Robert P. Lamont, Secretary of Commerce, on Oct. 14, 1929 denied that "a severe depression in business and industrial activity was impending . . ."

Charles M. Schwab, chairman, Bethlehem Steel Corporation, on Oct. 25, 1929:

"In my long association with the steel industry I have never known it to enjoy a greater stability or more promising outlook than it does today."

President Herbert Hoover on Oct. 25, 1929:

"The fundamental business of the country, that is production and distribution of commodities, is on a sound and prosperous basis."

And the *Times* of London, whose nation had been off gold for a year and a half, pronounced that the prospect of the United States taking a similar course now was "so unlikely that it may almost be left out of account." But we did go off the gold standard from 1933 to 1934.

Then note the performance of some respected publications on advice and reports to investors:

The Securities and Exchange Commission in the early 1960s disclosed that the Business News Editor of *Time* would buy shares of a company, then assign a writer and researcher to put together a story on that company. Upon publication the company's stock would often experience a sharp price rise, whereupon the editor would unload his stock for a profit.

In 1968, *Fortune* wrote a favorable article on the Bank of the Commonwealth of Detroit for which the reported earnings showed excellent growth. But by the early 1970s the bank was kept from bankruptcy proceedings through the intervention of the FDIC.

And in 1967 the *Financial Analysts Journal*, Pierre R. Bretey, a leading Wall Street railroad analyst, concluded that "interesting possibilities exist for both Pennsylvania [Railroad Co.] and New York Central [Railroad Company] stockholders as this merger, at long last, nears consummation. . . . consolidated earnings on the new company's stock should reach $13.50 per share in 1975." But in 1970 the merged company went bankrupt.

The investor may well wonder to whom he should listen.

Although he may listen to advice, he should seldom take it, preferring to make his own balance sheet and earnings analysis.

FORMULA PLANS

Investing by a formula plan aims toward reducing investor effort.

Here are some types of formula plans:

1. Dollar Averaging. In this plan the investor would invest a fixed dollar amount in stocks at definitely spaced periods, say every 3 months, buying more shares in low markets.

Such a policy implies staying invested continuously, and buying stocks at any price—not a very conservative policy.

2. Constant-Dollar Plan. Here the investor would keep

a fixed amount in the stock account, say $25,000, and make sales and buys at definite periods in the bond account to keep the dollar value of his stock account constant.

3. The Constant-Ratio Formula. In this plan the investor would adjust his portfolio of stock and bonds periodically, say once a year, to keep both parts, stocks and bonds, at a predetermined ratio, usually 50–50.

The appealing aspects of this plan are that as the market rises, the investor sells stocks and places funds in a less volatile medium (assuming that short-term high-grade bonds make up the other part of the portfolio), but when stock prices are low, the investor would reverse the procedure, selling bonds and buying stocks.

If the investor buys stocks of soundly financed companies at reasonable prices and has at least 20 of different industries, this plan would approach our method of investing except for the fixed-ratio aspect.

According to our system of investing, Chapters VII and VIII, the investor could be out of stocks and into short-term high-grade bonds 100%, if he found no common stocks at bargain-priced levels.

PUTS AND CALLS

Investors use these options to help "insure" a profit or to help limit a loss.

Here's a frequently presented example showing how an investor might use an option to limit a loss:

Buy 100 Common ABC @$40	$4000 + commission (a)
But, just in case, buy a put to deliver 100 ABC @$40 for	750 (1 year)
for a total cost of	$4750 + commission (a)
Results:	
1. If goal price is $50, sell 100 ABC @$50 and let option expire.	$5000 − commission (b)
Net result is a profit of	$ 250 less (a) and (b) commissions

2. If goal price is $50, but ABC falls to $10, deliver 100 ABC to option writer @$40	 $4000
Net result is loss of	$ 750 + (a) commission

In the last instance the investor lost only $750 plus commission, as against a possible $3,000 plus commission because of an adverse turn of the market.

Yet, we should keep in mind that these options are for a limited period only. If the price goals set by the investor are not reached by the option expiration date, the investor will no longer be protected unless he buys another option. That could turn out to be expensive.

The time limit factor should dissuade him from using options for any purpose.

INDUSTRY ANALYSIS AND TECHNOLOGY ASSESSMENT

If the investor had a sound assessment and prediction of the future potential of an industry or of a new technology, his investment problem for the long term would be over. Recall the superior growth records of Tampax, IBM, Polaroid, and Xerox?

But note these forecasts and predictions:

1. In 1974, Roger S. Ahlbrandt, chairman of Allegheny Ludlam Industries, Inc. predicted that "for the next five years, steel supplies will remain tight." "Even in a recession, the domestic steel industry may be sold out because it is now among the lowest-cost producers in the world."

By the end of 1977, however, a study showed that productivity on a tons-per-man-year basis was 50% greater in Japan than in the United States, giving Japan a significant edge on cost. And as for steel remaining tight, Bethlehem Steel Corp. closed several plants in 1977. (As for a footnote on the Japanese with an 11-point edge in median IQ over the U.S.', their disposition to working hard, and their propensity for a high rate of saving, we should expect them to gain an edge in other business areas.)

2. The U.S. Atomic Energy Commission in the 1950s had indicated that "lithium—the lightest metal, heat resistant, and a good energy absorber—would play a significant role in its programs."

3. And the National Aeronautics & Space Administration thought that cesium demand would be as much as 4 x 10^6 pounds per year by 1970.

Neither prediction materialized.

4. "In 1891, the U.S. Geological Survey (USGS) testified that America would soon run out of oil."

Again in 1919 the USGS "warned that the world supply of oil would be 'exhausted within 20 years.'" And in 1946, "another shortage was purported to be on the horizon." (Will their next forecast be correct?)

5. As Peter F. Drucker pointed out, in 1948 no one predicted the impact of the computer in business. At that time the most extensive market research study "reached the conclusion that the world computer market would, at most, be able to absorb 1000 computers by the year 2000." By 1977 there were "some 170,000 computers installed in the world." And there were 1.2×10^6 computers in operation in the U.S. alone in 1981.

What it comes down to is that forecasting which technology will have a significant economic impact is "almost always beyond anybody's imagination." "It is impossible to predict the impacts of technology." And those that "the experts predict almost never occur."

Consequently, industry forecasts and technology potential are of minimum value in our assessments of securities. Our system calls for investing in sound companies at bargain prices. Any growth from technological prospects would be bonus items for us. Don't pay extra for prospects.

BLUE CHIPS

Buy blue chips and hold them? So many think this is a profitable idea that we should explore it.

Here are the results of buying and holding some blue chips.

TABLE V–1

A PRICE SCAN OF THE 30 STOCKS IN THE DOW JONES INDUSTRIAL AVERAGE, 1964–1980

THE PRICES OF THESE 23 WERE HIGHER, ONCE, THAN THEIR 1980 HIGHS	NUMBER OF YEARS AGO PRICE WAS HIGHER THAN 1980 HIGH
American Can	16
Amer. Tel. & Tel.	16
Bethlehem Steel	16
Du Pont	16
Eastman Kodak	12
General Electric	9
General Foods	16
General Motors	16
Goodyear	16
IBM	12
Inco Ltd	16
Int'l Harvester	16
Int'l Paper	7
Johns Manville	13
Merck & Co.	8
MMM	9
Owens-Illinois	14
Proctor & Gamble	8
Sears, Roebuck	16
Union Carbide	16
U.S. Steel	16
Westinghouse	14
Woolworth	15

Obviously, it was not a profitable idea to buy any blue chip at any time and hold it.

PSYCHOLOGY AND THE STOCK MARKET

In the aggregate, over a long period, a large part of the time, earnings and stock prices follow a fairly similar track, up and down.

But note the performance of a sample of individual securities from the *3-Trend CYCLI-GRAPHS*, for the period of 1966 to 1977 (Table V-2).

TABLE V-2

	APPROX. LOW AND HIGH EARNINGS	AND	EARNINGS RATIO	APPROX. LOW AND HIGH PRICE	AND	PRICE RATIO
Adams Express	$ .44/sh	(1966)		$21	(1968)	
	.58/sh	(1970)	1.32	7	(1974)	3.00
American Air Filter	.75/sh	(1968)		49	(1972)	
	2.30/sh	(1977)	3.07	5¾	(1974)	8.52
American Building	.38/sh	(1966)		2½	(1967)	
Maint. Ind.	1.86/sh	(1977)	4.90	51	(1972)	20.42
American Brands	3.00/sh	(1966)		50	(1971)	
	5.75/sh	(1977)	1.92	28	(1974)	1.78
American District	1.15/sh	(1968)		67	(1972)	
Telegraph Co	2.67/sh	(1977)	2.32	15	(1974)	4.47

In this example price fluctuation in the 12-year period for 4 of the stocks was greater than earnings fluctuation. We attribute the phenomenon to investor psychology, which regularly drives prices below and above a "reasonable" value. The investor can take advantage of it by buying on the low side and selling on the high side, according to the system outlined in Part Two.

A review by the investor of the data for the securities in this example and for any others he may care to put together should convince him that *any time* is not a good time to buy securities. Clearly, there are times when security prices are too high and just as clearly there are other times when security prices are at bargain levels. The investor should wait for the bargains even if the wait is for several years.

THE FUTURES MARKET

This type of "investing" has to do with guessing the future price of those commodities traded.

Business Week (June 11, 1979) reported that "Albert D. Hanser, a senior vice-president with Dain, Kalman & Quail Inc., says a study done in 1976 found that 92% of futures traders lose rather than profit from their investment."

Knowledgeable investors, such as the Hunts of Dallas, experienced an extraordinary drop of their one-time net worth of hundreds of millions in the silver futures transactions in the early 1980s.

We mention this story since it is the most prominent to date on results of dealing in futures contracts.

The conservative investor should almost never deal in futures contracts in spite of the extraordinary successes of Commodities Corp. of Princeton, N.J.

FOREIGN COUNTRIES' STOCKS

The conservative investor who plans to invest in the stocks of a foreign country will have to become as familiar with the history of that country's stock market as he is familiar with that of the United States. There are differences.

For example, "the British idea of a sound P/E ratio . . . falls well below what an American with the American market in mind would judge to be sound."

And the information dispensed in foreign companies' reports is sparse by U.S.' standards, making for an investor handicap.

The investor will also have to determine the prospects for devaluation. He will avoid investing in securities of those countries where the prospect of devaluation is high, even if he has found sound bargain-priced issues there.

Let's go through the statistical exercise of determining devaluation prospects for Mexico.

On August 31, 1976, Mexico stopped supporting the peso at 12.5 to the dollar and allowed the peso to float. The peso, reduced to about half its previous value, caused losses for investors who bought Mexican securities.

The trick, of course, is to predict a devaluation.

The investor could have predicted that Mexico would devalue its currency sometime. To make that assessment he could have used several prospectuses for Mexican government bond issues, starting with the February 19, 1976 issue and going back to others issued prior to that date. These prospectuses contain useful economic data.

These showed that Mexico's foreign reserves were $\$1.5 \times 10^9$ in August 1975 and had been rising steadily since 1970. This appeared to be a favorable sign until the investor checked the balance of payments section and discovered that their reserves had been rising because Mexico had been taking on increasing amounts of debt—not a very solid way to improve the balance sheet.

Then he would have noticed that public-debt interest plus debt amortization amounted to 10×10^9 pesos in 1971, increasing to 31×10^9 pesos by 1976, which turned out to be 20% of the 1976 projected revenues, an onerous burden for any country.

Comparing this debt service to exports he would find that in 1972 it was 22.6% but rose, considerably, to 64% for 1976, when compared to the 1975 exports data. (Data for 1976 exports were not available then.)

Looking further he would have found that the current account payments balance was a deficit of $\$726 \times 10^6$ in 1971, which had risen annually to a projected deficit of $\$3.5 \times 10^9$ for 1975, a pretty good signal for devaluation.

Mexico's consumer price index had risen 3.5% in 1969 and increased fairly regularly to 24% in 1974, with an additional increase of 15% for 1975. These rates of inflation were higher than those for the U.S., Mexico's largest trading partner.

These three factors, continuously heavier debt load, steadily worsening balance of payments, and high inflation rate pointed to devaluation sometime in the future.

In early 1976 the statistics pointed toward that conclusion but they also did so in 1975 and in 1974. There may not be a way to pinpoint a devaluation date exactly.

Would the investor have invested in Mexican securities after the devaluation? Not until he had a few subsequent years of data to evaluate, since he would want to be sure that Mexico was correcting its problems; otherwise, he would expect another devaluation. He would also take time to evaluate the social-political climate and note any impediments to free enterprise. By 1982 Mexico devalued her currency again.

For another twist in determining devaluation prospects, keep in mind that, although a country's statistics may not indicate that devaluation is imminent, the country could devalue for other reasons. Argentina, for example, devalued her currency 12.5% in 1970, even though, on the face of it, devaluation did not make sense: exports were greater than imports by $\$210 \times 10^6$ in the first quarter of 1970, and the balance of payments showed a surplus of $\$102 \times 10^6$ in the same quarter, and the rate of inflation, 7.5%, was down from 9.6% in 1968.

Then, take the investor who might bet on a country that has just had a military takeover. Who would have thought that when the military took over the government of Peru in 1968 that it would promulgate liberal as opposed to conservative policies? The investor expecting a more favorable free enterprise outlook would have been disappointed.

Obviously, a statistical analysis will not always tell the investor everything. There will be risks even after he has done his work.

How about investing in securities of countries whose currencies float against the dollar?

In these instances of floating exchange rates, where currency values adjust daily, the investor will not be concerned about an abrupt, sizable devaluation, but here are some changes in currency values in relation to the dollar from Dec. 31, 1969 to Jan. 28, 1975, about a 5-year period:

Swiss Franc	up	72%
West German Mark	up	50%
Dutch Guilder	up	44%
Spanish Peseta	up	28%
Japanese Yen	up	20%
Canadian Dollar	up	8%
U.S. Dollar	at	0
Pound Sterling	off	3%

These are 6 instances of revaluations against the dollar rather than devaluations; but sometime later the reverse could be true. Nevertheless, the point is that daily, small devaluations could add up to a significant devaluation for the U.S. dollar over time. The investor, therefore, will have to be as circumspect about devaluations and revaluations for floating-exchange-rate countries as for the fixed-exchange ones in his analyses.

He will have an easier time making his determination for a country with a fixed-exchange rate since he will be evaluating actual past data in forecasting future exchange rate changes. For the floating-rate country, he will need to make some forecasts for the inflation rate for both the foreign country and the U.S., the balance of payments trend, the debt service to exports trend, plus the trends against free enterprise. Because he will be forecasting, he should expect to make some errors in his investment decisions.

The currencies of those countries with a slower inflation rate vs. that of the U.S. will rise against the dollar, usually, but not always. The statistics may indicate one direction, but the opposite might happen, as so many curreny speculators have discovered.

But putting it all together on the matter of investing in

securities of a foreign country, the investor should hold off until he evaluated a long history of stock market activity of that country, was sure the published data for any company was adequate for analysis, that the currency relationship between the foreign country and the U.S. was stable or in the investor's favor, and that the political climate was not adverse to free enterprise.

And as a final note on speculating in foreign bonds or foreign currencies, the investor should be aware of the record of the U.S. Treasury and of the Federal Reserve Board, two agencies that probably have more data available to them than the private investor has.

Professor Dean Taylor of the State University of New York at Albany studied the results of U.S. agencies' speculation in foreign currencies. His study, reported in the *Wall Street Journal*, showed "65 transaction decisions by U.S. agencies between 1973 and 1978, with 60 of these resulting in losses."

EFFICIENT MARKET THEORY, RANDOM WALK, BETA COEFFICIENT

The efficient market theory implies that stock prices adjust pretty quickly to new information. So don't expect to gain from buying a particular stock because of a recent announcement of an earnings increase, since the price will reflect the increase in earnings before you buy. Or, a managed portfolio cannot consistently beat the market; so, why try.

The random walk theory indicates that subsequent price changes are independent of previous price changes. In other words, no previous price change pattern of any common stock will suggest the direction of its next move in price.

The beta coefficient of a common stock or of a portfolio of stocks indicates the price volatility of the stock or portfolio in relation to the general market.

A common stock or portfolio with a beta of 2.0 will move at twice the fluctuation rate of the general market, up or down. If the market advances 20%, for example, the stock or portfolio will advance 40%.

The application of these theories and beta may be more useful to those investors who stay fully invested in common stocks, expecting the general market rise to make it for them, and to those who make very short term transactions, than they are to us.

Our theory is closer to the buy-low-and-sell-high system. If there are no bargains available, we buy no stocks. Or, we do not expect the market to make it for us automatically.

SELLING SHORT

If stock prices are too high for buying, why not sell short in the expectation of covering the short sale, later, at a lower price and profiting in a market decline as well?

For the conservative investor, selling short is too risky: At 50% margin the most the short seller can make is 200% on his investment, but his potential loss can exceed this by several times if the stock price keeps rising, whereas in a straight buy the investor's potential loss is 100%, or 200% on 50% margin, while his potential gain is from zero to large.

As usual, take note of the potential loss possible and rule out using those systems that could break the investor, on the basis that it will be hard for him to make that pile once he's broke.

Those enterprising investors who intend to short sell should note certain caveats:

1. Find stocks that are going down. We're willing to take credit for this brilliant idea, but are unable to suggest a certain method of spotting these. For example, high P/E ratio stocks ought to be on the list of those about to go down, but note the performance of Polaroid which sold at a low of 54 and its low annual P/E ratio of 36 in 1966, then

rose to 146 per share in 1969, before dropping to a profit-making price in 1974, when it recorded a low of 14, for a nerve-wracking 74% gain in 8 years, on the initial investment.

2. Remember that you must pay the dividends on the shorted stocks as the company declares them. Look for companies that pay a small dividend or no dividend.

3. In a short sale your broker must borrow that stock from his firm's customers. Make sure that there is plenty of stock to borrow—far more than you need.

4. A corner could develop in the shorted stock, sending the price so high that on a forced covering the investor could lose more than a lifetime of earnings and profits. So, short only those stocks that have a very large dollar value outstanding. Such stocks should be harder to corner.

PLAYING ON MARGIN

Borrowing from a broker to establish a margin account will permit the investor to buy more shares than if he invests only to the extent his own funds permit.

A 50% margin account will permit him to double up, so to speak, thus more than doubling his profits if his portfolio of stocks rises in price.

Should the market decline, taking his stocks along, the investor will have to post more funds with his broker. Or, should the value of his portfolio decline 50%, and the investor be unable to post additional funds, the broker will sell out the investor's portfolio for a 100% loss to the investor.

With that possibility looming, do not buy on margin.

VI
MUTUAL FUNDS AND OTHER INSTITUTIONAL INVESTORS

INSTITUTIONAL FUND PERFORMANCE VS. MARKET AVERAGES

Comprehensive studies on the performance of mutual funds by the Securities and Exchange Commission (1927–1935), The Wharton School (1953–Sept. 30, 1958), and the Twentieth Century Fund (1960–June 1968) conclude that mutual funds as a whole do not do any better than the market averages. But then the Investment Company Institute pointed out in an ad in the *Wall Street Journal* that $10,000 invested in funds in 1950 would have amounted to $113,500 by the end of 1972, assuming reinvestment of dividends but *not* taking into account sales charges.

However, Assistant Professor Martin E. Zweig of the City University of New York determined that a like investment in the DJIA or the NYSE composite index would have grown to $129,964 or $151,427 respectively, more in each instance than the funds returned.

Our 10-year study, ending in 1975, of 159 funds taken from Wiesenberger's data of those funds with at least a 10-year record that were graphed, distributions reinvestd and sales load charges taken into account, showed that the funds gained 2.4% per year for the 10-year period as against 2.7% per year for the DJIA, dividends reinvested quarterly.

Should the mutual fund investor have expected the term "professional money manager" to connote superior performance, he would have been disappointed for the past half century, as these studies show.

The pension funds do no better, according to a study by A. G. Becker & Co. where "the results of 300 major pension funds for 10 years ended Sept. 30, 1972 show that they only matched the 10.5% annual gain (capital gains plus dividend income) of the S&P 500" index.

And Edwin W. Hanezaryk's study (1963–1968) shows that bank trust departments did worse than the mutual funds or the market as a whole. While Marshall E. Blume and Irwin Friend's paper covering a 21-month period, Jan. 1968 through Sept. 1969, of the performance of bank trust departments, investment advisors, life insurance companies, property and liability insurance companies, and self-administered portfolios broken down further as to corporate employee benefit plans, educational endowments, and foundations concluded "that there are no sizable differences among investment performances of various institutional groups or between the investment performance of these groups and that of the market as a whole."

How do the universities do with their endowment funds?

A study completed in 1972 by J. Peter Williamson of the Amos Tuck School at Dartmouth College on the investment performance of 36 colleges found that on a total return basis 89% of these funds did worse than the Standard & Poor's 500-stock index over the 10-year period ending June 30, 1971 with but 4 performing better.

Obviously, the professionally managed funds, as a whole, do not do a superior job for the investor or for the institution.

But what may be more damaging to the purported quality of portfolio management is the Twentieth Century Fund's conclusion that there was no evidence that the securities purchased outperformed those sold.

And *Fortune* found "some evidence that casts serious doubt on the trading skills of the go-go funds." A 20-month study, ending August 1967, of 5 funds of unusually high turnover: Fidelity Capital, Fund of America, Ivest, Keystone K-2, and Oppenheimer, showed that "only one of the funds—Ivest—did better by active trading than it would have done by leaving its portfolio alone. And the difference was only slight. Ivest showed a gain of 35.6% in its net asset value/share, while shares in the unmanaged fund would have appreciated by 34.5%. . . . Oppenheimer did virtually the same with active management as it would have done with minimal management, while Keystone K-2, Fidelity Capital, and Fund of America did much worse by managing their portfolios than they would have done by leaving them intact."

Now let's check on how the funds have performed against other criteria.

MUTUAL FUND PERFORMANCE

Table VI-1 shows the results of a 10-year study comparing mutual fund performance with the performance of other investment mediums for the same period, from the end of 1965 to the end of 1975.

In perusing these data, the investor will discover that in this 10-year period he would have made more by not only neglecting mutual funds but also by passing up the stock market, if his policy was to buy and hold, and by keeping his money in savings banks or in Treasury bills. Over as long a period as ten years one might have expected that professional money managers would have at least beaten the savings bank rate.

We've discussed the performance of funds in the aggregate. Let's discuss a few details:

Is there a way to select a top performer ahead of time? Does the size of a fund make a difference in performance?

TABLE VI–1

PERFORMANCE OF MUTUAL FUNDS AND OTHER INVESTMENT MEDIUMS YEAR-END 1965–1975

	COMPOUNDED ANNUAL RATE OF GROWTH
190 open-end, load, and no-load mutual funds; capital gains reinvested and dividends added back	= 2.6%
Savings banks	= 4.95
Treasury bills, turned over every 90 days	= 5.7
DJIA, dividends reinvested quarterly	= 2.7
S&P 500-stock index, including dividend income	= 3.3
High-grade bond yields	= 7.13
Reference only (The investor in bonds may have a current high yield based on current bond prices but he could be losing his shirt on price.)	
Consumer price index	= 5.7
Wholesale price index	= 6.1

Does the sales charge for the load funds make a difference? Do certain types of funds perform better than others?

1. *Selecting a Top Performer*

Professor Eugene Fama of the University of Chicago showed in a study that not one of the 39 major funds ranked in the top half of the group consistently over a 10-year period from 1951 through 1960.

Then note the results on the performance of 39 no-load open-end funds for two 5-year periods, 1966 through 1971 and 1971 through 1976. (We added to the year-end price at the end of the period the cash value of distributions and compared that total to the year-end price at the start of the 5-year period. See Tables VI-2 and VI-3, Appendix II-Chapter VI.) Here we want to determine if superior prior performance is a signal for similar subsequent performance.

Of the 39 funds, 30 gained 5.9% per year or more in the first 5-year period, the period an investor might use as a key to finding one to invest in in 1972. But in the second 5-year period only 4 of these 30 performed at 5.9% per year or better and 10 of these 30 showed losses in the second 5-year period. Yet, the DJIA data, computed in the same way as for the funds, gained about 5.9% per year in both periods.

Of the best 5 performers in the first 5-year period, 4 showed losses in the second while the fifth gained 2% per year.

Obviously, prior superior performance does not connote subsequent superior performance.

Of the 9 funds that had the worst performance, under 5.9% per year in the first 5-year period, 5 made the 5.9% per year in the second. Yet this group of 9 included one fund that produced the largest loss in the second period, −42.3%, and another that had the largest gain of the 39, 106.%—not a good enough record to suggest that selecting the worst performer of a previous period will automatically result in the selection of a fund that produces superior results later.

Evidently, the investor will have to rely on luck for selecting his mutual fund, an unpromising system for preserving one's capital as well as for realizing better than average gains.

2. *Size of Fund and Performance*

On whether or not the size of the fund makes a difference, the Twentieth Century Fund Study (1970) pointed out: "The basic reason for the difference in performance between the mutual funds and the random portfolio with equal weight given to each stock held seems to be that the weighting scheme implicit in fund portfolios gives greater weight to the larger issues, which had significantly different rates of return from the smaller issues."

And prior to that Janos Aranyi showed "that the bigger the company an investor puts money into, the less money he makes." In surveying 900 companies for dividends plus price appreciation over 19 years, 1948 through 1967, performance for the largest companies, judged by market value, would have been minus 1.4%, while for the smallest it was 37%.

And the data for the load funds (1966–1976) show similar results.

TABLE VI-4

PERFORMANCE OF LARGE VS. SMALL LOAD FUNDS

	10-YEAR GAIN
132 load funds	48.3%
34 load funds—large only ($200 × 10^6 assets or more in 1966 and 1976)	39.5
98 load funds—other	51.4
DJIA including dividends in final price	71.4

Note: Value of shares end 1976 plus cash equivalent of gains distribution plus dividends vs. initial $10,000 investment.

The smaller funds outperformed the large by a comfortable margin.

3. *Fund Sales Charges and Performance*

Then in checking out the load charge factor, we noted that "fund shareholders paying higher sales charges had a less favorable investment experience than those paying less," according to the Twentieth Century Fund Study.

We examined this phenomenon for the 10-year period ending in 1976, using Wiesenberger's data, as usual, for those funds that had a 10-year history on graphs. We added fund distributions to the final value of the fund shares and compared that to the initial $10,000 investment.

TABLE VI–5

PERFORMANCE OF LOAD, NO-LOAD, AND CLOSED-END FUNDS

	INCREASE FOR 10-YEAR PERIOD END 1966—END 1976
172 Open-end funds	52.6%
132 Load	48.3
40 No-load	66.8
[16 Closed-end funds]	[101.2]
14 Closed-end funds (Excluding ASA Ltd and Japan Fund which invest in foreign securities)	71.4
DJIA, dividends added to final price	71.4

The no-load funds, as Table VI-5 shows, outperformed the load funds by a comfortable margin.

Next, to compare the management capabilities of these two types of funds, we removed the actual sales charge from the 132 load fund group and found that the resulting performance would have been 61.5% as against the 48.3% with the load charge included for the 10-year period. That 61.5% is close to the no-load performance of 66.8% for the 10-year period, which prompts us to conclude that the fund managers of the load funds are equal in "ability" to those of the no-load fund managers.

The investor obtains nothing extra by buying a load fund, obviously. And that prompts us to conclude that the mutual fund selling function at a frequent 8½% sales charge is an economic waste: fund salesmen being paid to sell mutual fund shares that not only perform worse than the market but also do worse than the no-load funds.

4. *Closed-End Funds vs. Open-End Funds*

For the closed-end funds, the results are better than those of the open-end funds, load and no-load lumped together, but only slightly higher than those of the no-load funds separately, and the same as that of the DJIA, reckoned similarly.

The management performance for all types of funds appears to be about uniform. But we would expect a somewhat better performance from the closed-end funds because the closed-end funds frequently sell at a discount from asset value; therefore, a similar dividend payment could yield more to the closed-end fund investor.

We surmised that there may be a method of profiting from buying closed-end funds when the discount from asset value was relatively high, then selling when the market price rose to a smaller discount or to a premium above asset value. Here, the investor could determine the buy-sell range from a history of percent discounts and premiums below and above asset value by studying Wiesenberger's historical data for closed-end funds.

We tried out such a system on paper by listing those 16 closed-end funds for which Wiesenberger reported an 11-year history of asset value per share vs. market price in percent.

Of these 16 we were able tofind 2 funds, ASA Limited and Petroleum & Resources Corporation (nondiversified funds), that had a history of discounts and premiums with sufficient delineation for establishing buy and sell prices visually.

We could select 3 buy-sell cycles for ASA and 2 for Petroleum & Resources in their 11-year price history. We "bought" and "sold" these at the average annual price during the selected buy-sell periods. The results? For ASA we recorded 2 losses and one gain and for Petroleum & Resources 2 gains, one of them for 2.1%.

We conclude, therefore, that the investor will take undue risk in trying to make it by buying and selling closed-end funds by this method. So much for trying to find an easy way to make it.

WHY INSTITUTIONAL FUNDS RECORD A POOR RELATIVE PERFORMANCE

It may be instructive to the investor to review why mutual funds and other institutional funds do no better than the market and frequently do worse.

1. Lorie and Hamilton in their study offer that "since mutual fund managers must maintain a portfolio of at least 20 securities, and since these are usually widely diversified, it is not at all surprising or indicative of incompetence that on the average these portfolios do not do significantly better or worse than portfolios of equal riskiness selected from the market as a whole."

If that is the case, though, why not merely pick a diversified portfolio of 20 stocks and eliminate a possible fund sales charge and a definite management fee in the process?

We think the problem stems from the funds almost always being fully invested in stocks, leaving little room for taking advantage of price drops. The fund managers expect a rising market to make their performance for them.

However, from another viewpoint, if the mutual fund investors want to buy into a stock fund at whatever price, then, of course, the fund managers have to accommodate them by having a fairly full load of common stocks in the mutual fund portfolio at whatever price.

So, is the fault here with the fund managers or with the mutual fund investors? (Maybe the fund investors should be licensed by the SEC.)

2. Fund managers are reluctant to try something new,

such as being out of the market when P/E ratios are high, on the basis that it is preferable to make the same mistakes that other fund managers make, rather than turn in a poorer performance for one year based on a sound, conservative approach to investing in stocks and bonds.

3. The funds invest in pretty much the same securities.
4. In a market slump they dump their securities simultaneously, accelerating the downward market slide.

While we're at it, more recent data from *Forbes* (September 1979) states that ". . . 84% of the nation's equity managers have underperformed the S&P's 500 over the last decade."

Or taking a shorter period, one year, David Dreman noted in his study (1929–1977) that of 50 large samples of stocks and industries that professional money managers liked best, "almost 80% did worse than the market the following year."

Adding it up, with 50 years of mediocre performance, we expect similar results over the next 50 for the mutual funds.

Although mutual funds in general report a mediocre performance, no-load funds perform better than load funds and the closed-end funds perform better than the open-end funds. Smaller funds do better than the larger ones. And one item we had not yet covered, the diversified, as opposed to the specialized funds, are preferable since they *are* diversified while the specialized funds concentrate in one or a small number of industries that could be subject to violent price swings.

After this commentary on mutual funds and the various methods of investing, let's consider our own system of security analysis.

PART TWO
SECURITY ANALYSIS

VII
THE BALANCE SHEET

Whatever the economic outlook, invest only in companies that have a sound balance sheet. One characteristic of such a company is that it is likely to withstand a long recession or a depression.

The economic outlook over the short term and long term calls for a conservative investment policy which, in turn, means investing in companies of conservative balance sheets and then only when the price is at bargain levels, in keeping with our overall program of it being more important not to lose than to try making a pile immediately.

Let's start with a preliminary discussion. The balance sheet of a company shows what it owes and what it owns.

A simple example of one is on next page.

Current Assets (CA) are those that may be converted to cash within a year while current liabilities (CL) are those that are payable within a year.

The ratio of CA to CL, $210,000 to $100,000, is 2.1 to 1.

Working capital (WC) is the result of CA less CL.

CA = $210,000
CL = $100,000
WC = $110,000

Quick assets are current assets less inventory:
$210,000 − 80,000 = $130,000.

Net quick assets (NQA) are quick assets less current liabilties: $130,000 − 100,000 = +$30,000.

ASSETS			*LIABILITIES AND EQUITY*	
Current Assets			Current Liabilities	
Cash		$ 20,000	Accounts Payable	$ 70,000
Short-Term			Accrued Taxes	5,000
Securities		40,000	Short-Term Debt	15,000
Accounts Receivable		70,000	Long-Term Debt Due	
Inventories		80,000	in One Year	10,000
Total Current Assets		$210,000	Total Current	
			Liabilities	$100,000
Plant & Equip.	990,000			
Depreciation	100,000		Long-Term Debt	250,000
Plant & Equip., Net		890,000	Pres. Val. Noncancel.	
Other Assets		200,000	Capital Leases	100,000
Goodwill		100,000	Preferred Stock	
			1,000 Shares	100,000
			Common Stock	
			100,000 Shares	200,000
			Surplus	650,000
Total Assets		$1,400,000	Total Liabilities and	
			Equity	$1,400,000

We prefer as potential investments those companies showing positive NQA as one criterion.

On debt, note that this balance sheet has $250,000 of long-term debt and $100,000 of equivalent debt in the form of present value of noncancelable capital leases (the amount of money that must be set aside now at a certain interest rate to make the lease payments as they come due over the years), totaling $350,000.

Note also that short-term debt, that listed in current liabilities, amounts to $15,000 and $10,000 for a total of $25,000.

In our computation for company debt we add the short-term and long-term debt, in this case $25,000 and $350,000, for a total debt of $375,000.

To the total debt we would add the prsent value of noncancelable operating leases, as we've done for noncancelable capital leases, which are not shown on this balance sheet. We discuss how to determine this item a few pages later.

The company's equity or net worth is the total of preferred stock, common stock, and surplus, \$100,000 plus \$200,000 plus \$650,000 or \$950,000.

Now, notice on the asset side of the balance sheet the item of \$100,000 for goodwill. Deduct such items from net worth (\$950,000 − \$100,000 = \$850,000) to arrive at tangible net worth of \$850,000.

A computation always used is percent of total debt to total tangible captial:

$$\frac{\$375{,}000}{\$375{,}000 + 850{,}000} = \frac{375{,}000}{1{,}225{,}000} = 30.6\%$$

Book value for common stock is the total of common stock (\$200,000), plus surplus items (\$650,000), less intangible items, such as goodwill (\$100,000), or \$750,000. When divided by the number of common shares outstanding (100,000), we arrive at tangible book value of \$7.50 per share.

This computation would be adjusted further if the market value or the call price is higher than the par value of the preferred stock. Deduct the highest excess over par value of these from tangible book value.

EVALUATING THE BALANCE SHEET

Here is how to evaluate a company's balance sheet. To start with, use Moody's manuals and note the following:

1. *Debt*

For industrials, short-term and long-term debt, plus the present value of all noncancelable leases, should be no greater than one-third of total capital (total capital being the debt and lease items listed above plus tangible net worth). As we've pointed out, tangible net worth is common and preferred stock, plus surplus items, less intangible items, such as goodwill. Moody's manuals do not contain sufficient data on leases, so for the time being compute the debt ratio without that item.

If total debt to total capital is greater than one-third, eliminate the security from consideration. For utilities, however, the debt ratio may be 50% or less. (We show the basis for these criteria in Chapter X.)

We have found, from the viewpoint of saving time, that by checking out the debt ratio first many companies can be eliminated from further consideration.

2. *Current Assets and Current Liabilities*

For industrials current assets should be at least twice current liabilities.

However, there are several types of companies that carry no product inventory. For these, current assets should at least equal current liabilities. Here is a list of these companies:

M/G FINANCIAL WEEKLY INDUSTRY GROUP NO.	COMPANIES IN THESE INDUSTRY GROUPS SHOULD HAVE CURRENT ASSETS EQUAL TO OR GREATER THAN CURRENT LIABILITIES
021–022	Airlines
091	Advertising Agencies
092	Insurance Brokers
095	Waste Management
111	Communications (including Telephone Companies)
221	Trucking Companies
223	Air Freight
225	Freight Forwarding
411	Newspapers
421	Railroad Systems
473	Sporting Events
474	Other Entertainment
591	Electric Companies (Electric Utilities)
601	Gas and Oil Pipelines
602	Gas Utilities
604	Water Utilities

Certain categories of companies do not report current assets or current liabilities. Here's a list of these along with reasons for our reluctance to invest in them.

M/G FINANCIAL WEEKLY INDUSTRY GROUP NUMBER	WHY WE SELDOM INVEST IN THESE
041–049 Banks	Quality of loans made not reported. Market value of portfolio rarely reported.
131 Personal Credit	Too much debt.
132 Business Credit	Too much debt.
261 Life, Accident and Health Insurance	Their method of portfolio management may not agree with ours.
262 Fire, Marine, Casualty and Title Insurance	Their method of portfolio management may not agree with ours.
273 Investors, Brokers and Bankers	Too much debt.
431 Mortgage Investment	Too much debt.
432 Real Estate Investment Trusts	Too much debt.
442 Real Estate Subdividers and Developers	Too much debt.
551 Savings and Loan Associations	Interest rate fluctuation interferes with stability of deposits, profits, and viability of the S&L.

3. *Net Quick Assets* (NQA)

Working capital less inventory = NQA, while current assets less current liabilities = working capital.

Net quick assets should be positive or zero.

4. *Cash Items vs. Current Debt*

There should be enough cash plus short-term investments to pay current debt. But the investor may usually overlook this item if total debt is one-third or less of total capital, on the basis that, with such a conservative debt structure, the company may borrow long-term, fairly easily, to replace the short-term debt.

5. *Adjustments*

If the current assets are less than 2 times current liabilities or if the net quick assets are negative, take the largest deficiency of these and add it to debt. If the adjusted debt is more than one-third of total capital, reject the security, otherwise approve it for further analysis.

6. *Fixed-Charge Coverage*

Net interest expense, annual payments on noncancelable leases, and amortized portion of debt discount constitute fixed charges.

Divide the quantity of profit *before* taxes plus fixed charges by fixed charges to determine fixed-charge coverage *before* taxes.

In like manner divide the quantity of profit *after* taxes plus fixed charges by fixed charges to determine fixed-charge coverage *after* taxes.

(Debt discount is the excess of face value over that collected from a bond sale. A company amortizes this deficiency over the life of the bond issue.)

In setting requirements for fixed-charge coverage we noted W. B. Hickman's comprehensive study on bond defaults (1900–1943) which showed that, in general, the greater the number of times fixed charges were covered the fewer were the number of defaults.

For example, of those bond issues of $5,000,000 or more whose fixed charges were covered 3.0 times or more after taxes, 4.0% of the industrial bonds and 5.5% of the railroad bonds defaulted. A lesser fixed-charge coverage produced many more defaults.

On the basis that a 3.0 covrage after taxes for industrials produced some defaults in this period, we have elected the requirement that fixed charges must be covered 4.0 times after taxes or 7.0 times before taxes, based on a 50% corporate tax rate:

INDUSTRIALS—EXAMPLE

Profit before taxes	=	$60,000
Profit after taxes	=	$30,000
Fixed charges	=	$10,000

If a company's coverage after taxes (30,000 + 10,000) ÷ 10,000 = 4.0 times, or equivalent coverage before taxes, (60,000 + 10,000) ÷ 10,000 = 7.0 times, the investor may consider that the company has met this part of the criteria.

However, if a utility covers its fixed charges at least 2.5 times after taxes, it meets our fixed-charge coverage requirement.

If the future corporate tax rate should drop to 40%, revise the fixed-charge coverage requirements for industrials to 4.0× after taxes and 6.0× before taxes. And for a 60% corporate tax rate use 4.0× after taxes and 8.5× before taxes as equivalent criteria.

Notice that the after tax fixed-charge coverage is kept constant at 4.0× but the before tax coverage requirement is varied with the corporate tax rate in the evaluations.

Of significance is what is left for a company's use and that is the money after taxes rather than money before taxes.

And Hickman in his study related bond defaults to after-tax coverage for the 1900–1943 period when corporate tax rates varied from 0% to 40%.

At those corporate tax rates the before-tax coverage would have to have varied from 3.0 to 4.3 times in this period to yield the same results in Hickman's study as the constant 3.0 times coverage after taxes did for the entire period.

Now let's make clear the difference in what constitutes fixed charges for our system and for that of Moody's Investors Service.

Use the net of interest income and interest expense. Moody's considers interest expense only in its fixed-charge coverage computation.

Make a definite attempt to find and include annual charges for noncancelable leases. Moody's does not include these for its fixed-charge coverage computation.

COLGATE-PALMALIVE COMPANY—1978

$\times 10^6$	
$16.650	Interest income
48.167	Interest expense
31.517	Net interest expense
4.219	Payment 1979 for noncancelable capital leases (Operating lease payments were not material)
175.572	Net income (after taxes)
322.238	Income before taxes

FIXED-CHARGE COVERAGE BEFORE TAXES

Moody's Computations:				Our Computations:		
$322.238	=	Income before taxes	=	322.238		
48.167	=	Interest expense		31.517	=	Net int. exp.
370.405	÷	48.167 = 7.69×		4.219	=	Annual payment noncancelable leases
				357.974	÷	35.736 = 10.0×

FIXED-CHARGE COVERAGE AFTER TAXES

$175.572	=	Income after taxes	=	175.572		
48.167	=	Interest expense		31.517		
223.739	÷	48.167 = 4.65×		4.219		
				211.308	÷	35.736 = 5.9×

As for preferred dividends of subsidiaries, Moody's includes these plus other fixed charges in "Times over-all Charges Earned."

Do not include preferred dividends of the parent company in the fixed-charge calculations since payments on these are not so mandatory as those for interest and noncancelable leases.

Determine the fixed-charge coverage for the latest three years and average these, placing the greatest stress on the latest year for the evaluation.

7. *Investment Value and Buy Price*

If the balance sheet data, as extracted from Moody's manuals, meet the criteria, determine the investment value and buy price according to the method outlined in the next chapter.

Then, if the actual price is at or below the computed buy price, list this security on your tentative buy list but you will need to do some more figuring before investing, as indicated in the following.

8. *Annual Report*

Before investing in a security, look over the latest annual report of the company.

These reports, in most instances, contain certain data not found in Moody's manuals, such as noncancelable lease obligations and annual payments for these.

Find the present worth of these leases at an 8% discount and add this discounted value to debt since this is an obligation to pay just as debt is. Failure to pay either of these could lead to foreclosure by the lessor or the lender.

9. *Present Value of Noncancelable Leases*

The method for computing the present value of noncancelable leases is easy.

Table VII-1 shows an example of the computation for

TABLE VII-1

NONCANCELABLE LEASES
HOUDAILLE INDUSTRIES, INC.

(1)	NONCANCELABLE LEASES $\times 10^3$ (2)	DISCOUNTED AT 8% WHAT $1.00 DUE IN THE FUTURE IS WORTH TODAY (3)	PRESENT WORTH OF THESE LEASES $\times 10^3$ (2) × (3)
1977	$1880.	.925	$1740.
8	1319.	.857	1130.
9	757.	.793	600.
0	463.	.735	340.
1981	266.	.680	181.
2		.630	
3		.583	
4	339.	.540	183.
5		.500	
6		.463	
7		.428	
8		.397	
9	89.	.367	33.
1990		.340	
1		.315	
Total	$5113.		$4207.

Houdaille Industries, Inc. using data from its annual report of Dec. 31, 1976.

The present worth of noncancelable leases for Houdaille Industries in 1977, discounted at 8%, was $\$4.2 \times 10^6$. This amount set aside at the beginning of 1977 and invested at a compounded rate of 8% would pay off all of the noncancelable lease obligations as they became due. (That is assuming, of course, that interest rates will have a weighted average of 8% to 1991.)

Another method some analysts use to determine the equivalent debt needed to acquire the property under lease is to multiply the annual noncancelable lease payment for the latest year by 10 and call that determination equivalent debt.

Using that basis for Houdaille whose noncancelable lease payments were 1.880×10^6 for 1977 would have shown an equivalent additional debt of $\$18.8 \times 10^6$.

We have opted for the discounting method since that amount set aside, generating interest, will pay off the noncancelable lease obligations.

In many instances the analyst will save time by omitting the discounting calculation and using the total noncancelable lease figure, in this instance $\$5.113 \times 10^6$, and regarding that, temporarily, as equivalent debt.

Doing the calculation for Houdaille in this way, one would have added $\$5.1 \times 10^6$ to debt, which total debt including this $\$5.1 \times 10^6$ equivalent would have been under the maximum limit of one-third of total capital, thus approving this security for further analysis, while saving the analyst calculating time.

However, should the analyst discover that using this quick method results in debt plus equivalent to be just over the one-third maximum, he should go through the discounting calculation for a more accurate determination of debt to total capital.

The Financial Accounting Standards Board (FASB) Statement No. 13, "Accounting for Leases," requires that companies determine the present value of noncancelable *capital* leases and include this figure in the debt section of the company's balance sheet. The investor will find that companies do calculate the present value of capital leases but do not, in most instances, calculate or include in company debt the present value of noncancelable *operating* leases.

The notes section of the annual report frequently shows

the amount of noncancelable operating lease payments to be made over succeeding years. The analyst will have to compute the present value of noncancelable operating leases and include these in the company's debt structure.

The author has suggested to the FASB that Statement No. 13 be amended to require the present value computation for the noncancelable operating leases as well as for capital leases and that both of these be included in company debt.

If the FASB and companies adopt the suggestion, Moody's will include such data in its manuals, thus saving the analyst calculating time.

EXAMPLE OF BALANCE SHEET ANALYSIS

Here's how those balance sheet calculations would have worked for Houdaille Industries, using their annual report for Dec. 31, 1976 (Appendix II—Chapter VII).

1. Debt as a percent of total capital					
Debt		$\times 10^6$			
Short-term	=	\$ 1.3			
Long-term	=	24.0			
Lease obligations	=	.2			
Discounted value of noncancelable lease obligations	=	4.2			
Tot. debt + equiv.	=		\$ 29.7	=	18.4%
Stockholder interest (Net worth)	=	\$143.3			
Less intangible items	=	11.0			
Tangible net worth	=		\$132.3	=	81.6%
Total tangible capital	=		\$162.0	=	100.0%
			Debt to total capital is less than ⅓		
2. Current assets	=	\$134.3			
Current liabilities	=	37.0			
Working capital	=	\$ 97.3	CA are greater than 2 × CL		
3. Inventories	=	−62.9			
Net quick assets	=	\$+24.4	NQA are positive		

4. Cash items vs. short-term debt

Cash	=	$ 7.6	
Certificates of deposit and Treasury bills	=	20.9	
Total cash items	=	$28.5	
Short-term debt	=	1.3	
Difference	=	$ +27.2	There is enough cash to cover short-term debt

Let's mention again, however, that the investor should be more concerned about the total debt vs. total capital. If that is one-third or less, he would assume that the company could borrow long and eliminate or reduce short-term debt so as to bring it in line with cash.

5. Adjustments

There were no adjustments necessary here.

6. Fixed-charge coverage before taxes

Income before taxes =		$45.201
Interest expense	$1.638	
Interest received	2.577	
Net interest expense	−.939	
Noncancelable lease payments for 1977 (Notes to financial statements)	1.880	
Total fixed charges		.941
Income before taxes plus fixed charges		$46.142

Fixed-charge coverage before taxes = 46.142 ÷ .941 = 49. Times

This fixed-charge coverage is greater than our required 7.0 times before taxes.

7. Fixed-charged coverage after taxes

Profit after taxes	$24.821
Total fixed charges	.941
Profit after taxes plus fixed charges	$25.762

Fixed-charge coverage after taxes = 25.762 ÷ .941 = 28.2 Times

This fixed-charge coverage is greater than our required 4.0 times after taxes.

This balance sheet meets our criteria statistically and the computations constitute our simple basis for analyzing a balance sheet.

But the investor should take note of several other balance sheet elements.

OTHER BALANCE SHEET FACTORS

1. *Accounts Receivable*. Are these increasing as a percent of sales? May the company have to borrow? If so, a company that already has debt close to one-third of total capital, may, in the event of having to borrow, not meet the criterion for this element later.

The investor might do well to search for another potential investment in such an instance.

2. *Cash*. A company must have enough cash to run its business. But there is no solid way to determine cash adequacy from the balance sheet, except in those instances where short-term investments are sizeable.

The investor should note the cash trend over a few years. If the cash items have been decreasing and the company has close to maximum debt, according to the criteria, the investor should make allowance for future borrowing in his computations for debt.

3. *Contingent Liability*. From the notes appearing after the balance sheet of the company's annual report, the investor should evaluate the potential effect on the company of any pending lawsuit it might lose.

4. *CPA Opinion*. Read this opinion and note any "subject to" statements. Evaluate the conditions these refer to for potential effect on profitability.

The investor will have to keep in mind that there is a limit to what the CPAs can do, consequently, they may not uncover all deficiencies that may exist in a company.

The investor, however, will have to rely on these reports. His "out" is diversification, many securities in his portfolio.

5. *Materiality*. Whether or not the auditors will disclose an accounting transaction will depend upon whether it is important to the investor.

Auditors consider that an item is material if it will affect the earnings by 5 to 10%.

However, each item in itself may not be material, but an accumulation of separate items or the cumulative effect over several years of one immaterial item may very well be material to an investor.

For example, an "instance of nondisclosure of material items came to light on March 16, 1971, when Ampex [Corp.] revealed that it had adopted a change in accounting policy . . . [in writing off] $10.7 million of previously deferred engineering expenses. But prior to this disclosure, security analysts believed Ampex had been expending all R&D costs and had no hint that the company was capitalizing some research and engineering outlays. . . . This specific sum was nowhere to be found in the balance sheet. It was 'buried' in inventory."

We'd like to make our standard comment that the investor will have to watch for these things but may not find out about them. Again, the way around an unwelcome surprise in the investor's portfolio is diversification.

6. *Fraud*. There is no protection for the investor against fraud. The only way out is to have many securities in a portfolio.

7. *Deferred Expenses*. Some companies follow a less conservative approach in treating costs as they occur:

Using a long depreciation period
  Computer leasing companies depreciated IBM computers over more years than IBM was taking for the same product.
Reporting long-term leases as immediate sales
Capitalizing research and development, marketing expense, interest, exploration costs, and mailing-list costs

Companies frequently use the liberal approach in accounting for costs in order to boost reported profits. If the investor finds too many of these "profit improving" items from a reading of the annual report, he should pass up the company as an investment candidate.

8. *Unfunded Pension Liabilities*. How should the investor take into account unfunded pension liabilities in analyzing a balance sheet? In the same manner as he takes into account noncancelable leases?

First, noncancelable lease payments, like interest payments on debt, must be paid or foreclosure might result.

But if a company does not earn enough in any year to make its payments into its pension fund, "the Treasury Department is authorized to waive the funding requirements," although waived contributions must be funded later.

Consequently, a failure to contribute to the company's employee pension fund is not as serious a matter as is a failure to make lease and interest payments. Therefore, do not treat unfunded pension liabilities as stringently as lease and debt liabilities, such as determining the present value of unfunded vested liabilities and including these as equivalent debt, or regarding the annual portion as a fixed charge when calculating fixed-charge coverage.

Nevertheless, what about those companies whose unfunded pension benefits are a significant portion of their net worth:

Obviously, the second group of companies is in better financial shape relative to pension liabilities than the first.

Consequently, do give positive weight to a company of low pension liabilities *visually* when you select one company over another for your portfolio. This point is brought up in the chapter on diversification.

How a company computes its pension liabilities will determine the size of its current pension fund deficiencies: Whether or not or to what extent future pay increases for current employees are taken into account and whether the

	UNFUNDED PENSION LIABILITIES AS A % OF NET WORTH—1979
American Motors (1980)	79
Bethlehem Steel	46
Fairchild Industries	46
General Motors	32
Goodyear Tire	21
International Harvester	41
Lockheed Corp.	117
Republic Steel	35
In contrast to those of some other companies:	
American Home Products	0
Cameron Iron Works	0
ConAgra (1980)	2
Dayton Hudson	2
Fed. Dept. Stores	0
Merril Lynch	0
Pillsbury (1980)	0
Standard Brands	0
Stokely Van Camp (1980)	4
Todd Shipyards	0
Union Carbide	3

selected rate of return on the fund is, say, 5% or 10%, will make a significant difference in the reported pension liability.

The investor will usually not find these data in the annual report. If he needs it, he should check with the company's treasurer.

If the company that already reports large pension fund deficiencies is using, say, an assumed rate of return of 12% and increases of 3% in salaries and wages, the investor should expect larger real pension fund liabilities in subsequent years.

9. *Deferred Taxes*. These stem from reporting in one way to the IRS for tax purposes in order to minimize immediate taxes and in another way to indicate higher earn-

ings to shareholders. Generally, do not adjust earnings for this item.

10. *Goodwill*. On a purchase of one company by another, the difference between purchase price and book value of assets is classified on the asset side of the balance sheet as goodwill. If the purchase price is in excess of book value, the goodwill is positive. But this goodwill could be negative as when McDonough Co. bought Edicott Johnson Corporation in 1970 for less than book value, where the goodwill item appeared as a negative on the assets side of McDonough's balance sheet.

Companies normally amortize these costs over a period of years in order to reduce them eventually to zero. Apply this goodwill item to shareholders' equity in order to determine tangible net worth.

11. *Investment Tax Credit*. Taking this credit all in one year or over the life of the equipment will make a difference in profit and loss reporting.

The investor will not, normally, make adjustments for this item, taking the results as the company reports them in his evaluation.

12. *Unconsolidated Subsidiaries*. Check the notes to the financial statements in the annual report to determine if the parent company has unconsolidated subsidiaries. Since the debt and net worth of these will not appear in the consolidated statement, the investor will have to consolidate these data to obtain a true picture of the debt ratio.

PACCAR, Inc. does have an unconsolidated finance subsidiary. Consolidating these reports for 1979 showed a debt to total capital of 29.1% vs. 5.6% without the finance subsidiary. Next year the debt may be over our limit of one-third of total capital.

13. *Joint Ventures*. In this instance a company that owns 20% to 50% of a joint venture may report only its share of earnings but none of the joint venture's guaranteed debt.

Again, the analyst will have to search the annual report

notes to determine the unconsolidated debt and net worth applicable and adjust the company's consolidated statements for a true picture of its debt ratio.

14. *Noncancelable Leases*. We have made a pretty specific point of including the present value of not only the noncancelable capital leases but also the noncancelable operating leases in company debt and the annual payments for these in computing fixed-charge coverage.

15. *Acquisitions*. A company may worsen its balance sheet by acquiring another company. Harper & Row, Publishers, Inc. had a relatively more conservative balance sheet at fiscal year end, April 30, 1978, than after it bought J. B. Lippincott Company, when the debt plus debt equivalents ballooned to 65% of total tangible capital in fiscal 1980.

The investor may not be able to spot these subsequent adverse developments even after perusing the *Wall Street Journal* and other business publications for such data before he buys a company for his portfolio.

The conservative investor should eliminate such securities from his portfolio.

VIII
INVESTMENT VALUE AND BUY PRICE

If a company's balance sheet meets the criteria, the investor establishes an investment value for the company and from that determines a buy price.

As a first step we'll outline the system of calculating investment value and buy price, then discuss the back-up for it, after which we'll show the results of using the system in the 1973–74 market drop and during the Depression, then show several actual examples of how to compute investment value and determine buy price, and wind up with some general comments.

CALCULATING INVESTMENT VALUE (I.V.) AND BUY PRICE

The investor computes investment value for any company in the same manner but pays less for smaller companies.

He determines the I.V. of a company on the basis of past average earnings and multiplies these by a price-earnings ratio applicable to the growth rate of the company (Table VIII-2).

The first 5 years' earnings total \$20.90 while the second 5 years' total \$15.90, for an overall total of \$36.80 per share for 10 years. The average per year is \$3.68 per share.

EXAMPLE:

	EARNINGS/ SHARE DILUTED		
1977	\$5.00		Working capital = $\$18.2 \times 10^6$
6	4.30		
5	4.00		
4	4.00		
3	3.60		
2	3.50	20.90	
1	4.00		
1970	3.00		
9	2.80		
8	2.60		
		15.90	
7	1.50 down	36.80,	\$3.68/share average
6	3.50 up		
5	1.90		
4	2.00		
1963	1.50		

Compute earnings growth from the two 5-year earnings totals: $\frac{20.90 - 15.90}{15.90} = \frac{5.00}{15.90} = 31.\%$ or $\frac{20.90}{15.90} = 1.31$ or 31% growth in 5 years, which translates to a 6.2% growth per year on a simple (not compounded) basis.

Table VIII-2 on earnings growth vs. P/E ratios shows that a 6% annual growth, on a simple basis, calls for a price-earnings ratio of 12.

So, INVESTMENT VALUE (I.V.) = AVERAGE EARNINGS × P/E RATIO—\$3.68 per share × 12 or \$44.16 per share.

From this point determine buy price according to company size.

Note that we have divided companies into 3 sizes: small, medium, and large (Table VIII-1).

TABLE VIII-1

COMPANY SIZE VS. BUY PRICE

WORKING CAPITAL $\times 10^6$	COMPANY SIZE DESIGNATION		WHAT TO PAY OFF INVESTMENT VALUE (I.V.): IF NON-FLUCTUATING OR MILDLY FLUCTUATING EARNINGS	IF WIDELY FLUCTUATING EARNINGS IN A 15-YR. PERIOD (WFE)
up to $25	small	S	⅔ off I.V.	⅘ off I.V.
25–200	medium	M	½ off I.V.	⅔ off I.V.
200–plus	large	L	⅓ off I.V.	½ off I.V.

The company used in the example has working capital of $18.2 $\times$ 10^6, making it a small company. But note from the 15-year earnings record that earnings doubled or more from 1963 to 1966, and then dropped 50% or more from 1966 to 1967. Erratic earnings such as these in a 15-year period place the company in the widely fluctuating earnings (WFE) category. From Table VIII-1 the investor would pay four-fifths less than the investment value for such a company. That is, if the price dropped to one-fifth of $44.16 per share or $8.83 per share, he would buy it, then sell it at investment value of $44.16 per share. An important point in this system is that the investor computes a new I.V. (selling price) each year when the company issues new earnings. Sell whenever the price hits the latest investment value.

For those companies that have no product inventory and consequently have no working capital, such as the transportation group and utilities group, use total assets divided by 4 to obtain equivalent working capital for determining company size. For example, an electric utility that has assets of $800 $\times$ 10^6 or equivalent $200 $\times$ 10^6 of "working capital" ($800 $\times$ 10^6 $\div$ 4 = $200 $\times$ 10^6) would place this company in the large-company category.

TABLE VIII-2

EARNINGS GROWTH VS. PRICE-EARNINGS RATIO

EARNINGS GROWTH RATE/YEAR (SIMPLE BASIS)	PRICE-EARNINGS RATIO
0	8
1	9
2	9
3	10
4	11
5	12
6	12
7	13
8	13
9	14
10	15
11	16
12	17
13	18
14	19
15	20
16 & over	20

The foregoing is the gist of the system as it has to do with establishing investment value and buy price. The following outlines the basis for it.

BASIS FOR THE SYSTEM

In a market decline prices of smaller companies drop more than those of the larger. From the author's study of 500 companies for the 1973–1974 market decline, he determined the cut-offs in size of decline for small, medium, and large companies. From these data he compiled Table VIII-1, Company Size vs. Buy Price.

For companies whose earnings fluctuated widely, the investment value varied considerably from year to year; consequently, the buy price for such companies is less than for companies whose earnings do not fluctuate erratically.

As for earnings growth and price-earnings ratios, he took note of the low P/E ratios for each year since 1870, compared these to common stock price growth, and established that a growth in earnings of 3% per year is worth a P/E = 10. From there it was easy enough to establish the other points for Table VIII-2, Earnings Growth vs. Price-Earnings Ratio.

(The analyst will find the analytical data including references and tables for the basis for this system in Appendix II—Chapter VIII.)

SECURITY EVALUATION SYSTEM TRYOUT

Using the criteria the author tried out the system for the 1973–1974 market drop by analyzing the first 500 common stocks listed in Standard & Poor's *Stock Guide*, year-end 1974, and to them adding the stocks in the DJIA for a total of 516 investigated.

He found 25 that fitted his balance sheet and buy price criteria. This group contained 3 oil companies, so he eliminated 2 of these for a final portfolio of 23 stocks, each in a different industry.

That portfolio gained about 100% in 2 years.

Then he developed a portfolio for the Depression, 1929–1932, which gained 73.5% in 2.4 years.

(The reader will find the details for this exercise of several pages in Appendix II—Chapter VIII.)

Now let's run through some actual examples using the system.

ACTUAL EXAMPLES OF I.V. AND BUY PRICE COMPUTATION

Each of the following 3 examples meets the balance sheet criteria.

Being a large company with working capital of over $\$200 \times 10^6$ of non-widely-fluctuating earnings, the investor

LARGE COMPANY—TEXTRON INC.

	DILUTED EARNINGS PER SHARE	
Dec. 31, 1976	$3.23	
5	2.58	
4	2.62	
3	2.72	
2	2.30	
1	2.03	13.45
1970	1.86	
1969	2.02	
8	1.98	
7	1.97	
		9.86
1966	1.67	23.31 or $2.33/share/average
5	1.26	
4	.98	
3	.83	
2	.71	

Working capital = 625×10^6

$\frac{13.45}{9.86} = 1.37$ or 37% increase in 5 years
7.4%/yr (simple basis)

From Table VIII-2 this growth calls for a P/E ratio of 13.

$ 2.33/sh × P/E of 13 =
$30.29/sh investment value
Buy @ ⅓ off I.V. = $20.20/share
(Table VIII-1)

would buy the company at one-third off I.V. or $20.20 per share.

This buy price for Textron would have been in effect the second, third, and fourth quarters of 1977 and the first quarter of 1978.

Houdaille's earnings fluctuate widely: down 50%, up 100% or more within a 10 to 15-year period. Consequently, the investor would buy it, a medium-sized company, at two-thirds off investment value of $11.00 per share.

MEDIUM-SIZED COMPANY—HOUDAILLE INDUSTRIES, INC.

	DILUTED EARNINGS PER SHARE	
Dec. 31. 1976	$2.88	
5	2.02	
4	2.12	
3	2.01	up
2	1.48	
1	.92	10.51
1970	.76	down
9	1.47	
8	1.50	
7	1.38	
		6.03

16.54 or $1.65/sh average.
$1.65/sh × P/E of 20 = $33.00/sh investment value
Buy @ ⅔ off I.V. = $11.00/share

Working capital = $\$97.3 \times 10^6$

$\frac{10.51}{6.03} = 1.75$, 75% increase in 5 yrs or 15%/yr (simple basis) This growth calls for a P/E ratio of 20.

This buy price would have been in effect the second, third, and fourth quarters of 1977 and the first quarter of 1978.

The buy price for Esquire Radio (next page) would have held for the second, third, and fourth quarters of 1977 and the first quarter of 1978.

FURTHER STEPS IN SECURITY ANALYSIS

After the investor has found his potential investments from an analysis of the balance sheets and determined the buy prices from earnings data in Standard & Poor's "Stock Reports" and Moody's manuals, he should read the latest

SMALL COMPANY—ESQUIRE RADIO & ELECTRONICS, INC.

	EARNINGS PER SHARE	
Dec. 31. 1976	$1.97	
5	1.90	
4	1.28	
3	1.63	
2	1.45	
1	1.17	8.23
1970	1.41	
9	1.40	
8	.80	
7	.50	
		5.28
		13.51, $1.35/share average
1966	.45	
5	.40	
4	.37	
3	.25	
2	.17	

Working capital = $\$10.1 \times 10^6$

$\frac{8.23}{5.28} = 1.56$, 56% growth in 5 yrs or 11.2%/yr (simple basis) This growth calls for a P/E ratio of 16.

$1.35/share × P/E of 16 =
$21.60/sh investment value
Buy @ ⅔ off I.V. = $7.20/share
(non-widely-fluctuating earnings)

annual reports. These reports contain more data than the reports from S&P and Moody's.

The previous chapter covered what to look for in these annual reports relative to the balance sheet.

Here we discuss items that affect the profit and loss statement, although many will also affect the balance sheet.

Nonrecurring items

Do not agonize over whether to include nonrecurring

items in the earnings report. Include them, generally. They are part of what it takes to run a company:

1. Security transaction profits and losses
2. Tax refunds
3. Extraordinary write downs of inventory, accounts receivable, sales of divisions, or other items
4. Lawsuit gains or losses

Standard & Poor's "Stock Reports" include these data in the footnotes of their reports but a look at the annual reports will confirm this. If these nonrecurring items have not been included in earnings, the analyst should include them when determining investment value.

Deferred Expenses

The importance of looking for deferred expenses is that some companies use this method for boosting current reported profits:

1. Capitalizing research and development costs
2. Capitalizing exploration costs
3. Taking smaller than normal depreciation costs (computer leasing companies)
4. Capitalizing sales development costs
5. Reporting total value of sales as having been made when they are paid for over an extended time period (land companies)
6. Valuing inventory on first-in first-out (FIFO), in lieu of last-in first out (LIFO), during a period of rising wholesale prices

With material costs and prices increasing during inflationary periods, a company using FIFO, that is, charging off earlier purchased materials at their lower costs, will report higher earnings than if it used LIFO valuation of material costs.

7. Changing the assumed rate of return for a pension fund to a higher rate

Chrysler changed its assumed rate of return on its pension funds to 7% from 6%, thus reporting greater earnings than if it had used the previous rates.

The change from 6% to an expected 7% return on pension funds does not appear unreasonable. But the analyst should note the increase in reported earnings that such a change caused.

He should check the notes in the annual report to determine if a company has been using many tricks in adjusting upward its reported earnings. He should then either readjust the earnings to a more conservative stance or overlook the security as an investment candidate.

Here are some other items to watch for on the profit and loss statement:

1. A company's taxes and net earnings, on a 46% taxable income basis, will be about 50–50, but remember that
   long-term capital gains are taxed at less,
   some dividends are taxed at 15%,
   prior year losses will affect current year profits, and
   interest on municipal bonds is not taxed.
2. On retrospective adjustment of earnings, take note of whether such an adjustment gives the impression of rising earnings.
3. Can the investor spot everything? Back in 1965 Brunswick Corporation wrote off $\$129 \times 10^6$ in receivables. "In many cases, perfectly good equipment was written down to scrap value." Later sales of this equipment produced inventory rather than operating profits, misleading the analyst. For its fiscal year ended January 1970, Mattel, Inc. included $\$10 \times 10^6$ in reported profits that it expected to, but did not yet, receive from insurance companies. (The information on this was in the report's footnote section.) That activity showed reported profits to have increased over the previous period, but without the $\$10 \times 10^6$ inclusion profits had actually declined.

Even the gambler who bought or hung onto the stock

when at year-end 1971 its P/E ratio was 65 and at year-end 1972, 28, would have been alerted to adverse prospects had he read the notes in the annual report. So, always read the annual report notes!

4. T. W. Phelps in his *100 to 1 in the Stock Market* points out that "opportunities for profiting by capital leverage are easy to find. What is hard is deciding whether the added profit potential outweighs the added risk." In one such example he notes: "The kind of situation to look for is a severe but temporary slump in the business and profits of a large company with a very high proportion of senior securities in its capital structure. Obviously if one can buy the equity for 5 to 10% of the value of the total enterprise, a doubling of the value of the total enterprise may result in a 10 to 20 fold increase in the market price of the equity."

This is not the kind of situation to look for. If the slump is long enough (no one can forecast the length of a slump), this is the kind of company, with high debt, that could go broke.

After having listed many securities that qualify for investment, how should the investor select one out of many in an industry? Note growth rate, dividends, previous high price, and percent of unfunded vested benefits to net worth. More on this in the chapters on diversification.

ADJUSTING EARNINGS

If the investor needs to make adjustments in earnings due to stock dividends and stock splits, here's an example of how to do it.

List the common shares outstanding, stock dividends, stock splits, and unadjusted earnings per share as in Table VIII-14. By way of example note that year 1, when the company split the stock 3 for 2, has an earnings divisor of 1.00 (column 5); adjust prior years' earnings by 1.50 (1.00 × 1.50). Year 3, when the company declared a 10% stock dividend, has an earnings divisor of 1.50; adjust prior year earnings by 1.65 (1.50 × 1.10). Year 4, when the company split the stock 2 for 1, has an earnings divisor of 1.65; adjust prior year earnings by 3.30 (1.65 × 2.00).

Moody's manuals give the data on stock splits and stock dividends.

TABLE VIII-14

ADJUSTING EARNINGS FOR STOCK SPLITS AND STOCK DIVIDENDS

1	2	3	4	5	6
YEAR	COMMON OUT. $\times 10^6$	STOCK DIVIDENDS STK SPLITS	PER SHARE EARNINGS UNADJUSTED	EARNINGS DIVISOR	PER SHARE EARNINGS ADJUSTED (4 ÷ 5)
1	120.000	3 for 2	$10.00	1.00	$10.00
***2	80.000		11.00	1.50	7.35
3	79.200	10%	8.10	1.50	5.40
4	72.000	2 for 1	7.00	1.65	4.25
5	36.000	50%	6.00	3.30	1.82
**6	24.000		6.00	4.95	1.21
7	24.200	10%	5.00	4.95	1.01
8	22.000	100%	5.00	5.45	.92
*9	11.000		4.00	10.89	.37
10	10.000		2.00	10.89	.19

*Bought a company for 1,000,000 shares.
**Co. bought back 200,000 shares.
***Co. sold 800,000 shares to public.

} Make no adjustments for these.

IX

WARRANTS—CONVERTIBLE SECURITIES—STRAIGHT INTEREST PREFERREDS

Now that we have elaborated on how to evaluate common stocks, what about warrants, convertible bonds, and convertible preferreds as investments?

You might invest in these if, first, the common stock of the company meets the balance sheet criteria and, second, if your calculations show that you may make more on one of these than on the common.

Here's how to evaluate these using Textron Inc. as an example.

EVALUATING WARRANTS AND CONVERTIBLE SECURITIES

The balance sheet for this large company was in good shape and the investment value of its common stock for 1974 was $24.80 per share, making $16.52 a buy price at one-third off investment value.

The company had warrants and two convertible issues outstanding. Compute the potential gains for these and the common.

The sell price of the common was $24.80, therefore the equivalent sell price of the 2.08 convertible preferred, since it is convertible into 1.1 common shares, would be 10% more than the common ($24.80 + 2.48 = $27.28).

TABLE IX-1

TEXTRON INC.

	SHARE PRICE ON 12/11/74	EQUIVALENT SELL PRICE PER SHARE	POTENTIAL GAIN %
Common stock	\$13⅞	\$24.80	79%
2.08 pfd cv into 1.1 common	21	27.28	30
1.40 pfd cv into .9 common	15¾	22.32	42
Warrants to buy common at \$10 —these expire in 1984	8¾	14.80	70

(The common equivalent price of these warrants would be \$13⅞ (price of the common) minus \$10 (the cost of conversion) or \$3⅞ per warrant. Since these warrants sold at \$8¾, the premium for the warrants is \$8¾ minus \$3⅞, or \$4⅞ per warrant.)

On the basis of the data in Table IX-1, considering no premiums for the warrants or the convertible preferreds, you would buy the common and pass up the other 3, since the potential gain is greater for the common.

The enterprising investor, though, might have assumed that the warrants would continue to be priced at a premium of at least one dollar and bought these instead of the common.

But a conservative investment policy calls for passing up such a program, since warrants may not always sell at a premium even if they have once.

WARRANTS

Although the investor should not consider warrants unless he would buy the common, some have used a method of finding warrants that will expire in, say, 2 years, selling these short and buying some common long in a combination play.

E. O. Thorp and S. T. Kassouf have outlined the system

they have used but point out some impediments to profit making:

1. The common could drop all the way to zero.
2. The stock could rise a number of points in one day, beyond the break-even combination of short warrants and long common.
3. The warrants could rise without a concomitant rise in the common.
4. An extension of the warrant expiration date may work adversely in the hedge.
5. A corner might develop in the shorted warrants, wiping out all prior and possibly all future gains.

Consequently, the conservative investor should pass up this method of trying to make it in warrants.

PREFERRED STOCKS, STRAIGHT INTEREST

The dividend on preferred stock is fixed (unless it is a participating preferred), thus increasing profits will not influence the preferred's price or dividend payment.

Should the company report small or negative earnings, the preferred dividends will usually be omitted (but will accumulate to be paid in the future if the security is a cumulative preferred stock).

Preferred stock usually has no maturity date, so a general rise in interest rates will cause the price of preferreds (as well as for bonds) to decline.

The investor will be better off buying stocks or short-term bonds of sound companies rather than preferred stocks.

X
ANALYZING FIXED-INCOME SECURITIES

The investor will have that portion of his portfolio not in common stocks invested in fixed-income securities, such as bonds, Treasury bills, money market instruments, and savings deposits.

SHORT-TERM VS. LONG-TERM BONDS

Invest in high-grade *short-term* bonds of a maturity of 5 years or less, rather than the long-term bonds, in order to reduce the effect of interest rate fluctuation on bond prices.

Let's discuss this point.

Investors have lost money in high-grade bonds.

That has happened when the investor bought low coupon long-term bonds at par and held on while interest rates rose, as note the Northern Pacific Railway Company 3% bonds issued in 1897 and maturing in 2047, rated BBB by Standard & Poor's.

The price of this bond fell to 36¾ in March 1978, to accommodate a current yield of 8.2% on this grade of bond ($30 interest ÷ $367.50 = 8.2%). That price represents a decline of 63% from purchase price for the investor who paid $1000 for this bond at the offering or in the 1950s when interest rates were about 3%.

There were several bonds in this category, long-term bonds selling considerably below their issue price, causing losses for investors who hung on.

So, what does the term "a safe bond" mean? It means only that the interest payments and payment at par on the maturity date are *reasonably* assured, and not that the price of the bond can't fluctuate considerably between issue date and maturity date.

Note how interest rates have fluctuated over the past half century.

MOODY'S AVERAGE YIELD ON Aaa CORPORATE BONDS

1980 = 11.94%	1950 = 2.62%
1976 = 8.43	1945 = 2.62
1974 = 8.57	1940 = 2.84
1968 = 6.18	1935 = 3.60
1965 = 4.49	1930 = 4.55
1960 = 4.41	1925 = 4.88
1955 = 3.06	1920 = 6.12

Obviously, a long-term bond bought at $1000 in 1950 to yield 2.62% would sell at a good deal less in 1978 in order to yield the current 8% or so, as the example showed.

To avoid this type of loss, that due to fluctuating interest rates, buy high-grade *short-term* bonds, since any change in interest rates will have a minimum influence on the price of a bond that will mature in 1 to 5 years.

Now let's discuss bond ratings and other bond features.

BOND FEATURES

1. *The Agency Rating*. Moody's bond ratings of Aaa, Aa, A, Baa and Standard & Poor's ratings of AAA, AA, A, BBB are "investment grade," meaning that, at the time of rating, the interest payments and principal are considered secure.

Both Standard & Poor's and Moody's consider that income to debt service, that is, fixed-charge coverage, is more significant than total assets of a company being rated. (Fixed-charge coverage = profit after taxes but before fixed charges ÷ fixed charges.)

For this characteristic the Standard & Poor's ratings for industrial bonds are as follows:

Bond Rating—Fixed-Charge Coverage

AAA if after-tax coverage is 5 times
AA if after-tax coverage is 4 times
A if after-tax coverage is 3–3½ times
BBB if after-tax coverage is not less than 2½ times

Our own requirement of a fixed-charge coverage of 7 times *before* taxes or 4 times *after* for industrial companies coincides with the first two grades and sometimes with the third grade but not with the BBB grade.

Another statistic agencies consider to be significant is that of long-term debt as a percent of total capitalization. (Total capitalization in this instance being long-term debt plus common, preferred, and surplus.)

Bond Rating—Debt Ratio

AAA if long-term debt is 25% or less of total capital
AA if long-term debt is 30% or less of total capital
A if long-term debt is 35% or less of total capital
BBB if long-term debt is 40% or less of total capital

The reader will recall that before we consider an industrial company's common stock eligible for investment, that its total debt, short term, long term, plus the present value of noncancelable leases, may not exceed one-third of total capital, that its current assets must be at least twice current liabilities, and that net quick assets must be positive.

The agencies' criteria, then, will *at times* be adequate for many of those bonds rated AAA and AA and sometimes adequate for those rated A. But the BBB-rated ones may not meet our conservative criteria.

The bond rating agencies consider other criteria in rating bonds: cash flow to senior debt, tangible assets to long-term debt, the company's position in the industry, stability of earnings, and any positive or negative factors that might disturb these ratios in the future.

Use these agency ratings as a guide in listing bonds for further analysis, to find those that meet the criteria outlined here for personal investment.

The investor will consider other factors when buying bonds.

2. *Size of Issue*. Brokers point out that investors will have an easier time trading bonds of issues of $\$50 \times 10^6$ or over than those of smaller issues.

Nevertheless, for a short-term buy of, say, one or two years, which the investor normally intends to hold to maturity, the size of the issue won't matter, particularly if the smaller-issue bond pays a higher yield to maturity than that of the larger-issue bond.

3. *Call Provision on Bonds*. The bond issuer frequently includes a provision in the indenture to call the bond for payment at a stated price in a certain year. Should interest rates decline, the issuer may in such an instance issue a replacement bond with a lower coupon, saving itself interest charges.

The investor will notice that the call feature will have a more prominent influence on prices of long-term bonds than for the shorter-term ones. Should interest rates drop, the bond price will rise, yielding a profit to the holder, if the bond has no call provision. The call provision will usually hold down the price rise to the call price, limiting gains for the investor of long-term bonds.

The holder of short-term bonds should check the call provision also.

For example, if the bond price is below the call price, the call feature will not be an impediment to a rise in the bond price, as note Standard Oil of California 4⅜, 1983, which sold for 85⅛ (3–10–78) rated AAA, with a call feature giving the company the OK to buy the bonds from the investor at $100.80 in 1978 (and for lesser amounts later).

There is little chance that the company would buy back

these 4⅜% bonds only to issue duplicates at 8+%. Even if the company did, the investor in these bonds would gain.

Take another example: Baltimore Gas & Electric Company 10⅛s, 1983 @ 105¾ on 3–10–78 for a yield to maturity of 8.8%. The call is at 105.59 starting in 1978, and decreasing to $100.00 by 1982.

The bond price here is not too far from the call price and by maturity date, 1983, each would have decreased to 100.

There is not much chance of the investor losing out on yield to maturity here either because of the call feature.

Now note Union Pacific Corporation 8.6s, 1983, priced at 101⅝ on 3–10–78, rated AA, with a call price of 100 beginning in 1981 and a yield to maturity of 8.2%.

The bond price is higher than the call price. But even this situation doesn't pose much danger of extensive loss for the investor either, when the price of the bond over the next 5 years will decline to 100 anyway, while yielding 8.2% to maturity.

Nevertheless, the investor, when compiling a potential list of short-term high-grade bonds for investment, should determine the call provision from Moody's manuals and favor those bonds for investment whose price is not over the call price.

4. *A Round Lot—An Odd Lot*. A round lot consists of 100 bonds or $100,000 of face value. But as time goes on that 100 may rise to 500 or 1000 bonds.

A smaller lot may be harder to buy or to sell, but the odd-lot investor should set a price with his broker, at which he is willing to buy or sell, and wait.

Also, he should be aware that he may have to pay ⅛ more per bond for his odd lot.

Brokers charge $2.50 per bond in commission but some houses charge $5.00 per bond and also have a minimum charge.

HIGH-GRADE VS. LOW-GRADE BONDS— A HISTORY OF DEFAULTS

Now let's discuss a short history of bond defaults and why the investor should prefer high-grade over low-grade bonds.

Referring to W. B. Hickman's study on bond defaults (1900–1943), note the data in Table X-1:

TABLE X-1

AGENCY RATING	EQUIVALENT S&P RATING	PROPORTION OF BONDS IN DEFAULT BEFORE 1944 TO THE TOTAL PAR AMOUNT OF THAT CLASS OF BOND, 1900–1943
I	AAA	5.9%
II	AA	6.0
III	A	13.4
IV	BBB	19.1
V–IX	BB-C	42.4
No Rating		28.6

What Table X-1 shows is that even the highest-grade bonds did not escape some defaults. But equally important is the fact that the lower-rated bonds suffered more defaults than did the higher-rated ones in the 1900–1943 period.

However, since World War II (to 1975), "no industrial or utility bond has gone into default while still rated 'investment grade' by Moody's or Standard & Poor's."

But "several investment-grade issues went into default" in the rails and "only two tax-exempt issues with 'investment grade' ratings have defaulted."

Although the ratings record of these two agencies has been far better in this later period than it was during the period that included the Depression, we have not had, in this latest period, a drastic, long-lasting economic downturn for an in-depth test of the security rating system for the postwar period.

But W. B. Hickman's data for the 1900–1943 period, the worst of the 2 periods since it included the Depression, show that bonds earned their fixed charges after taxes by 3.0 times and over had fewer defaults than those earning fixed charges fewer times. For example, see Table X-2.

TABLE X-2

PROPORTIONS OF OFFERINGS 1900–1943 IN GIVEN CLASSES OF TIMES-CHARGES-EARNED RATIO AT OFFERING THAT WENT INTO DEFAULT BEFORE 1944

	TIMES-CHARGES-EARNED RATIO				
	UNDER 1.0	1.0–1.4	1.5–1.9	2.0–2.9	3.0 AND OVER
Larger issues:					
All industries	35.0%	34.1%	17.9%	4.0%	2.1%
Utilities (except Street Railways)	38.4	4.1	0.4	0	0
Railroads	55.2	49.4	28.0	15.1	5.5
Industrials	9.7	16.0	16.5	7.4	4.0

Note: (Times charges earned: Average annual income after taxes but before charges over the five-year period preceding offering date was related to the fixed charges for the first full year following offering.)

In scanning these data, it will become obvious to the analyst that the agency ratings, which stress in their evaluation the times-charges-earned ratio, are worth considering, particularly as a starting point in making a list of potential bond investments.

What the investor would like, of course, is a 100% reliable rating, which, once made, would hold to maturity.

But, "during most business cycles the agencies upgraded some issues in good times and downgraded considerably more in bad, with the result that the net volume of high-grade outstandings expanded and contracted with the business cycle."

And that "the errors in rating corporate bonds can be traced principally to the business cycle and to the difficulty of forecasting industry trends." But anybody has trouble forecasting.

So, one should expect, therefore, that the agencies will continue to have the same problems as previously but that the highest-rated bonds will continue to experience the lowest default rates.

But the matter of fluctuating ratings is a further inducement to favor the short-term bonds, on the basis that the shorter the term to maturity, the less the chance of adversity overtaking a company before bond payoff time. And because there have been fewer defaults for those bonds rated high grade, the investor will favor buying high-grade bonds.

Now let's discuss how to analyze various bonds: industrial, utility, municipal, U.S. government, federal agency, and defaulted bonds.

ANALYZING BONDS

1. *Industrial Bonds*

Bonds with identical ratings and similar maturity dates vary in yield to maturity. The idea is to find bonds of the highest yield to maturity that are also high grade and short term.

Compile a list of AAA- or AA-rated bonds having similar maturity dates. For example, pick a year from 1 to 5 years away, and list the straight-interest bonds of the same maturity along with their yield to maturity (from the *M/G Financial Weekly*).

Then check out more data from the company's annual report for each bond:

(a) *Fixed-charge coverage*. Recalculate the fixed-charge

coverage by including the latest annual charge for noncancelable leases with net interest and debt discount payments. If that fixed-charge coverage is less than 7 times before taxes, eliminate this bond from the potential investment list.

(b) *Debt ratio*. Next, determine the percent debt to total capital by including in debt the short-term debt and the present value of noncancelable leases. If that total debt is over one-third of total capital, remove this one from the list.

(c) *Working Capital* (current assets (CA) less current liabilities (CL))
Current assets should be at least two times current liabilities. As for those companies that carry no product inventory, CA should at least equal CL.

(d) *Net Quick Assets* (working capital less inventory) These should be zero or positive.

(e) *Adjustments*. If the "c" and "d" items are deficient, take the largest deficiency and add that to debt to determine if the "adjusted debt" is one-third or less of total capital. If not, cross this security off the potential investment list.

(Notice that the analyst is to use the same criteria for analyzing industrial bonds as for analyzing the balance sheet of industrial common stocks.)

You will now have a list of industrial bonds of similar short-term maturity dates, that meet the investment criteria, to select from for your portfolio. Invest in those of the highest yield to maturity.

2. *Utility Bonds*

Table X-2 shows that utilities, except street railway companies, that had a fixed-charge coverage after taxes of 2.0 or more, experienced no defaults in the 1900–1943 period.

Another section of Hickman's data shows that no large

utility issues, those of over 5×10^6, rated grade I (AAA), went into default in the 1900–1943 period, while 0.1% of the large issues rated grade II (AA) went into default.

And note again that since World War II (to 1975) no utility bond has gone into default that was rated investment grade, AAA to BBB.

This is a 75-year record worthy of the investor's consideration.

Yet, the high debt ratio for the utilities is bothersome.

Here is the debt ratio for the 15 utilities in the Dow Jones utility average for 1976 and for 1929:

	TOTAL DEBT TO TOTAL CAPITAL %
1976	52.5
1929	33.7

The debt ratio for the utilities was lower once.

Five of these companies in 1929 had debt below one-third of total capital, where the conservative investor likes to see it. Yet, two of the 15, Pacific Gas & Electric Co. and Philadelphia Electric Co., had debt ratios of 50 to 51% in 1976 *and* in 1929, while only one of the 15, Houston Industries, had a higher debt ratio in 1929 than in 1976, although it was a fairly small company in 1929.

But even though the utilities have a high debt ratio now, should the investor accept that as the norm? How high may this debt ratio go before we experience some defaults for the utilities?

Nevertheless, even with the adverse portent in mind about high debt for the utilities, recall that the earnings for utilities are fairly steady, that a prewar utility having a fixed-charge coverage after taxes of 2.0 or more, or in later years, an investment grade rating, had not gone into default—an exemplary record.

Also, since one may feel confident about a one-third debt to total capital for *industrials* whose earnings fluctuate more than those of utilities, shouldn't the investor be willing to accept a higher debt ratio for the utilities whose earnings are more stable?

Adding it up, even without knowing how high that debt ratio may prudently be for utilities, invest in the higher-grade utility bonds, but of the short-maturity issues only, if the fixed-charge coverage is 2.5 or more after taxes, debt is 50% or less of total capital, and working capital or net quick assets are positive. (Utilities have no inventory, so these two items may be equal. If working capital is negative, add this negative amount to debt to determine adjusted debt.)

In making the calculations for fixed-charge coverage, the investor should deduct from reported earnings an item, now appearing frequently, called cost of borrowed funds for construction. Such earnings are not real, although Moody's and Standard & Poor's include such "earnings" in their fixed-charge coverage calculations.

3. *Municipal Bonds*

How well have state and municipal bonds performed for the investor?

George Hempel noted: "During the early years of American independence, the idea prevailed that no economic unit should go into debt." Consequently, there were no defaults until the panic of 1837, which signaled the depression lasting into the 1840s.

In "1842 and 1843 over 50% of the total outstanding state indebtedness of approximately $232 million was in default." During that period two local governments defaulted but these finally repaid their debts in full; however, "not one of the 9 states that defaulted in 1841 and 1842 paid its bonds in full."

Then "from the beginning of the Civil War through the

early 1880s there was a regular flood of defaults." The \$220–250 $\times$ 10^6 in default from 1873 to 1879 "represented approximately one-fourth of the net minicipal indebtedness in the United States."

Next, the depression of 1893 brought defaults of "approximately 10% of total municipal bonds outstanding."

"By far the largest number and most severe minicipal defaults in the 1900s took place during the depression from 1929 through 1937." Then, 15.4% of outstanding debt was defaulted. But these were practically all cleared up by early 1941.

Investors lost about \$100 $\times$ 10^6 in principal and interest during this period, which amounted to .5% of the municipal bonds outstanding.

"From 1947 through 1964 there were approximately 200 defaults on minicipal bond issues," which totaled "approximately \$280 $\times$ 10^6" or "less than ⅓ of 1% of the total municipal debt outstanding" in 1964.

How about relying on agency ratings for assurance as to pay off of principal and interest? Hempel found that during the 1929 Depression "48.1% of these defaulting issues were rated Aaa in 1929 and, in the same year, 78.0% of the defaulting issues were rated Aa or better."

Of the dollar value of these defaulted issues, "94.4% were rated Aa or better."

Since then the rating quality has improved considerably, as note that since World War II "only two tax-exempt issues with investment grade ratings [AAA/Aaa to BBB/Baa] have defaulted. In addition, \$1.6 $\times$ 10^9 in New York City notes, which had only recently been rated investment grade by Moody's, suffered a de facto default [in 1975]."

And Standard & Poor's had a AAA rating on Development Corporation of Evergreen Valley, Maine, which defaulted in 1972.

Well, nobody's perfect.

Yet, adding it up for his study which ended in 1964,

Hempel's data indicate that "the overall quality of municipal bonds has weakened in the post war period."

And the Advisory Commission on Intergovernmental Relations (ACIR) in its study in 1972 pointed out why cities are in poorer shape fiscally these days:

1. Growing use of short-term debt for operations is "perhaps the major problem of the Depression thought to be relevant today."

2. "Poor financial planning, budgets that are not truly balanced . . . make the true condition of the cities almost impossible to ascertain."

3. "The condition of state and local employee retirement systems and the accumulation of unfunded pension fund liabilities" usually is a mystery in the budget and in some instances "exceeded the bonded debt or the current operating budget."

Nevertheless, in spite of the adverse comments so far on municipal bonds, the investor in the 50% tax bracket will be interested in these tax-free bonds since the income from a 6% municipal will be equivalent to that of a 12% industrial bond after taxes, for example.

So, let's continue.

In keeping with a conservative approach to investing, the investor should investigate only those short-term minicipals that have been audited independently and have a AAA/Aaa or AA/Aa agency rating.

There are four factors important in judging the credit worthiness of general obligation bonds according to *The Rating Game:*

1. Ratio of tax-supported debt to the assessed value of taxable real estate

"When possible, it is better to get a ratio of net debt to full market valuation of taxable realty. Generally, a 'full value' ratio of 6% is considered the dividing line between higher and lower quality debt (assuming a 50% assessment, the debt to assessed value ratio would be 12%)."

2. Debt per capita

"The dividing line between better and lesser credits was reported in 1967 at about $200 for cities of under 25,000; $250 for cities between 25,000 and 250,000; and $300 for cities over 250,000. Generally per capita debt levels of $100 to $150 above these are considered to be problems deserving careful examination."

But these figures are "obviously affected by the price level."

3. Annual debt service payments as a percent of the total current-revenue budget expenditures

"This ratio measures the weight of the current payment of principal and interest in the current-revenue budget. . . . A ratio of 10% is felt to be the separation between better and lesser credit worthiness, 15% warrants concern, and it should never exceed 20 to 25%."

4. The legal opinion

Have the taxing authorities provided for the necessary taxes to pay off the bonded debt?

Also, the analyst will have to consider, as the bond-rating agencies do, several subjective factors: Is industry in the community diversified? What portion of total taxes does industry pay? Are any contemplating moving? And, is the community paying its own way or is it overly dependent on outside sources to balance its budget?

These are some of the objective and subjective factors the analyst will be concerned with when evaluating general obligation bonds, that is, those that are secured by the states' and cities' "unlimited" authority to tax.

But a new impediment to municipal-bond analysis has been added by California's Jarvis-Gann Initiative to *limit* local taxation.

The best bet for the conservative investor is to wait until the dust settles before investing in bonds of communities that have placed a limit on legislative taxing power.

The other class of municipal bond is the revenue bond, which is secured by a particular source of revenue, such as turnpike revenues, airport revenues, and sports arena income. On these, many investors feel that a 1.2 times coverage of debt service is adequate. We are not in that group and would be uncomfortable owning a bond with such a small coverage.

In the 1970s there were about 120,000 municipal bond issues, representing borrowings of 34,000 entities, that make up the two categories.

There is no central market place for these $\$250 \times 10^9$ outstanding municipal bonds. Consequently, the investor in buying or selling these will be at the mercy of the bond dealers—all the more reason why he should analyze the prospectus.

Investors should be aware of the Municipal Bond Insurance Association (MBIA), which insures certain municipal bonds of issues of up to $20,000,000.

"The insurance is provided by 4 large insurance companies, which irrevocably—and unconditionally—guarantee payment of principal and interest. The quality of the companies [that provide the insurance]—Aetna Insurance, Aetna Casualty and Surety, St. Paul Fire and Marine, and U.S. Fire—is such that all bonds backed by the MBIA automatically enjoy an AAA from Standard & Poor's Corp."

The investor should make a point of searching for these when the bond maturity date reaches the 1- to 5-year range in spite of the smallness of the issue size of under $\$50 \times 10^6$.

The minimum denomination of a municipal bond is $5000 but many older issues are in $1000 denominations. The minimum sale is for $5000.

4. *U.S. Government Securities*

Treasury issues (bills, notes, and bonds) represent the ultimate in safety since they are backed by the full faith and credit of the U.S. government.

Every Monday the Treasury auctions off 90-day and 180-

TABLE X-3

FEDERAL SECURITIES

	ISSUING MATURITY RANGE	MINIMUM PURCHASE	GUARANTY	STATE AND LOCAL TAX STATUS	BEARER OR REGISTERED	CALL FEATURE
TREASURY ISSUES (available from brokers, banks, or from a branch of the Federal Reserve)						
Bills	To 1 Year	$ 10,000	By	Exempt	Bearer	
Notes	1–20 plus	$ 1,000	U.S.	Exempt	Bearer or	
Bonds	Years	$ 1,000*	govt.	Exempt	registered	Some callable
KEY FEDERAL AGENCIES (available from brokers, some banks)						
Banks for Cooperatives	6 Months	$ 5,000	By issuing agency	Exempt	Bearer	Noncallable
Export-Import Bank	1 Month– 7 Years	$ 5,000– $100,000	By U.S. govt.	Not exempt	Bearer or registered	Noncallable
Farmers Home Administration	1–25 Years	$ 25,000	By U.S. govt.	Not exempt	Bearer or registered	Noncallable
Federal Financing Bank	1–20 Years	$ 1,000– $ 10,000	By U.S. govt.	Exempt	Bearer or registered	
Federal Home Loan Bank	1 Month– 20 Years	$ 10,000***– $100,000	By issuing agency**	Exempt	Bearer	Noncallable
Federal Intermediate Credit Bank	9 Months– 5 Years	$ 5,000	By issuing agency**	Exempt	Bearer	Noncallable
Federal Land Bank	1–10 Years	$ 1,000	By issuing agency**	Exempt	Bearer or registered	Most Noncallable
Federal National Mortgage Assn. debentures	1 Month– 2–25 Years	$ 10,000	By issuing agency**	Not exempt	Bearer	Noncallable
Govt. National Mortgage Assn. participations	1–25 Years	$ 5,000	By U.S. govt.	Not exempt	Bearer or registered	Noncallable
Govt. National Mortgage Assn. pass-throughs	1–25 Years	$ 25,000	By U.S. govt.	Not exempt	Registered	

*Some long-term Treasury bonds are redeemable at par for estate taxes, regardless of market price. These "flower" bonds have lower yields because of this provision.

**These issues are not expressly guaranteed by the U.S. government, but there is a strong implied government guaranty.

***Some outstanding issues are available in $5,000 denominations.

TABLE X-3 (cont'd)

ADDITIONAL FEDERAL SECURITIES.

	ISSUING MATURITY RANGE	MINIMUM PURCHASE	GUARANTY	STATE AND LOCAL TAX STATUS	BEARER OR REGISTERED	CALL FEATURE
Federal Home Loan Mortgage Corp. mortgage backed bonds (FHLMC)	12–25 Years	$ 25,000	Not directly backed by U.S. but by Govt. Nat. Mtge Assn. which is	Not exempt	Bearer or regist.	Some are callable
Federal Housing Admin. (FHA)	1–40 Years	$ 50	By U.S. govt.	Not exempt	Regist.	Callable
TVA bonds	3–25 Years	$ 1,000	By TVA— First claim on "Net Power Income"	Exempt	Bearer or regist.	Callable
U.S. Postal Service	10 Years	$ 10,000	The Sec. of Treas. may guaranty at his discretion	Exempt	Bearer or regist.	Callable
Washington Metro. Transit Authority	40 Years	$ 5,000	By U.S. govt.		Bearer or regist.	Callable
World Bank	10–26 Years	$ 1,000	Bank has the right to call on its member govt's to meet its debt obligations	Not exempt	Bearer or regist.	Some are callable
General Services Administration	30 Years	$ 5,000	By U.S. govt.		Regist.	Callable
Dept. of Housing and Urban Development	10–20 Years	$ 5,000	By U.S. govt.		Regist.	Callable
Small Business Administration	10 Years	$ 10,000	By U.S. govt.		Regist.	Non-callable

day bills. In addition, every month it auctions off one-year bills. The minimum investment is $10,000.

The Treasury offers notes and bonds several times a year for which the minimum investment is $1,000.

The only "analysis" the investor needs to make here is to note if the yield to maturity is the same or higher than for short-term high-grade bonds of nongovernment securities.

5. *Federal Agency Issues*

"Most agency issues are just a smidgen less safe than Treasury issues because most carry an implicit, not explicit, guaranty by the U.S. government."

Five federal agencies dominate the field: Federal Home Loan Bank, Federal National Mortgage Association (Fannie Mae), Federal Intermediate Credit Banks, Banks for cooperatives, and Federal Land Banks.

There may be times when the Treasury and agency securities' yield to maturity equals or surpasses the yield to maturity for corporate bonds. The investor should always compare the return from these against those from corporate bonds.

Pages 108–9 list government securities along with useful information compiled from *Business Week*, *The Complete Bond Book*, *Handbook of Securities of the United States Government and Federal Agencies*, and *Moody's Municipal & Government Manual*.

6. *Defaulted Bonds*

W. B. Hickman, in his study of bond defaults for 1900 through 1943, found that "yields realized on bonds purchased at default and held to extinguishment were usually attractive, averaging 20%/annum for the combined industries, 17% for public utilities, 19% for rails, and 26% for industrials." Then Hickman also deduced from that same study that "almost without exception . . . unsecured issues had poorer records than secured issues as to cash payments after default, and had poorer life-span yield experience. From the evidence, secured issues generally fared better than unsecured issues in corporate reorganization."

With these data in mind the investor might be tempted to try his luck in defaulted bonds.

But the above record is the result of investing in all of the defaulted bonds over that 43-year period. The result over the next 43-year period may not be at all similar. Besides, the investor in such an experiment would have to be a well-endowed one so as to have the means for investing in all of the defaults and be young enough for a 43-year siege of investing in these.

Take note of how New York Central Railroad Company gold 4s of 1998 have worked out since the parent company filed for bankruptcy proceedings on June 21, 1970.

	PRICE RANGE
1969	61½—44¼
June 19, 1970	33½
June 22, 1970	23
1970	50⅛— 9½
1971	15½— 9⅝
2	13¾— 6¼
3	10½— 5⅛
4	11 — 3½
5	9½— 3¾
6	19 — 9½
7	43 —18¾
Sept. 6, 1978	74⅛

Buying these at 23 after the bankruptcy announcement and holding until 1978 would have resulted in a 15.3% per year compounded gain for the 8.2-year hold period. But note that from the time of purchase the price was considerably lower for 7 of those years, and then who could have foretold how these bankruptcy proceedings would have worked out.

The soundest approach is to try to determine what the sales value is of the assets behind the defaulted bonds and from that, what the pay-off might be, but to buy the bonds at a price that permits a several times theoretical gain for each bond purchase, as a margin of safety.

But the conservative investor will shun defaulted bonds.

The less conservative investor might try them with a portion of his capital if he develops the expertise in evaluating defaults himself and has the time for the extraordinary effort that such evaluations will require.

SHORT-TERM MONEY MARKET INSTRUMENTS

The investor should be familiar with these as a means for parking his money while analyzing securities for his portfolio.

1. *Bankers' Acceptance*. The bankers' acceptance finances the import, export, and storage of goods.

It has "strong credit backing, derived not only from the guarantee of the draft by the accepting bank, but also by the implicit backing of the firm drawing the check and the underlying merchandise involved in the transaction." The face value of these is $5,000 to $1,000,000.

"In its 66 years of usage [to 1980] in the United States, the bankers' acceptance has come through the trials of war and economic depression with no known principal loss to investors. Courts have held that the letter of credit agreement . . . is based on the principle that the acceptor bank holds the agreement not for its own benefit or the benefit of its general creditors, but in trust for the holder of the acceptance."

2. *Certificate of Deposit*. A certificate of deposit is a receipt from a bank for a deposit of money that matures in one to 12 months. It is backed by the bank doing the issuing. While $100,000 to $1,000,000 and more is the usual denomination, certificates for $25,000 may be available.

The Federal Deposit Insurance Corporation (FDIC) insures $100,000 maximum of a bank depositor's combined funds per bank, such as the regular type of bank deposits plus his certificates of deposit.

Virtually all commercial banks are members of the FDIC.

3. *Commercial Paper*. Commercial paper is a promissory note, sold by a corporation, which matures in 5 to 270 days. The usual denomination for one of these is for $100,000, $500,000, and $1,000,000 but some are for $25,000 for which the investor will pay a $25 transaction charge.

A maturity of over 270 days is rare since a corporate security of over 270 days' maturity must be registered with the SEC in order to be offered to the public.

TABLE X-5

RATINGS ON COMMERCIAL PAPER

STANDARD & POOR'S	MOODY'S	FITCH
A-1 Highest Investment Grade	Prime-1	F-2 Highest
A-2 High Investment Grade	Prime-2	F-2 Investment Grade
A-3 Medium Investment Grade	Prime-3	F-3 Good Grade
B Medium Grade	Not	F-4 Not Recommended
C Speculative	Rated	
D Expected to default		

Source: *The Complete Bond Book* by David M. Darst. Copyright © 1973 McGraw-Hill, Inc. Used with the permission of McGraw-Hill Book Company, p. 181.

Moody's Bond Record, issued monthly, contained commercial paper ratings for about 700 companies in October 1978. Only 10 were rated P-3, while two-thirds were rated P-1, the top grade. The investor has plenty to choose from for further analysis.

As for analyzing commercial paper, the investor would start with a list of the highest rated ones, then analyze each issuing company's balance sheet as he would for stocks and bonds, rejecting those that do not fit the criteria. Of the 3 money market instruments, we would feel most comfortable with commercial paper since these lend themselves to our method of analysis.

The investor would skip the certificates of deposit, except for the FDIC-guaranteed amount of $100,000 per bank, since he would not know how to analyze a bank adequately (quality of loans made and value of the bank's portfolio are usually unknown quantities).

The bankers' acceptance, because of the backing, appears to be a reasonably safe investment. The investor would want to evaluate the balance sheet of the importer who had written the check, nevertheless.

4. *Money Market Funds*. These funds invest in short-term dividend-yielding investments, such as bankers' acceptances, certificates of deposit, commercial paper, and other types of bills, notes, and bonds that also mature in less than one year.

We prefer to make up our own fund of short-term maturity items that would contain Treasury bills, notes, and bonds; commercial paper, bankers' acceptances, industrial bonds and notes that meet the balance sheet criteria; and certificates of deposit of up to the FDIC-insured amount of $100,000 per bank.

But let's comment on the Scudder Cash Investment Trust for March 31, 1981, which had $\$900 \times 10^6$ invested in 94 securities of 43 different banks and companies.

Sixty percent of the fund was invested in commercial paper of credit companies (39%) and in certificates of deposit (21%), types of investments that do not fit into our system even though Moody's gave the commercial paper of the credit companies a P-1, its highest rating (although Moody's did not rate the paper for Ingersoll-Rand Financial Corporation or for Ingersoll-Rand Company).

The fund had an average portfolio maturity of but 20

days. With such a fast turnover the investor might assume that the chance of adversity overtaking one of the invested-in companies before pay-off time was slim; and that, at a 14½% return, 5 of the banks or companies represented in the portfolio would have to default within a 20-day period and pay nothing on capital or interest before the investor's capital losses equalled the fund's dividend payments for the year.

In spite of the brevity of the 20-day maturity period adversity could overtake a bank within that time.

Invest in money market funds that buy only short-term government securities that are backed by the full faith and credit of the federal government. Such funds should pay off the investor however adverse business conditions become.

SELECTING BONDS FOR INVESTMENT

By way of example here's how to go about listing and selecting bonds for a portfolio.

First make up a list of prospects from, say, the *M/G Financial Weekly*, selecting AAA-rated bonds with a similar maturity date, such as 1983 in this example. Note the fixed-charges data and debt ratio for these from Moody's manuals.

Remember that for industrials debt should not be over one-third of total capital, current ratio should be 2.0 or more, net quick assets should be zero or positive, and that the fixed-charge coverage before taxes should be 7.0 times (or 4.0 times after taxes). For utilities debt should not be over 50% of total capital, current ratio be 1.0 or more and that fixed-charge coverage be at least 2.5 times after taxes.

From this list eliminate the bank. Also eliminate the pipeline and Sears, Roebuck and Co. because of high debt. When you adjust the debt for the two oil companies so that current assets equal two times current liabilities, the adjusted debt will be over one-third of total capital—decline investing in these. The oil companies had more solid

TABLE X-6

STANDARD & POOR'S BOND RATING: AAA DUE 1983

	COUPON RATE %	AMT. OUT. $\times 10^6$ $	PRICE AUG. 1978 $/SH.	YLD. TO MAT. %	DEBT TO TOTAL CAP. %	FIXED-CHARGE COVERAGE TIMES EARNED AFTER TAXES			CALL PRICE	CALL DATE
						1976	1975	1974		
Exxon Pipeline	7.65	150.	96⅜	8.5	84.	4.93**	5.03**	—	100.	1981
First Bank Syst.	8¾	50.	100	8.7	—	—	—	—	100.	1982
Sears, Roebuck	4¾	166.	87	8.0	45.	3.67	2.92	2.37	101.97	1978
So. Cent. Bell	8.2	100.	99⅛	8.4	41.	2.64	2.50	2.80	100.	1980
S. W. Bell Tel.	3⅛	100.	76⅝	9.3	44.	2.86	2.69	2.73	100.	1978
Std. Oil Calif.	4⅜	120.	84⅞	8.2	41.a	8.32	10.60	16.02	101.	1977
Std. Oil Ind.	4½	95.	87¼	7.6	37.a	7.18	7.00	9.55	100¼	1978

** = *Before* income taxes

a = Adjusted debt. An amount was added to debt to make current assets = 2 times current liabilities or to make quick assets positive.

TABLE X-7

STANDARD & POOR'S BOND RATING: AA DUE 1983

	COUPON RATE %	AMT. OUT. $\times 10^6$ $	PRICE 9-1-78 $/ SHARE	YLD. TO MAT. %	DEBT TO TOTAL CAP. %	FIXED-CHARGE COVERAGE TIMES EARNED AFTER TAXES 1976	1975	1974	CALL PRICE	CALL DATE
Arco Pipeline	8⅜	250.	96⅝	8.7	91.	1.3**	1.4**	—	100.	1981
Balt. Gas & E.	10⅛	50.	106⅝	8.5	51.	2.51	2.38	2.54	105.59	1978
Clev. Elec. Illum.	8.85	50.	102	8.3	58.	2.44	—	—	100.	1980
Comm. Edison	9	125.	101⅝	8.6	54.	2.36	2.31	2.25	100.	1980
Duquesne Lt. Co.	3⅝	12.	*78⅛	9.1	53.	2.24	2.45	2.33	100.94	1978
First Int'l Bank	9	65.	*100	9.0	—	—	—	—	100.	1981
Ford Motor Cr.	8⅝	125.	100⅝	8.5	90.	1.3**	1.3**	1.2**	100.	1981
Gen. Motors Acc.	4⅝	150.	85¾	8.5	91.	1.4**	1.3**	1.2**	100.60	1978
Kerr-McGee	8	75.	96⅞	8.8	26.	6.91	10.28	11.84	100.	1981
Sohio/BP Pipe	8⅝	250.	99¼	8.8	99.9	—	—	—	100.	1981
Texas Co.	3⅝	150.	82½	8.2	40.4a	4.76	5.50	11.78	101.	1978
Union Pacific Cp	8.6	100.	100¾	8.4	37.5a	4.09	4.07	4.26	100.	1981

a = Adjusted debt
* Price: close on 8-4-78
** Finance Cos and Pipeline Cos: Times charges earned *before* taxes.

banace sheets once. Wait for an improvement. Of this group of 7 select, as candidates for annual report investigation, the two utilities, South Central Bell Telephone Co. and Southwestern Bell Telephone Company, favoring the second one since the yield to maturity is higher. Also the investor would have a bonus at pay-off time, a long-term capital gain, when the company redeemed the bond at a price higher than he paid.

Next, let's try our luck on bonds rated AA due 1983 (see Table X-7).

From this group of 12 select for annual report investigation Baltimore Gas & Electric Company and Kerr McGee Corporation, favoring the last one because of its higher yield to maturity. The others have too high a debt ratio or inadequate fixed-charge coverage.

Our third try was for A-rated bonds due 1983 (see Table X-8).

From this group of 14 select for further annual report analysis, Deere & Company and Tektronix, Inc., favoring the last one because of its higher yield to maturity. As for Consolidated Edison Co. of New York and Long Island Lighting Company, look at another year of fixed-charge coverage data to be sure the trend continues in the right direction. Corn Products Company has just a bit too much debt, 34.0% vs. our requirement of not over 33.3%. As for Asarco, Inc., the debt ratio is OK and the 3-year average fixed-charge coverage is OK but because the two latest years by themselves are inadequate, place Asarco toward the bottom of your potential investment list.

(In the annual report for Long Island Lighting Company (LILCO) for 1976, income before interest charges of $\$184 \times 10^6$ was inflated by $\$60 \times 10^6$, allowance for funds used during construction.

Do not include such "income." Recomputed, the 1976 fixed-charge coverage after taxes is 1.72 times rather than 2.54 times as Moody's has it, thus the investor would cross off LILCO from his potential investment list.)

TABLE X-8

STANDARD & POOR'S BOND RATING: A DUE 1983

	COUPON RATE %	AMT. OUT. $\times 10^6$ $	PRICE 9-1-78 $/ SHARE	YLD. TO MAT. %	DEBT TO TOTAL CAP. %	FIXED-CHARGE COVERAGE TIMES EARNED AFTER TAXES 1976	1975	1974	CALL PRICE	CALL DATE
Asarco	8.8	50.	99⅞	8.8	33.2a	2.25	2.12	11.60	100.	1981
Consol Edison	3½	40.	79⅝	9.2	48.	2.67	2.45	2.07	100.91	1978
Corn Products	4⅝	31.	83	8.8	34.0a	5.09	3.86	3.93	100¾	1979
Deere & Co.	4½	19.	87½	7.6	31.3	5.25	3.66	5.71	100½	1978
Delmarva P&L	9⅜	30.	100⅝	9.2	53.	2.23	2.08	2.20	109.23	1978
Dominion Bank	9½	25.			—				100.	1982
First Mary. Bank	9¾	25.			—				100.	1981
Fruehauf Fin.	9.15	60.	101½	8.7	79.	1.9**	2.0**	1.8**	100.	1981
Int'l T&T	9⅛	75.	101⅝	8.7	51.a	2.57	2.16	2.23	100.	1981
ITT Finan'l	9.7	50.	*103	9.0	82.	1.4**	1.4**	—	100.	1982
Long Island Lt.	9¼	80.	101¼	8.9	50.	2.54	2.40	2.22	100.	1980
Montgomery W. Cr.	9½	60.	101⅝	9.0	81.	1.5**	1.5**	1.5**	100.	1981
Tektronix Inc.	8⅞	35.	*99⅞	8.9	15.	7.4	6.6	18.7	100.	1981
Trans. Am. Fin.	9⅜	50.	102	9.1	80.	1.9**	1.7**	—		

* Price: close 8-18-78.
a = Adjusted Debt.
** Finance Cos: Times charges earned *before* taxes.

TABLE X-9

STANDARD & POOR'S BOND RATING: BBB DUE 1983

	COUPON RATE %	AMT. OUT. $\times 10^6$ $	PRICE AUG. 1978 OR 9-1-78 $/SHARE	YLD. TO MAT. %	DEBT TO TOTAL CAP. %	FIXED-CHARGE COVERAGE TIMES EARNED AFTER TAXES			CALL PRICE	CALL DATE
						1976	1975	1974		
Appalachian Pr.	11⅛	40.	105½	9.6	61.	1.72	1.95	1.84	107.85	1978
Chrysler Fin.	9½	100.	89	10.5	85.	1.3**	1.3**	1.3**	100.	1982
Columbus & S.Oh.E.	11	30.	104⅜	9.8	51.	2.36	2.20	1.72	100.	1981
Columbus & S.Oh.E.	3⅝	8.			51.	2.36	2.20	1.72	101.01	1978
Cont'l Tel Corp.	10½	75.	103	9.7	63.	2.08	2.00	2.02	100.	1981
Indiana & Mich El.	11	60.	105½	9.6	59.	1.72	1.77	1.48	107.34	1978
Kidde, Walter	10½	50.	104⅞	9.3	34.	3.46	2.84	2.61	100.	1982
Kroger Co.	9⅞	50.	104	8.8	50.a	5.20	3.63	4.25	100.	1981
Ohio Elec. Co.	11	75.	104¾	9.8	55.	2.43	2.10	1.78	108.22	1978
Pennzoil Co.	10⅝	75.	103⅞	9.6	51.	4.83	4.10	4.44	100.	1981
Puget Sd P & L	10¾	30.	106	9.3	57.	2.12	2.02	1.90	104.25	1980
So. East Banking	10	40.	103	9.2	—	—			100.	1982
Spiegel Inc.	5¼	40.	84	9.6	70.	2.4**	2.2**	2.1**	100.70	1978
Williams Cos	10¼	100.	103	9.4	51.	2.19	4.33	4.49	100.	1981

a = Adjusted debt.
** Finance Cos: Times charges earned *before* taxes.

Finally, we made a list of BBB-rated bonds maturing in the same year (see Table X-9).

The conservative investor would not select any of the above 14 bonds in Table X-9 for investment. The industrials have too much debt, the utilities do not cover their fixed charges at least 2.5 times, while the finance companies have more debt than we like to see in any of our investments. The banks we automatically eliminate.

In sum, only the first three grades of bonds yielded some possible candidates for investment. Again, the selections made from the first 3 lists are for further investigation rather than immediate investment. The investor should check out the annual reports of these companies for total debt, being sure it includes short-term debt and present value of noncancelable leases, and for fixed-charge coverage to be sure it includes the annual charge for noncancelable leases.

YIELD TO MATURITY

Here's a quick method for computing yield to maturity.

Example:
Bond due date = 6 years
Price = 90% or $900
Coupon rate = 6%
Current yield = $\frac{60}{900}$ = 6.67%
Yield to maturity = 8.42%
Due price = $1000
Current price = 900
To be collected in addition to buy price
in 5 years = $100 ($1000–900)
or $ 20/year
$60 interest/year
20 amortization/year
$80 theoretical gain/year

$$\frac{80}{\text{Avg. Price } \frac{(1000 + 900)}{2}} = \frac{80}{950} = 8.42\% \text{ yield to maturity}$$

This formula is inaccurate for long-term bonds.

It is reasonably accurate for the shorter-term bonds.

The investor might like to try out a few computations on bonds of various maturities and compare his data with the yield to maturity data listed in the *M/G Financial Weekly* for which a computer with a proper program makes an accurate determination of yield to maturity.

PART THREE

PORTFOLIO MANAGEMENT

XI
DIVERSIFICATION

Now that we have established a method for evaluating stocks and bonds, let's develop a system for building a portfolio of these. First, let's discuss the common stock portion of the portfolio.

Lawrence Fisher and James Lorie show that a portfolio of 16 securities, each of a different industry, will act as the general market does 90% of the time, while 32 will do it 95% of the time, and 128 will perform the same as the market 99% of the time.

And when we recall Ben King's study which showed that 50% of the price fluctuation of a common stock was due to general market activity, we have the basis for setting up a portfolio that won't do much worse than the market as a whole, at least.

These are handy data since we want to avoid doing worse than the market.

The Depression portfolio of 26 stocks (p. 238) had 4 losers in it, yet the overall portfolio results were quite satisfactory, stressing the value of diversification.

Let's start with pinpointing the number of industries there are to invest in.

INDUSTRIES LIST

Moody's Industrial Manual, *Moody's Transportation Manual*, and *Moody's Utility Manual* list 166 industries and also in the blue pages section of the *Industrial Manual*,

Moody's lists the industrial companies under each industry, making for investor convenience in separating his potential investment list of securities by industry. Standard & Poor's *Stock Guide* lists the principal business of each company, making it a handy guide for diversification.

The *M/G Financial Weekly* lists 60 numbered groups of industries. Including the subgroups, the total is 176 industries.

This paper also lists about 3300 common stocks and in one section lists these according to 176 industries, making that list handy for the investor to check out the diversification requirement for his portfolio.

But from this *Weekly*, we made up our own industry diversification list: First we crossed off 9 bank classifications, then 2 credit, 2 insurance, 3 financial, 2 investment, 2 real estate, and one savings and loan association industry class for a total deduction of 21 industry classes at this point.

Then we crossed off others within an industry group that we thought were too closely related, such as 031 Auto Manufacturers and 032 Automotive Parts and Accessories. We would invest in one company of either group but not in one of each. The 05 group of industries contains 9, from 051 through 059. Here we would be wary of having a company of each of these nine in a portfolio of 25 stocks, say.

We found one industry group, 241, Hotels, Motels, Camping Facilities, that we would expand to two investments rather than one: Hotels or Motels for one and Camping Facilities for the second.

In this matter we deducted another 30, giving us a list of 126 industries (Table XI-1), the companies of which we would invest in if they met our balance sheet and buy price criteria.

TABLE XI-1

M/G FINANCIAL WEEKLY INDUSTRY CLASSIFICATION

Code	Industry	
011	Aerospace Industries	1
012	Aerospace Components	x
013	Aircraft Mfgrs, Services	1
021	Trunk Airlines	1
022	Regional Airlines	x
031	Auto Manufacturers	1
032	Automotive Parts and Accessories	x
041	New England Banks	x
042	Middle Atlantic Banks	x
043	South Atlantic Banks	x
044	East North Central Banks	x
045	East South Central Banks	x
046	West North Central Banks	x
047	West South Central Banks	x
048	Mountain States Banks	x
049	Pacific States Banks	x
051	Residential Construction	1
052	Lumber and Wood Products	x
053	Cements	x
054	Clay Products	x
055	Glass	x
056	Paints	1
057	Other Building Materials	x
058	Plumbing and Heating	1
059	Air Conditioning	1
061	Contractors General	1
062	Contractors—Special	x
064	Materials and Components Mfgrs	1
071	Computers, Subsystems & Periferals	1
072	Computer Software, Data Process	x
073	Computer Leasing	x
081	Office Machines	1
082	Copying Machines	x
083	Other Business & Industrial Equip.	x
084	Office Supplies	1
091	Advertising Agencies	1
092	Insurance Brokers	1
093	Printing	1
094	Other Business Services	1
095	Waste Management	1
101	Chemicals, Synthetics	1
102	Sulphur and Nitrates	1
103	Specialty Chemicals	1
111	Communications	1
121	Cosmetics and Grooming Aids	1
131	Personal Credit	x
132	Business Credit	x
141	Distillers	1
142	Brewers, Wineries	1
151	Drug Manufacturers	1
161	Electrical Equip. Mfgrs.	1
171	Electronic Equip. Mfgrs.	1
172	Radio, TV, Phonograph, Stereo	1
181	Farm Products	1
182	Canned, Cured and Frozen Foods	1
191	Soaps and Cleansers	1
192	Grain Mill Products	1
193	Bakery Products	1
201	Livestock	1
202	Meat and Poultry	x
203	Dairy Products	1
211	Sugar Companies	1
212	Confectioners	x
213	Soft Drinks	1
221	Trucking Companies	1
222	Water Transportation	1
223	Air Freight	1
225	Freight Forwarding	1
227	Truck, Rail Leasing	1
231	Medical Instruments & Supplies	1
232	Institutional Services	1
241	Hotels, Motels, Camping Facilities	2
243	Restaurants	1

251	Appliances	1
252	Fixtures	x
253	Furniture & Home Furnishings	x
254	Housewares	x
255	Rugs and Carpets	x
261	Life, Accident & Health	x
262	Fire, Marine, Casualty and Title	x
271	Financial, Fund Management	x
272	Closed-End Funds	x
273	Investment Brokers & Bankers	x
281	Farm, Construction, Handling, Mining	1
282	Special Industry Machines	1
283	General Industry Machines	x
284	Railroad Equipment	1
285	Engines and Turbines	1
286	Pollution Controls	1
291	Machine Tools and Accessories	1
292	Small Tools	x
293	Screw Machine Products	1
294	Machine Accessories	x
295	Light Machine Equipment	x
301	Fabricated Metal Products	1
311	Iron Mining	1
312	Iron and Steel Furnaces, Mills, Foundries	1
321	Copper Mining	1
322	Copper Refining	x
324	Aluminum Refining	1
325	Lead, Ni. Tin, Zn, Mining & Ref.	1
327	Uranium Mining	1
328	Other Mining Including Coal	1
329	Other Metal Refining	1
331	Rare Metals Mining	1
332	Rare Metals Refining	x
341	Multi-Industry Companies	1
351	Oil & Gas Field Services	1
352	Offshore Drilling	1
353	Oil Exploration	x
361	Oil and Natural Gas Producers	1
371	Oil Refineries & Marketing Cos.	1
381	Paper Products	1
382	Metal Cans	1
383	Paperboard Containers & Boxes	x
384	Glass Containers	1
385	Specialty Containers	1
391	Personal Services	1
392	Educational Services	1
393	Automotive Services	1
395	Photographic Services	1
396	Vending Machine Suppliers	1
401	Scientific Instruments	1
402	Mechanical Devices	1
403	Electronic Controls & Instruments	1
404	Photographic Equip & Supplies	1
411	Newspapers	1
412	Periodicals	1
413	Books	1
421	Railroad Systems	1
431	Mortgage Investment	x
432	Real Estate Investment Trusts	x
441	Real Estate Operators & Lessors	x
442	Real Estate Subdividers & Develop.	x
451	Toys and Games	1
452	Sporting Goods	1
453	Sport Vehicles	1
454	Musical Instruments & Equip	1
456	Jewelry	1
457	Watches & Clocks	x
458	Mobile Homes	1
461	Broadcasting	1
462	CATV Systems	x
471	Motion Picture Production, Distribution and Theaters	1

473	Sporting Events	1
474	Other Entertainment	1
481	Apparel & Accessories Stores	1
482	Shoe Stores	1
491	Department Stores	1
501	Drug & Proprietary Stores	1
502	Discount & Variety Stores	1
511	Food Chain Stores	1
521	Automobile and Automotive Parts	1
522	Building Materials Sales	1
523	Drug Wholesalers	1
524	Electrical Equip. Distributors	1
526	Radio, TV Distributors	1
527	Grocery Wholesalers	1
528	Metals Distributors	1
529	Other Importers, Wholesalers & Retailers	1
531	Tires & Inner Tubes	1
532	Rubber and Plastic Products	1
541	Savings & Loan Associations	x
551	Leather Tanning, Finish & Prod	1
552	Footwear	1
561	Weaving Mills	1
562	Knitting Mills	x
571	Textile Manufacturers	1
581	Cigarettes	1
582	Other Tobacco Products	1
591	Electric Companies (Utilities)	1
592	Electric & Gas Companies	1
601	Gas & Oil Pipelines	1
602	Gas Utilities	1
603	Propane Gas Suppliers	1
604	Water Utilities	1

Note on "1" and "x":

By way of example, take 561 weaving mills and 562 knitting mills; if we invested in a company of one of these, "1," we would not invest in a company of the other, "x."

SELECTING SECURITIES WITHIN AN INDUSTRY

Having separated securities by industry with the aid of the above list, we are then ready to select one out of several candidates of an industry for a portfolio.

Assuming the investor has a long list of common stocks that meet the criteria for investment, he should consider several factors in selecting one security over another from this list:

1. *Dividend rate and dividend consistency over a long period*. Being compensated while waiting for the price to rise to investment value is a significant point.

2. *Earnings growth rate*. Prefer a company with a reasonably steady earnings growth to one of widely fluctuating earnings or to one of flat earnings, however do not rule out securities of the last two categories if the price is right.

3. *Highest previous price*. We are not so certain of what part this item should play in the selection process for a company whose investment vaue is higher than the stock's previous high price. A growing company may not as yet have posted its highest price. But a company of an industry long in disfavor among investors may not in the past have risen to investment value and may not rise to that for many more years. Therefore, the investor should give this factor some weight in picking one company over another for his portfolio. That is, he should favor those companies that have, in the past, recorded a price higher than investment value.

4. *Greatest Potential Gain*. After computing investment value and buy price of a security, the investor knows at that point what he *expects* to make on a purchase—50%, 100%, 200%, or 400%—depending upon the company size, the extent to which earnings fluctuate, and in some instances, the price at which he may buy a security that may be lower than his computed buy price.

The greater potential gains from the samller companies reflect our view of the greater risk involved in buying smaller companies. If the investor buys them, he does so at a greater discount from I.V. than for the larger companies and in this manner adjusts his buys for the risk factor.

Yet, does the investor choose a large company over a small one, in the same industry, in spite of the greater potential gain from a small or medium-sized company?

Our primary view is conservatism in investing. So, the investor should be leery of a portfolio with no large companies in it, even though Janos Aranyi, whose study is quoted in Chapter VI, showed that from 1948 to 1967 the smaller companies showed greater returns as a group than did the larger.

5. *Pension Liabilities*. The unfunded vested pension benefits as a percentage of net worth is another item to

consider in selecting one security over another. The smaller that ratio is, the better, obviously.

6. *Percent Debt to Total Capital*. Although the common stock investments will not have more than one-third debt to total capital, we prefer less.

With less than a one-third debt ratio our company could borrow more with less chance of exceeding the debt limit, while the investor holds it for disposal at investment value.

The investor will make his selection of one company over another in the same industry by considering the above 6 factors visually.

Also, he'll use the same approach in selecting securities for his portfolio for one security over another in different industries.

TRANSACTIONS VS. PRICE CHANGE

Now let's wrestle with another one. How much money may we put into each stock?

The investor with a small account will have no trouble with this question.

Since the system calls for investing uniform amounts in each security in a portfolio of common stocks, the investor with a few hundred million will have a question about the amount to invest in each.

We looked at this question from the viewpoint of what portion of a company's stock might one buy (or sell) but not change the price more than 2%.

The *M/G Financial Weekly* compiles weekly data on percent market value of stocks traded and percent price change.

The *Weekly* compiles such data for each stock and industry and for all stocks combined. The trouble is that the ratio of percent market value of securities traded to percent price change varies considerably, zero to 20, according to one observation.

Nevertheless, Table XI-2 shows data for two weeks of trading for the composite of all stocks traded on the NYSE, ASE, and OTC.

TABLE XI-2

	MARKET VALUE TRADED VS. TOTAL MARKET VALUE %	FROM PREVIOUS WEEK, PRICE CHANGE %	PERCENT MARKET VALUE TRADED AND PERCENT PRICE CHANGE RATIO
Week ended 3-12-82	.91	−1.3	1: 1.43
Week ended 3-19-82	.71	+1.8	1: 2.53

(On 3-19-82 total value of all common stocks traded on NYSE, ASE, and OTC = $\$1.160 \times 10^{12}$)

So as to give *some* aid to the investor, we will use, as an extremely rough guide, the basis that a trade of 1% of outstanding shares of a stock will change its price 2%.

For example, see Table X1-3.

TABLE XI-3

IF SHARES OUTSTANDING ARE	A TRADE OF 1% OF THESE	AT A PRICE OF	FOR A TOTAL TRANSACTION VALUE OF*	WILL PROBABLY CHANGE THE PRICE 2%.
1,000,000	10,000	$25	$ 250,000	$0.50
10,000,000	100,000	$20	$2,000,000	$0.40

*Commission omitted.

Because our basis for the 1% trade causing a 2% price change is flimsy, the investor should expect some surprises in his large value transactions for common stocks. But he should work with his broker on these, since it may take several days to buy or sell a large batch within a small price range.

PORTFOLIO SIZE—NUMBER AND DOLLARS

Now for another phase of our program of setting up a portfolio of common stocks.

TABLE XI-4

1973–1974 PORTFOLIO
DOLLAR VALUE OF 1% OF OUTSTANDING SHARES

1	2	3	4	5	6
	NO. SHARES OUT. $\times 10^6$	1% OF SHARES $\times 10^6$	PER SHARE BUY PRICE	TOTAL DOLLAR VALUE (3×4) $\times 10^6$	COMPANY ACTIVITY
Johns Manville	L 18.484	.185	$16.	$ 2.960	Mining, Industrial Build. Prod.
Akzona	12.429	.124	11.63	1.440	Synth. fibre, cable, salt, chem.
Alberto Culver	4.273	.043	8.13	.350	Hair care, beauty aid, food
Altamil	S 1.685	.017	1.25	.021	Truck hdware, boxes
Amer. Broadcasting Cos.	L 17.186	.172	14.50	2.495	TV, Radio networks, theatre
Amer. Greetings	13.630	.136	6.88	.935	Cards & gift wrap
Amer. Rubber & Plast.	S .450	.004	3.38	.015	Sponge, rubber, plastic foam
Amer. Smelt. & Ref.	L 26.737	.267	15.	4.000	Nonferrous metals, copper
Anchor Hocking*	6.853	.068	19.38	1.320	Glass, tableware, containers
Anderson Clayton	6.228	.062	10.25	.635	Foods & related prod.
Angelica Corp.	6.141	.061	5.00	.305	On-the-job apparel/uniforms
Assoc. Coca Cola Bot.	6.036	.060	5.50	.330	Soft drinks, bott. distr.
Avon Prod.	L 57.991	.580	19.25	11.200	Cosmetics distr. by housewives
Ball Corp.*	4.635	.046	10.50	.482	Glass cont'r, metal, rubber
Basset Furn.	7.636	.076	11.88	.900	Mfg. wood furniture/houses
Binks Mfg.	1.873	.019	9.	.170	Mfg. coatings applic. equip.
Borg Warner	L 18.266	.183	17.38	3.180	Widely divers. prod.
Bowne & Co.	S 1.973	.020	5.50	.110	Finance Corp. printing
British Petroleum	L386.100	3.861	6.	23.200	Oil
Brockway Glass*	4.764	.047	12.	.565	Glass containers
Brown Forman Dist.	11.976	.120	7.50	.900	Largest independent distiller
Brush Wellman	2.261	.022	7.63	.168	Makes beryllium alloys
Bundy Corp.	2.702	.027	6.38	.172	Steel tubing, eng'd plast.
Total				$55.853	

*Although these companies make glass products, the *M/G Financial Weekly* lists each of the 3 in a different industry.

How many common stocks in a portfolio?

That will depend upon the number of securities that fit our investment criteria that we expect to find in a market decline and the amount of money available for investment.

Although we have 126 industries from which to choose stocks for a diversified portfolio, we found, through a projection for the 1973–1974 market decline of 45%, 163 large, medium, and small companies that qualified for investment.

Continuing, we compiled Table XI-4 (using the stocks in the 1973–1974 portfolio), which shows total shares outstanding for each company, 1% of these, buy price, and the total of 1% of the outstanding shares times buy price.

From these data we compiled Table XI-5 showing the dollar amounts of the portfolio by company size that we could buy but not exceed 1% of the total value of any company in each size class.

TABLE XI-5

1	2	3	4	5	6
CO. SIZE	NO. IN PORT-FOLIO	A 1% INVESTMENT IN SMALLEST OF GROUP $\times 10^6$	TOTAL (2×3) $\times 10^6$	IF WE CHECKED OUT ALL SECURITIES IN *STOCK GUIDE*, WE EST. WE WOULD HAVE 7.1 TIMES TOTAL IN (4) $\times 10^6$	PROJECTED POTENTIAL NO. IN PORTFOLIO $7.1 \times (2)$
L	6	$2.495	$14.970	$106.287	43
M	14	.168	2.350	$ 16.685	99
S	3	.015	.045	.320	21
	23	.015	.345	2.450	163

According to data in Table XI-5, we could have invested $15,000 in each of the 163 for a total of $\$2.5 \times 10^6$ in a portfolio and probably not have bought more than 1% of any company. Then, projecting that to not more than 5% in any one company, our portfolio could have grown to over $\$12 \times 10^6$ for the common stock portion.

Although we had 163 securities to choose from for our portfolio in the 1973–1974 market drop and could accommodate a 12×10^6 common stock portfolio, the picture changes somewhat when we have a large portfolio and need to invest, say, 10×10^6 in each security.

According to our 1973–1974 portfolio data, an investment of 10×10^6 in a medium-sized company, where $168,000 represented not over 1% of any one company of that size, might have meant buying 60% of that company. But we shun investing in more than 5% of a company. So, what we would do here is buy several medium-sized companies at not over 5% of the smallest of this size class until the total of these equaled the 10×10^6 equivalent investment in a single large company.

For example, for the 1973–1974 portfolio we found a projected total of 99 medium-sized companies of which an investment of $168,000 in the smallest of these was not over 1% of that size company. A 5% investment would, therefore, be $840,000 per medium-sized company. So, we would need about 12 medium-sized companies in the portfolio to equal the 10×10^6 investment in a large company as we show in Table XI-6.

If the goal is 25 companies for our portfolio, and we find 24 large ones and 12 mediums, we would have a total of 36 companies in the portfolio, but consider that we had the equivalent of 25 large companies in our package.

In a large-dollar-value portfolio the investor will have a hard time finding 133 small companies to fulfill an equivalent 10×10^6 buy of a large company, but he might find 11 to make up the equivalent of one medium-sized company ($.840 ÷ .075 = 11).

Using these data, here's how we would have invested portfolios of various dollar amounts for the 1973–1974 market drop when we found 163 companies of various sizes but limited our buys to 5% of any company (see Table XI-7).

Notice from Table XI-7 that for an account of 2×10^6 or

TABLE XI-6

NUMBER OF SMALLER COMPANIES EQUIVALENT TO ONE LARGE COMPANY

	1	2	3	4*
COMPANY SIZE	NO. OF BUYS WE EXPECTED TO FIND IN THE 1973–1974 MARKET DROP	A 1% INVESTMENT IN SMALLEST COMPANY OF GROUP $\times 10^6$	A 5% INVESTMENT (5 TIMES COLUMN 2) $\times 10^6$	NO. OF SMALLER COMPANIES NEEDED TO EQUAL AN INVESTMENT OF $\$10 \times 10^6$ IN A LARGE COMPANY ($\$10 \times 10^6 \div$ COLUMN 3)
Large	43	$2.495	$12.475	
Medium	99	.168	.840	12
Small	21	.015	.075	133
Total	163			

*Example of Computation: Medium, $= \dfrac{\$10 \times 10^6}{.804 \times 10^6} = 12$,

and Small $= \dfrac{\$10 \times 10^6}{.075 \times 10^6} = 133$.

Data for columns 1 and 2 extracted from Table XI-5.

less we were able to use all 163 stocks on our potential buy list for selecting up to 25 for our portfolio, but not buy over 5% of any company.

As the amount to invest per security increased, the fewer were the equivalent number of large companies we had to select from.

According to the number of securities we found for the 1973–1974 market drop (on a projected basis), we could have accommodated a common stock portfolio of $\$625 \times 10^6$ composed of securities that met our investment criteria. The limit on the common stock portfolio size will have to do with the number of stocks we can find for investment that meet our qualifications.

One reason we were limited to a potential 163 companies

TABLE XI-7

BUYING NOT MORE THAN 5% OF ANY COMPANY

COMMON STOCK PORTFOLIO SIZE VS.
SECURITIES AVAILABLE
DATA BASED ON THE 45% MARKET DROP, 1973–1974

COMMON STOCK PORTFOLIO SIZE $	NO.	AMOUNT IN EACH SECURITY $	NO. OF EQUIVALENT LARGE COMPANIES TO SELECT FROM L	M	S		POTENTIAL BUY LIST TOTAL EQUIVALENT LARGE COMPANIES TO SELECT FROM TO BUILD PORTFOLIO
5,000	15	333	43	99	21	=	163
10,000	20	500	43	99	21	=	163
25,000	25	1,000	43	99	21	=	163
50,000	25	2,000	43	99	21	=	163
100,000	25	4,000	43	99	21	=	163
250,000	25	10,000	43	99	21	=	163
500,000	25	20,000	43	99	21	=	163
1,000,000	25	40,000	43	99	21	=	163
2,000,000	25	80,000	32	99	21	=	163
10,000,000	25	400,000	43	99	4	=	146
100,000,000	25	4,000,000	43	21	0.4	=	64
200,000,000	25	8,000,000	43	11	0.2	=	54
200,000,000	50	4,000,000	43	21	0.4	=	64
500,000,000	50	10,000,000	43	8	0.2	=	51
625,000,000	50	12,500,000	43	7	0.1	=	50

in the 1973–1974 market decline was that many of the other 3700 companies listed in Standard & Poor's *Stock Guide* had inadequate balance sheets.

If balance sheets continue to deteriorate, we should expect to find fewer than the 163 in the next substantial market decline. Of course, if balance sheets improve, we would expect to have a longer potential buy list to build our portfolio from and therefore be able to handle larger accounts with our system, if the market declines enough.

Also, at any time, the greater the market decline the

more securities would we expect to find for our potential buy list.

For the 45% market decline our retrospective study showed that we had 163 stocks to choose from but that at lesser declines we had fewer than that number, as we've noted in Appendix II—Chapter VIII.

At the start of a decline the investor will not know how big a dip the market will take.

So, what he should do is, first, decide on the number of stocks he will have in the common stock section of his portfolio, say 25. Then, as he finds stocks that fit the criteria, while the market declines, he should buy them as he finds them.

If he finds 10 of his goal of 25 when the market turns around toward a new high, he would have to be satisfied with that number and keep the cash for the other 15 in his bond portfolio.

Should the investor have aimed for a portfolio of 50 stocks and found but 10 before the market started up again, he would have had funds for 40 allocated for but uninvested in stocks.

Consequently, in many instances, the investor will be better assured of completing his portfolio if he aims for a limited number of securities in it, say, 25 rather than 100.

However, in those instances of a sudden, steep market drop when the investor discovers something like 300 stocks that meet our criteria, there is no good reason why he should limit his portfolio to 25.

A batch of money spread over 100 as against 25 stocks will permit individual transactions of smaller amounts, making it easier to buy and sell at desired prices, although transaction costs may be slightly higher.

BOND PORTFOLIO—DIVERSIFICATION

The investor will make up his bond or fixed-income portfolio with savings accounts, Treasury bills, Treasury notes,

Treasury bonds, federal agency bonds, bankers' acceptances, commercial paper, and industrial bonds and notes including those for transportaton companies and utilities.

There are many ways he may distribute these funds. We suggest that he place three-quarters of his fixed-income portfolio into items maturing in one year or less and the other quarter into high-grade issues maturing in 2, 3, and 4 years.

One compilation from Moody's manuals and First Boston's *Handbook of Securities of the United States Government and Federal Agencies* showed that the investor had $\$500 \times 10^9$ of short maturity issues to select from, such as public utility, transportation, and industrial bonds; Treasury bills, notes, and bonds; and commercial paper and bankers' acceptances.

XII
FUNDS DISTRIBUTION—STOCKS AND CASH ITEMS

In setting up a policy for managing a portfolio, we take into account not only the need for diversification but also the need for dealing with the significant matter of subsequent price drops after we have bought a common stock portfolio.

It is unsettling for the investor to see his excellent bargain-priced selections, bought for a price rise, decline substantially at times.

Our 1973–1974 portfolio of 25 stocks experienced an average price drop of 20% from buy price to low before rising to the sell price, with a range of individual price declines of 3.3% to 51.0% from buy to low.

The Depression portfolio of 26 stocks experienced an even worse result by declining 54% after our purchases, with individual declines ranging from 2.7% to 89.5% from buy to low.

For additional perspective we compiled the price declines of Cowles P-2 industrials index and the Dow Jones industrial average for a 100-year plus period and found that there were 25 major market declines in this period. Eight of these were of 40% or more, while another 3 were close to that, 36% to 38%, as we note in Table XII-1.

It is during these times of severe market drops that the

TABLE XII-1
MARKET DECLINES 1870–1978

COWLES P-2 INDUSTRIALS INDEX

	HIGH	LOW	% DECLINE
1873	23.7	19.3	19
1874	24.0		
1877		14.9	38
1881	24.7		
1884		18.7	24
1889	34.3		
1890		25.1	27
1892	33.4		
1893		20.2	40
1895	26.4		
1896		18.6	30
1899	37.8		
1900		29.9	21
1901	43.3		
1903		24.3	44
1906	48.9		
1907		26.8	45
1909	55.8		
1911		41.7	25
1912	54.1		
1915		39.0	28
1916	77.3		
1917		49.4	36
1919	82.5		
1921		46.5	44

DOW JONES INDUSTRIAL AVERAGE

	HIGH	LOW	% DECLINE
1929	381.		
1932		41.	89
1937	194.		
1938		99.	49
1939	156.		
1942		93.	40
1946	213.		
1949		162.	24
1952	292.		
1953		256.	12
1956	521.		
1957		420.	19
1961	735.		
1962		536.	27
1966	995.	744.	25
1968	985.		
1970		631.	36
1971	951.	798.	16
1973	1052.		
1974		578.	45
1976	1015.		
1978		742.	27
1980	1024.		

investor may discover even better bargains than he bought for his portfolio.

Along with this conservative security evaluation system, carry the conservatism to managing a portfolio.

That means keeping some money in cash items ready for buying more stocks if the market continues to decline after you've bought your first round of common stocks.

FUNDS DISTRIBUTION POLICY

We've opted for a funds distribution policy of 25% bonds-75% common stocks for the first buy round. Here's how that 25%-75% funds distribution plan would work.

You have $10,000,000 to invest. Start with $2,500,000 in bonds and $7,500,000 in common. Say, also, that you want 50 stocks in your portfolio, making for a $150,000 investment in each common stock in the first buy round.

Let's assume that the market declines slowly, producing stocks that meet the criteria one or two at a time. Buy these as they show up until you have your 50. On this first buy round expect to make 50% on the large companies, whose earnings fluctuate mildly or not at all.

The market continues to decline. But you are ready for the second buy round by designating half of your cash items portfolio of $2,500,000 or $1,250,000 for the purchase of another 50 stocks at $25,000 each.

When to buy the second round? Not until prices dropped enough to enable you to make twice the expected gain of the previous buy round. For example, in a first buy round you expect to make 50% on our large company buys, but on a second buy round invest only when prices declined enough so that, theoretically, you could make twice that, or 100%, on each large company. Buy these one at a time, as they show up, until you have an additional 50 in your common stock portfolio.

Should the general market continue to drop repeat the process for the third buy round: half of remaining cash items, $625,000, into another 50 stocks at $12,500 each, on which you expect to make 200% on the large companies.

(For medium-sized companies of non-widely-fluctuating earnings expect to make twice what you expect to make on the large companies for each round, and for the small companies, twice what you expect to make on the medium-sized companies. See Table XII-2 for this program.)

TABLE XII-2

FUNDS DISTRIBUTION SYSTEM

STARTING WITH 25% BONDS—75% COMMON FOR FIRST BUY ROUND (AS THE MARKET CONTINUES TO DECLINE)

INVEST-MENT BUY ROUND	OF $10,000,000 IN ORIGINAL FUNDS, AMOUNT ALLOCATED TO: CASH ITEMS $	COMMON $	CASH ITEMS %	COMMON %	ADDITIONAL AMOUNT INTO COMMON $	AMT. INTO EACH OF 50 STOCKS EACH ROUND $	EXPECTED GAIN LARGE COMPANIES EACH ROUND %	PER SHARE BUY PRICE LARGE COS IF I.V. = $30 $
1st	2,500,000	7,500,000	25	75		150,000	50	20
2nd	1,250,000	8,750,000	12½	87½	1,250,000	25,000	100	15
3rd	625,000	9,375,000	6¼	93¾	625,000	12,500	200	10
4th	312,500	9,687,500	3⅛	96⅞	312,500	6,250	400	6
5th	156,250	9,843,750	1 9/16	98 7/16	156,250	3,125	800	3⅓

I.V. = Investment value (selling price)
Cash items: Bonds, Treasury bills, Treasury notes, money market instruments, cash.

Having cash ready for additional investment in stocks when prices decline further is conservative and, therefore, worry-free investing.

Instead of concern about a further market decline, the investor may welcome one so that he might buy more at better bargains than those of his previous buy round.

From the data in Table XII-2 the investor may expect to make $3,750,000 on the first buy round, then an extra $1,250,000, for each of the second, third, fourth, and fifth buy rounds, plus interest and dividends, on large companies.

BASIS FOR FUNDS DISTRIBUTION SYSTEM

We discuss in Appendix II-Chapter XII why we selected the 25% bonds-75% stocks plan (for the first buy round) over 4 other plans.

PART FOUR

GENERAL

XIII
COMPILING A POTENTIAL BUY LIST

Having established a security evaluation and portfolio management system, we need an efficient method for compiling a list of securities for evaluation in order to eliminate the need for analyzing 3500 or so.

STEP-BY-STEP LISTING AND EVALUATING

Let's start with our favorite method of making a potential investment list of common stocks, indicate the step-by-step analysis, then show the format for selecting one security over another for a portfolio.

1. The *M/G Financial Weekly*.

List companies whose P/E ratio is less than 10.0, whose equity per share is at least twice long-term debt per share, and whose current ratio is 2.0 or more.

This exercise in early 1979 produced a list of 747 prospects out of the 3300 listed in the *Weekly*. (This method of screening will eliminate companies that do not report current assets or current liabilities: finance companies, insurance companies, savings and loan associations, and banks. We seldom invest in these.

However, this screening method will also eliminate companies that carry no product inventory, whose current assets need but equal current liabilities: advertising agencies, utilities, railroads, airlines, and trucking companies. These could be candidates for investment.)

2. Moody's Manuals.

a. Refigure the debt ratio for the prospects by including short-term debt and by using tangible net worth. With this exercise 138 were eliminated from the initial list of 747.

b. Compute working capital (WC).

c. Determine net quick assets (NQA).

d. Adjustments. If current assets are not twice current liabilities or NQA are negative, add the largest deficiency of these to debt (and to WC and call it adjusted working capital), then note the new debt. Reject if over a third of total capital.

3. Standard & Poor's "Stock Reports" and Moody's "News Reports."

a. Determine investment value using diluted earnings, including extraordinary items. Reject if fewer than 10 years of earnings are reported (Chapter VIII).

b. Determine if company is in the widely fluctuating earnings category from a scan of 10 years of earnings. (Skip the 15-year scan for now.)

c. Determine buy price (Table VIII-1). If the buy price is close to the current price, continue the analysis.

4. Annual Reports.

a. Include present value of noncancelable operating leases as well as noncancelable capital leases in debt.

b. Compute ratio of unfunded vested pension benefits to net worth.

c. Determine fixed-charge coverage. Include annual payments for noncancelable leases. These to be 7 times before taxes for the average of the 3 latest years, but 2.5 times for utilities after taxes.

d. Read the notes to the financial statements noting adverse items.

5. Make a table of potential buys (Table XIII-1) to include the following data:

a. Company name

b. Industry group number (The *M/G Financial Weekly*)

c. Common stock outstanding (Standard & Poor's "Stock Reports")
d. Investment value (sell price)
e. Buy price
f. Widely fluctuating earnings notation
g. Expected gain, buy-sell, in percent
h. Percent debt to tangible capital
i. Ten-year average growth per year
j. Five-year average growth per year (The *M/G Financial Weekly*)
k. Fixed-charge coverage before taxes
l. High price since 1960 (Standard & Poor's *Stock Guide*)
m. Unfunded vested pension benefits as a percent of tangible net worth (Annual reports)
n. Dividend yield (The *M/G Financial Weekly* or the *Wall Street Journal*)
o. Latest price
Check this price with the current number of shares outstanding against the number outstanding when I.V. was computed. There may have been a stock dividend declared since you computed I.V.

6. List the stocks on this table of potential buys that meet the balance sheet criteria and whose buy price is close to the current price.

7. Decide on the number of stocks to be in the portfolio and select a diversified portfolio of these.

8. Recheck each company selected for widely fluctuating earnings by noting 5 additional years of earnings for a total of 15 (Moody's manuals).

9. Advertising Agencies and Transportation Companies. The *M/G Financial Weekly*, in one of its sections, lists companies by industry. From the advertising and transportation groups, list companies for additional screening from the advertising and transportation industries, whose equity per share is at least twice long-term debt. Next, follow the

steps from 2 through 8, adjusting, if necessary, current assets so they at least equal current liabilities, then adding this adjustment to debt. If the adjusted debt is greater than one-third of total capital, reject.

10. Utilities.

From the utility industry group, list those companies whose equity per share is equal to or greater than long-term debt per share; and, as in item 9 above, follow the steps from 2 through 8, adjusting current assets so that they at least equal current liabilities, then adding the adjustment to debt. If the adjusted debt is greater than one-half of total capital, reject.

11. Potential Buys—1979 (Partial Listing) (Table XIII-1).

To help in selecting a portfolio from this table, circle the adverse items: the high price since 1960 if it was lower than I.V., the high unfunded vested pension benefits to net worth, the fixed-charge coverage if it was less than 7.0 times before taxes for industrials or less than 2.5 times after taxes for utilities, and the 5-year growth rate if it shows flatness vs. a robust 10-year growth rate.

Favored investments from this list include:

CBS, Inc.
Colgate-Palmolive Company
Cummins Engine Company, Inc.
Hersey Foods Corporation
Monsanto Company
North American Philips Corp.
Textron Inc.
V. F. Corp.

As a final note on this method of finding securities for investment, the project that produced 60 stocks of adequate balance sheets and buy prices close to or lower than current prices (of which are listed 16 in Table XIII-1), took 104 man–hours to complete.

For an organization of security analysts, the effort of ana-

TABLE XIII–1

POTENTIAL BUYS—1979 (PARTIAL LISTING)

	INDUSTRY GROUP NO.	I.V. END 1ST Q 1979–1ST Q 1980 $	BUY PRICE $	COMMON OUT. WHEN I.V. COMPUTED × 10^6	EXPECTED GAIN %	DEBT TO TOTAL TANG. CAP. %	AVG. GROWTH PER YEAR (SIMPLE BASIS) FOR LATEST 10 yrs %	5 yrs %	NOTE IF WFE	1960–1978 HIGH PRICE $	UNFUND. PENS. BEN. TO TANG. N.W. %	DIV. YIELD %	FIXED CHGE. COVER. B.T. ×	PRICES 7/29/79 $
Anderson Clay.	192	35.40	23.60	13.561	50	9.3	36	13		26¼	0	5.0	10.9	20¾
Blue Bell	571	47.20	31.50	12.524	50	25.1	48	41		31⅝	0	6.0	11.1	26⅛
CBS	461	80.40	53.60	27.711	50	17.9	21	22		69¾	0	5.2	40.0	53½
Champ. Sprk. Plug	032	13.60	9.07	38.100	50	16.0	6	4		20¼	22	7.7	21.1	12
Colgate-Palm.	191	29.60	19.80	81.875	50	27.0	17	10		35⅜	0	6.4	15.2	16½
Cone Mills	561	60.20	40.14	5.794	50	18.6	73	39		33⅞	0	5.0	21.0	30¼
Cummins Engine	285	83.80	41.90	8.300	100	29.5	19	34	WFE	69⅜	4	4.2	6.6	33¼
Dana Corp.	032	44.00	29.30	32.611	50	27.6	23	25		32⅞	17	5.2	14.4	27½
Harsco Cp.	312	57.60	38.60	9.657	50	23.3	22	21		36⅞	5	6.2	20.8	29⅛
Hershey Foods	212	40.20	20.10	13.745	100	11.8	20	19	WFE	40¾	7	6.8	31.0	20
Johns Manville	057	39.80	26.27	21.642	50	25.0	8	26		46⅛	0	6.8	10.	25⅛
Monsanto Co.	101	120.20	80.14	36.150	50	31.7	27	−2.4		100	2	7.0	6.6	50⅞
No. Amer. Philips	161	53.30	26.65	12.941	100	31.6	12	22		60¾	2	5.8	8.9	28
Robins, A. H.	151	12.10	8.06	26.127	50	16.1	8	3		40¾	0	4.5	18.7	10⅛
Textron	341	41.60	27.73	35.586	50	17.2	10	14		57⅞	0	7.3	14.	26⅞
V. F. Corp.	562	42.60	28.40	9.909	50	18.0	15	5		34¼	0	7.7	13.3	17⅜

Notes: I.V. = Investment Value
WFE = Widely Fluctuating Earnings
B.T. = Before Taxes
Manville and A. H. Robins have large law suits pending.

lyzing several thousand securities according to a specific system will be no problem at all. But for the lone investor who works full time but plans on extracting some gains from his savings, analyzing several thousand securities part time could take a complete market cycle to investigate. So, let's find some shortcuts.

How might one select a smaller group of securities for investigation where a larger proportion of those investigated produced an adequate portfolio that meets the investment criteria?

Here are some ideas.

SHORTCUTS TO COMPILING A POTENTIAL BUY LIST

1. *3-Trend CYCLI-GRAPHS*. On these graphs the price scale is 15 times the earnings scale. Consequently, list from these graphs those companies whose price is some distance below the 15-times-earnings scale as candidates for investigation.

Of the 4 graphs on the page extracted from the *3-Trend CYCLI-GRAPHS*, Revlon, Inc. and Revere Copper & Brass, Inc. would not have been listed for investigation. Resistoflex Corp. would have been investigated for 1966, 1973, 1974, 1975, 1976, and 1977, and Revco D.S., Inc. in 1966 and 1974.

In actual practice the investor will examine the latest year of the graph only. He will find data on about 1000 securities graphed from which to make his initial potential investment list.

The investor would examine the balance sheet of each company he listed and cross off those from the list that did not meet that part of the security evaluation system.

For those that pass that part of the test, he would compute the I.V. and buy price of each and compare that to the current price. He would check the company's annual re-

FIGURE XIII–1

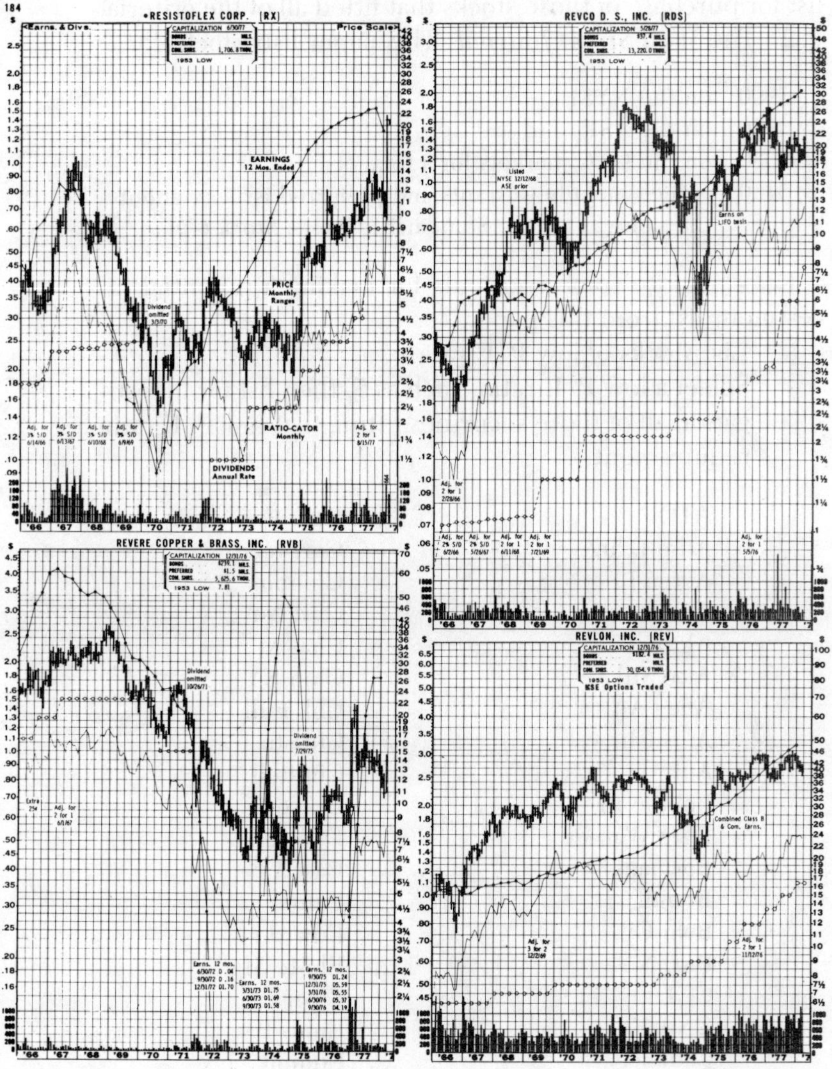

port of these tentative buys, then put together a diversified list for purchase of those stocks that fitted all of the criteria.

2. The *Wall Street Journal*. This paper lists stocks for

1900	on the NYSE,
930	on the ASE, and
2330	on the OTC markets for a total of
5160	(which include warrants and preferred issues), about the same as for the Standard & Poor's *Stock Guide*.

Let's explore some shortcuts for making a potential investment list from this paper.

a. List stocks of low P/E ratios.
Select a low P/E ratio, such as 5, then list for investigation all of those securities fitting that low P/E ratio requirement.

ATO		Caro Frg	
Adm Drug		Cert-teed	
Aetna Lf	x	Chmpin	
Ahmanson	x	Chrt NY	x
Alcan A		Chas M	x
Alco Std		Chm NY	x
Alleg Air		Chk Full	
Allis Ch		Christn	x
Am Air		Cin Bell	
Bobbie Br		Dorsey	
Borg Warner		Dyn Am	
Bormans		East Air	
Braniff		Eaton	
Bwn Gp		Edwrd	x
Burl No		El Me Mg	
CCI		Elixir	
CNA Fn	x	Ennis B	
Cadence		Equimk	x
Cd Pac		Ethyl	
Carlisle		Evan Prod	

Total = 40

36 THE WALL STREET JOURNAL, Monday, Feb. 5, 1979

Friday's Volume

28,986,110 Shares; 73,500 Warrants

TRADING BY MARKETS

	Shares	Warrants
New York Exchange	25,350,000	72,400
American Exchange	200	....
Midwest Exchange	1,203,800	....
Pacific Exchange	1,081,600	....
Nat'l Assoc. of Securities Dealers	689,110	1,100
Philadelphia Exchange	362,300	....
Boston Exchange	116,200	....
Cincinnati Exchange	100,100	....
Instinet System	82,800	....

NYSE–Composite

Volume since Jan. 1:	1979	1978	1977
Total shares	759,694,040	564,914,230	670,676,567
Total warrants	2,918,232	3,099,700	2,986,650

New York Stock Exchange

Volume since Jan. 1:	1979	1978	1977
Total shares	668,899,644	492,840,100	574,812,697
Total warrants	2,798,700	3,099,600	2,981,300

MOST ACTIVE STOCKS

	Open	High	Low	Close	Chg.	Volume
Carrier Cp.	27⅛	27¼	26⅞	26⅞	– ⅜	657,500
McGrw Hill	29½	31½	29⅝	30¼	+1¼	458,000
Gard Denv.	30⅜	30⅜	30	30¼	– ⅛	308,300
Boeing	76⅜	78⅛	76¼	76⅝	+ ¼	266,300
Firestone	13⅛	13⅛	12¾	13	– ⅛	260,000
ICN Pharm.	6⅜	6⅞	6⅛	6⅞	+ ⅜	215,100
McDer 2.60pf	30⅜	30⅝	30⅜	30½	+ ¼	213,100
SearsRoeb	21	21⅜	20⅝	20¾	– ⅜	205,200
Exxon	51⅛	51¼	50⅞	51	– ⅛	205,100
Saxon Ind.	5¼	5⅜	5¼	5⅜	....	204,900
AmExpress	29¾	29¾	29⅛	29⅜	– ⅜	204,700
LawterCh	11½	12⅛	11½	12⅛	+ ½	193,900
Transco Cos.	22⅛	24⅛	22⅛	23⅜	+1⅜	184,500
Texaco Inc.	24½	24½	24	24	– ¼	178,700
Asarco Inc.	19	19⅛	18⅝	19	– ⅛	177,500

52 Weeks High	Low	Stock	Div.	Yld %	P-E Ratio	Sales 100s	High	low	Close	Net Chg.
		– A–A–A –								
39½	28⅞	ACF	2.10	7.0	7	141	30¼	30	30⅛	– ¼
23⅜	15½	AMF	1.24	7.2	8	269	17⅜	17	17⅛	....
32⅞	14⅛	AM Intl	.28	1.3	8	145	23⅜	22	22⅛	–1⅛

NYSE-Composite Transact

Friday, February 2, 1979

Quotations include trades on the New York, Midwest, Pacific, Philadelphia, Boston and C exchanges and reported by the National Association of Securities Dealers and Ir

Of 300 securities in this excerpted section of the *Wall Street Journal* 40 had a P/E ratio of 5 or less. After crossing off the banks, insurance companies, real estate companies, and closed-end investment trusts, 31 remained.

Since there are 1900 securities listed in this section of the *Journal*, we might expect to find 6⅓ times 31 or 200 from the NYSE alone that would be worth the analyst's investigative effort.

b. List stocks reporting deficits.
Those stocks reporting deficits will show a blank in the P/E ratio column of the *Wall Street Journal* (Skip the preferreds, closed-end funds, real estate companies, finance companies, warrants, banks, and insurance companies.)

Aileen	Caro Co
Allied Prod	Chrysler
Bulova	Chelsea
Brns RL	Dillingham
Buttes	Dutch B

Ten were in this deficit category. Projecting that 10 by 6⅓, you would expect to find 63 deficit companies for investigation from the list of NYSE securities.

In another exercise, the *M/G Financial Weekly* (Mar. 5, 1979) yielded a list of companies reporting deficits on the NYSE (5), ASE (19), and the OTC (6), for a total of 30 that also had a current ratio of 2.0 or more and equity per share of at least twice long-term debt per share. Seven were rejected from this list after checking out the balance sheet of each of these from Moody's manuals in order to include short-term debt.

From Standard & Poor's "Stock Reports" and Moody's "Industrial News Reports" containing the latest earnings data, we determined investment value and buy price and found one selling at a price close to the computed buy price, Michigan Sugar Company. But we would shun investing in this company at our buy price which was inflated since the company reported extraordinary profits in 1974, 1975, and 1976, which were way out of line from their historical record. This project took 2¾ man–hours to complete.

c. Check out the new lows:
These are published daily in the *Wall Street Journal*. Sometimes this list is a source of buys.

3. Standard & Poor's *Stock Guide*. As for the *Wall Street Journal*, a. list stocks of low P/E Ratios and b. list stocks reporting deficits.

4. The *M/G Financial Weekly*. From the excerpted section of the *M/G Financial Weekly*, in another execise, we listed companies whose equity was at least twice long-term debt and whose current ratio was 2.0 or more. We found 20 out of the 52 companies listed or 38.5% (Table XIII-2).

The paper on April 3, 1978 listed

1560 stocks on the NYSE,
960 on the ASE, and
830 on the OTC market for a total of
3360.

Assuming that the .385 ratio would hold for the 3360, we would project, in this manner, 1290 for investigation.

To cut down this number, we eliminated from this list of 20 those that had a P/E ratio of over 10.0. We deducted 5 from the list of 20 for a remaining total of 15 or 29%. That would leave us with a projected total of 974 to investigate.

To reduce the list further, we deducted the 3 that had a negative growth rate bringing the total of this sample group down to 12, or 23% of the 52 in the excerpt. Projecting 23% against the total of 3360, we'd have 775 to investigate.

Then to cut down the list from there, we picked a dividend rate of 2.0% or less but found none to deduct. So we selected a dividend yield of 4.0% or less and found 4 more

FIGURE XIII–2

EXCERPT—THE *M/G FINANCIAL WEEKLY*

VEN-WIL NAME	IND GRP	5-YEAR ANNUAL GROWTH RATE %	P/E RATIO TODAY	DVD YIELD %	CUR-RENT RATIO	PER SHARE LONG TERM DEBT $	PER SHARE STOCK EQ-UITY $
Vendo Co	282	−57	NE	.0	2.3	2.21	13.09
Venice Ind	562	−37	NE	.0	3.7	4.90	7.85
Verex Corp	431	+20	10.5	.0	NA	8.79	13.48
Vestaur Secur	272	NA	NA	9.6	NA	NA	NA
V.F. Corp	562	+ 8	6.4	6.5	4.5	2.66	17.63
Viacom Intl Ind	462	+19	13.0	1.1	1.2	9.45	9.00
Va El & Pwr	591	− 2	7.4	8.8	1.0	27.09	18.89
Vornado Inc	502	−29	NE	.0	2.0	28.55	27.40
VSI Corp	012	+10	7.3	4.0	2.9	1.81	11.02
Vulcan Maters	057	+18	7.5	5.1	2.8	7.98	17.34
Wabash Inc	161	+29	6.3	3.2	2.8	13.35	9.74
Wachovia Corp	043	+10	8.0	3.7	NA	2.31	22.43
Wachovia Rlty	432	−72	NE	.0	NA	.00	10.55
Walgreen Co	501	+10	8.9	5.6	2.1	9.96	20.89
Walker, Hiram	141	− 1	8.0	5.6	3.9	2.87	35.42
Wallace B Fm	093	+13	7.6	3.6	3.1	1.64	17.07
Wallace Murr	058	+20	5.3	4.9	2.9	17.44	35.34
Wal-Mart St	502	+34	12.8	1.0	2.4	1.70	4.85
Walter, Jim	051	+11	6.1	4.9	2.3	36.27	36.91
Ward Foods	193	+32	7.5	.0	1.4	18.25	1.29
Warnaco Inc	571	−36	8.5	.0	2.0	14.72	16.25
Warner & Swas	291	+ 9	8.5	5.0	4.4	10.65	36.61
Warner Comms	471	+21	7.3	2.4	1.5	22.63	24.56
Warner-Lambert	151	+ 7	11.5	4.1	3.0	3.20	14.94
Wash Gas Lt	602	+ 2	8.5	8.0	1.7	44.14	31.80
Wash Natl Cp	261	0	6.8	4.8	NA	8.10	35.16
Wash Steel	312	− 2	6.6	5.6	2.4	10.60	28.76
Wash Wat Pwr	592	+ 7	9.2	8.4	1.3	36.27	22.17
Waste Mgmt	095	+21	11.4	1.9	1.1	7.39	9.37
Watkins Jhnsn	012	+ 6	11.3	2.0	3.4	5.35	16.80

FIGURE XII–2 (Cont'd)

EXCERPT—THE *M/G FINANCIAL WEEKLY*

VEN-WIL NAME	IND GRP	5-YEAR ANNUAL GROWTH RATE %	P/E RATIO TODAY	DVD YIELD %	CURRENT RATIO	PER SHARE LONG TERM DEBT $	PER SHARE STOCK EQUITY $
Wayne Goss	571	− 3	7.7	7.2	6.3	6.25	20.27
Wean United	282	+25	3.6	3.5	2.0	10.29	17.35
Webb Del E	241	+ 5	8.2	1.6	1.5	9.04	9.15
Weis Markets	511	+17	8.6	3.2	3.9	.00	19.33
Wells Fargo	049	+13	6.9	5.4	NA	13.54	27.08
Wells Far Mtg	432	−27	11.2	8.7	NA	2.74	17.36
West Point-P	561	+ 8	5.7	7.0	3.6	24.33	55.47
Westcst Trans	601	+ 8	9.0	6.2	1.3	28.72	24.74
Wstn Air Lines	021	− 1	8.6	4.8	.9	8.72	9.25
Wstn Bancorp	049	+ 9	6.5	5.2	NA	14.77	39.55
Wstn Co NA	351	+57	6.7	1.8	2.1	16.57	14.91
Wstn Pac Ind	421	+49	4.4	3.6	2.2	27.50	56.29
Wstn Publish	413	− 1	10.7	4.6	3.0	8.59	27.10
Wstn Union Cp	111	+ 3	6.7	8.6	1.3	42.44	36.69
Westinghouse	161	+ 7	5.4	5.8	1.3	4.72	26.34
Westvaco Cp	381	+ 9	7.0	4.8	3.3	14.96	27.58
Weyenbrg Shoe	552	+ 7	6.8	5.4	4.8	2.32	24.61
Weyerhauser	052	+ 8	9.8	3.6	2.1	8.60	14.04
Wheelabr-Frye	286	+22	10.9	3.6	1.7	6.17	16.47
Wheel Lk Erie	421	−22	NE	8.0	NA	25.29	192.06
Wheel Pitts St	312	−28	NE	.0	1.9	49.41	83.57
Whirlpool Cp	251	+10	7.2	5.5	2.5	2.39	15.29

TABLE XIII–2

POTENTIAL INVESTMENT LIST CONSTRUCTED FROM DATA IN THE *M/G FINANCIAL WEEKLY* EXCERPT

		1	2		3	4	5	6	7	8	9	10
			PER SHARE				5-YEAR ANNUAL	COLUMN NO. INVOLVED				
INITIAL LIST	IND. GROUP	CURRENT RATIO	LONG TERM DEBT	STOCK EQUITY	P/E RATIO	DIV. YIELD %	GROWTH RATE %	3	5	4	4	1
Vendo Cp	282	2.3	2.21	13.09	NE	0	−57	x	x	x	x	x
V. F. Corp	562	4.5	2.66	17.63	6.4	6.5	8					
VSI Corp	012	2.9	1.81	11.02	7.3	4.0	10				x	x
Vulcan Maters	057	2.8	7.98	17.34	7.5	5.1	18					x
Walgreen Co	501	2.1	9.98	20.89	8.9	5.6	10					x
Walker, Hiram	141	3.9	2.87	35.42	8.0	5.6	− 1		x			
Wallace B Fm	093	3.1	1.64	17.07	7.6	3.6	13				x	
Wallace-Murr	058	2.9	17.44	35.34	5.3	4.9	20					x
Wal-Mart St	502	2.4	1.70	4.25	12.8	1.0	34	x		x	x	x
Warner & Swas	291	4.4	10.65	36.61	8.5	5.0	9					
Warner-Lambert	151	3.0	3.20	14.94	11.5	4.1	7	x				x
Wash Steel	312	2.4	10.60	28.76	6.6	5.6	− 2		x			x
Watkins Jhnsn	012	3.4	5.35	16.80	11.3	2.0	6	x		x	x	
Wayne Goss	571	6.3	6.25	20.27	7.7	7.2	− 3		x			
Weis Markets	511	3.9	0	19.33	8.6	3.2	17				x	
West Point P	561	3.6	24.33	55.47	5.7	7.0	8					
Westn Pac Ind	421	2.2	27.50	56.29	4.4	3.6	49				x	x
Westn Publsh	413	3.0	8.59	27.10	10.7	4.6	− 1	x	x			x
Weyenbrg Shoe	552	4.8	2.32	24.61	6.8	5.4	7					
Whirlpool Co	251	2.5	2.39	15.29	7.2	5.5	10					x

Total = 20
Initial List = Current ratio is 2.0 or more and equity at least 2× debt.
Column 6 = Cross off if P/E is greater than 10.0.
Column 7 = Cross off if negative growth rate.
Column 8 = Cross off if dividend rate 2.0% or less.
Column 9 = Cross off if dividend rate 4.0% or less.
Column 10 = Cross off if current ratio is 3.0 or less.

to deduct. That gave us a remaining total of 8 out of the 52 in the excerpt or 15.4% for a projected total of 520 to investigate.

The investor could reduce the list further by eliminating those with a current ratio of 3.0 or less, in which case he could deduct another 4, leaving but 4 out of 52 in the excerpt, or 7.7%.

That 7.7% times the 3360 in the paper would result in a list of 260 to investigate.

The investor's next step would be to evaluate the balance sheet from Moody's manuals, determine fixed-charge coverage from data in the annual reports, then compute investment value and buy price from earnings listed in Standard & Poor's "Stock Reports."

5. The *Value Line Investment Survey*. The *Value Line Investment Survey* contains much useful data on 1700 companies which Value Line updates regularly.

The reports list the P/E ratio and dividend yield prominently at the top of the page for each security.

These reports also contain:

Fifteen years of earnings data, not diluted
Short-term and long-term debt
Current assets and current liabilities
Net worth and working capital
Interest coverage (not including noncancelable lease requirements)
Leases data (but not the present value of all noncancelable leases)

The investor may discover that he can make up his potential investment list faster from the *Wall Street Journal* or from the *M/G Financial Weekly* than from Value Line's sheets.

6. Standard & Poor's "Stock Reports". These Stock Reports contain the current ratio, long-term debt, shareholders' equity, working capital, and earnings.

7. *Barron's National Business and Financial Weekly*. Use the data in *Barron's* in the same manner as those from the *Wall Street Journal*. That is, list companies for investigation that have low P/E ratios for one list and companies that report deficits for another list. Then check out the balance sheet from Moody's manuals and earnings data from Standard & Poor's "Stock Reports."

XIV
OTHER PROMISING INVESTMENT PLANS

In a search for shortcuts to investing, let's explore some other promising methods.

STOCKS SELLING BELOW BOOK VALUE

(Book value is stockholders' tangible equity less the liquidating value of preferred shares.)

A test by Marine Midland Banks, Inc. over a 19-year period (1948–67) for 900 industrial stocks revealed that investing equal sums in all those stocks for which the book value exceeded the market value showed that this investment in stocks selling below book value outperformed Standard & Poor's index of 425 industrial stocks by 70% per year on the average.

Then note the 1973–1974 Portfolio, Table XIV-1. Of the 23 stocks in it, the buy price was below book value for 21, while 13 of these had a buy price of 40% or more below book value. However, we did not take book value into account in the security evaluation system, although we appear to endorse the system of investing in stocks selling below book value, indirectly.

Yet, the sell price was below book value for 8 of the 23 while higher for 15.

Obviously, our system of definite prices for buying and selling does not tie in very well with this book value concept of bargain-priced securities.

TABLE XIV–1

1973–1974 PORTFOLIO

BUY AND SELL PRICES VS. BOOK VALUE

	SIZE	BUY PRICE $	SELL PRICE $	1973 BOOK VALUE PER SHARE $	BOUGHT BELOW (−) OR ABOVE (+) BOOK VALUE %	SELL PRICE BELOW BOOK VALUE
Johns Manville	L	16.	24.	27.58	−42	√
Akzona	M	11.63	20.	24.43	−52	√
Alberto Culver	M	8.13	8.25	10.28	−21	√
Altamil	S	1.25	7.63	5.92	−79	
Am. Broadcast Cos	L	14.50	21.75	17.44	−17	
Am. Greetings	M	6.88	13.75	7.15	− 4	
Am. Rubber & Plast.	S	3.38	9.13	17.30	−81	√
Am. Smelt & Ref.	L	15.	20.50	29.00	−48	√
Anchor Hocking	M	19.38	26.38	25.09	−23	
Anderson Clayton	M	10.25	24.	17.70	−42	
Angelica Corp.	M	5.00	6.13	4.98	0	
Assoc. Coca Cola Bot.	M	5.50	11.	7.64	−28	
Avon Prod.	L	19.25	28.88	7.71	+149	
Ball Corp	M	10.50	19.25	17.83	−41	
Basset Furniture	M	11.88	20.	13.43	−12	
Binks Mfg.	M	9.00	18.	15.61	−42	
Borg Warner	L	17.38	23.75	33.47	−48	√
Bowne & Co.	S	5.50	10.88	8.80	−38	
British Pet.	L	6.00	16.50	12.24	−51	
Brockway Glass	M	12.00	32.75	26.28	−54	
Brown Fmn Dist.	M	7.50	14.25	9.95	−25	
Brush Wellman	M	7.63	18.25	22.50	−66	√
Bundy Corp.	M	6.38	10.25	12.86	−50	√

Note: Buy price and sell price extracted from Table VIII-10, p. 230.

A crucial point is when to *sell*. We do not feel that there is a *system* if that factor is missing, as it is for the book value idea.

Also, the bank made the study during a generally rising market. We would like to see one made during a flat market with an indication of how many work out profitably. In addition, we'd like to have some limits or signals for buying and selling, such as buy at 20% below book value and sell at

20% above book value for a potential gain of 50% with the results of such a plan over many years.

The furthest we would go, at this point, in treating stocks selling below book value is to examine a list of these for balance sheet and buy price analysis.

SECURITIES SELLING BELOW QUICK LIQUIDATING VALUE (Q.L.V.)

(Q.L.V. = Working capital minus the following: long-term debt, liquidating value of preferred, present value of noncancelable leases, present value of unfunded vested pension benefits, and any other liabilities except net worth.)

This figure, Q.L.V., shows the value of a company if it were liquidated quickly, disregarding fixed assets, such as plant and equipment.

We'll show four examples of companies that have sold at less than Q.L.V. and comment.

TABLE XIV–2

STOCKS THAT SOLD BELOW QUICK LIQUIDATING VALUE

	1977 BALANCE SHEET	I.V. PER SHARE	1978 BUY PRICE PER SHARE	1978 QUICK LIQUIDATING VALUE PER SHARE
Bond Industries	Not OK	0	0	$ 2.87
Craddock-Terry	Not OK	0	0	9.80
Esquire Radio & Elec.	OK	$21.70	$7.23	17.10
Publicker Ind.	Not OK	0	0	2.67

I.V. = Investment Value

The balance sheet of 3 of the 4 companies did not meet the usual investment criteria.

Esquire Radio & Electronics, Inc.

The investor would invest in only 1 of the 4 in Table XIV-2 according to the security evaluation system: Esquire Radio. He would buy at 7¼ and note the $17.10 per share of Q.L.V. as denoting additional value. Even if the inventory at $10.60 per share were to be written down to 25% of its value on the books, the *net* Q.L.V. would be $9.15 per share, making the company an excellent buy at $7¼ with that additional back-up in value.

The company, according to Form 10-K filed with the SEC, sells virtually all of its products to Montgomery Ward. Of course, this is an adverse factor, having but one customer. But the investor who bought the company at $7¼ with a back-up of $9.15 to $17.10 per share in Q.L.V. would have had a comfortable margin of safety in his investment.

(Also, in computing Q.L.V. the company's annual report did not contain data on leases. This was determined from the 10-K report, indicating that, after all, not all necessary data may be in the annual report. But many companies are generous about sending along a copy of the 10-K report as well as the annual report upon request.)

To comment further on investment value, buy price, and quick liquidating value, the investor will note readily that finding and investing in a diversified portfolio of securities as exemplified by Esquire Radio: growing earnings, sound balance sheet, increasing dividends, buy price appropriately below investment value *and* below a conservative interpretation of Q.L.V., that we will have a group of securities that could ride out a bad economic cycle and, by hanging on, make money in the process.

Bond Industries, Inc.

According to the annual report for 1977, Bond Industries is liquidating its primary business.

First, you would not have bought the company on the

basis of the security evaluation system since the company's fixed-charge coverage was negative.

Its stockholders' equity was $\$22.2 \times 10^6$, according to the annual report, but present value of noncancelable leases was $\$10.3 \times 10^6$, reducing that equity figure to $\$11.9 \times 10^6$ or $12.25 per share.

The Q.L.V. was $2.87 per share after making allowance for the $\$10.3 \times 10^6$ of noncancelable leases. But deducting 25% of the inventory would give a negative figure for Q.L.V.

We would pass up investing in this company because of our conservative bent.

Publicker Industries Inc.

Although the company's Q.L.V. was $2.67 per share in 1977, its stockholders' equity was $\$93.8 \times 10^6$ in 1974 and $\$80.2 \times 10^6$ in 1977, a loss of $\$13.6 \times 10^6$ in 3 years. At this rate of loss the equity could be down to zero in 18 years.

An article in the *Wall Street Journal* in 1972 pointed up adverse aspects of management's attitude about reversing losses. Several years later, after reading the annual reports, the investor has to assume that the company will continue to be run as before, selling its assets.

However, $2.67 per share represents the Q.L.V. for this company in 1977 ($\$21.8 \times 10^6$). In 1970 this value was twice that ($\$41.3 \times 10^6$). In another 7 years that value may be zero, at the current rate of decrease.

The investor would pass up investing in this company on any basis.

Craddock-Terry Shoe Corporation

For this company, debt as a percentage of total capital is just over one-third and the fixed-charge coverage is also inadequate, therefore the investor would not invest in this company on the basis of the usual analysis.

But the quick liquidating value for the company in 1977 was $9.80 per share and after deducting a fourth of the inventory, the net Q.L.V. was $7.00 per share.

The company's book value, in spite of reduced earnings and a regular dividend payment, has increased in each of the past six years, a plus.

The investor would buy this one at 5 and sell it at 10.

In summary, prefer to use the Q.L.V. per share as a plus factor in the security evaluation system rather than as something to look for in a company to the exclusion of the primary method of security evaluation.

STOCKS WITH LOW PRICE-EARNINGS RATIOS

There are several studies showing the results of buying low P/E ratio stocks:

1. Drexel & Company showed in a study, "that an original investment of $10,000 made in the low-multiplier issues [of the DJIA] in 1936, and switched each year in accordance with the principle [buying low P/E ratio stocks] would have grown to $119,200 by 1962. The same operations in high multiplier stocks would have ended with a value of only $10,800."

But, "in the early period, 1971–1933, this approach proved unprofitable."

2. And a study by the Cleveland Trust Company of the 30 stocks in the DJIA showed "that low price/earnings multiples were no protection during the decline of 1966" and "that from their 1965 highs to their 1966 lows, the tendency has been for stocks with low price/earnings ratios to fall the furthest—further than the stocks with higher price/earnings ratios."

3. Ben Graham's study indicated that the low multipliers comprising the DJIA showed a sharp *loss* but a good profit for the high multiplier selection from the end of 1968 to June 30, 1971.

4. And David Dreman's study from August 1967 to August 1976, 1000 plus stocks, 10 deciles, showed that "$10,000 invested . . . in the lowest P/E stocks and switched to the lowest P/Es quarterly would increase to $49,944," and "10,000 invested in the same manner in the top 10% of stocks would be worth only $8,650; $10,000 invested in the S&P 425 would have grown to $16,170."

Putting it all together, buying stocks purely on the basis of a *relatively* low P/E multiple has not worked out profitably every time for the investor in the past.

Consequently, do not invest in relatively low or in low P/E multiple stocks automatically without further analysis.

But, compiling a list of low P/E ratio stocks and analyzing these for balance sheet adequacy, investment value, and buy price should yield some sound prospects for investment.

COMPANIES REPORTING DEFICITS

Janos Aranyi, a financial consultant, studied the price action of stocks reporting deficits. His computer, "on surveying the records of 900 stocks from 1948 through 1967, reported that anyone who had invested in companies with a deficit, would, within an average of 2–3 years, have done better than in any other stock. For example, if he had invested $100 in the companies on the Big Board that had deficits in 1948, he would have been worth $3,032 by 1967—substantially more than if he had invested in any other group." The DJIA advanced 5.1 times in this period.

And, Marine Midland Banks, Inc. studied the performance of companies reporting deficits over approximately the same period but reported the results for one- to 5-year holding periods and compared these results to those of Standard & Poor's 425 index. In each instance the deficit group outperformed the general index.

The results were favorable. But be wary of buying but

not knowing when to sell. Again, let us emphasize that there is no system without a formula for setting a selling price.

Also, Aranyi and Marine Midland Banks made these studies for an economic growth period which included rising stock prices. The conservative investor should be skeptical, always, of investing in any system blindly.

The investor, however, might make up a list of companies reporting deficits for analysis, as was pointed out in the previous chapter.

PROSPECTIVE TURNAROUND CANDIDATES

These are companies that, because of new management, investors expect, will show an improvement in profit and, consequently, price.

Buy such companies only if they fit the investment criteria. Do not pay ahead of time for prospects, since not every turnaround candidate is turned around.

However, when you find a turnaround candidate that fits the investment criteria, you might hang onto it beyond the sell price signal in expectation of greater things later. But in this instance set a selling price, mentally, at 10% below the company's highest current price. Whenever its price retreated by 10%, sell.

Still conservative, you see.

XV
WHAT TO READ

The new investor (and probably those 85% of investors who lose playing the market) needs a steer in how to start to learn the investment game.

During an alumni meeting at M.I.T., with Professor K. J. Germeshausen presiding, a question came up on whether the way to stay in touch with what is going on is to read a lot. The professor thought that the best bet would be to have someone qualified pick out the material to be read since "most of what is written is trash."

The professor was not asked whether he had read any books on the stock market. But the investor reading 100 to 200 books on the subject will be disappointed to learn how few discuss the need for a sound balance sheet, how many have an interesting narrative but no method for analyzing securities, and others that discuss methods requiring an intuitive feel for highs and lows, which cannot be passed on to anyone else, then still others with systems based on forecasting that are hard to convert to profits.

Consider the problem of the prospective investor who has decided to become familiar with investing in the stock market and reads a dozen books on the subject. He has every reason to believe, at this point, that he knows more than before his reading program. Yet, should he have read the wrong ones, he would be worse off than had he read none.

The best way around the problem is for the investor to take the time to read 100 to 200 books on the subject. In that manner he will have the basis for a solid opinion of his own on what is sound investment advice.

In this connection this short reading list will set the conservative investor on the right track of evaluating properly anything else he might read on the subject of investing.

1. Benjamin Graham, *The Intelligent Investor*, 4th ed. (New York: Harper & Row, 1973). This one is easy reading. The conservative investor will be off on the right track by reading this one first.

2. Benjamin Graham and C. McGolrick, *The Interpretation of Financial Statements* (New York: Harper & Row, 1964).

3. Merrill Lynch, Pierce, Fenner & Smith, Inc., *How to Read a Financial Report* (pamphlet) (New York, 1979). From a reading of these last two, the investor will be off to a good start in learning how to analyze balance sheets.

4. Benjamin Graham, et al. *Security Analysis*, 4th ed. New York: McGraw-Hill, 1962). This book is hard going but a must for the serious, conservative investor.

5. James H. Lorie and Mary T. Hamilton, *The Stock Market: Theories and Evidence* (Homewood, Ill.: Richard D. Irwin, 1973). This book discusses many of the important studies related to stock market investing.

6. David M. Darst, *The Complete Bond Book* (New York: McGraw-Hill, 1975).

7. Robert Lamb and Stephen Rappaport, *Municipal Bonds: The Comprehensive Review Of Tax-Exempt Securities and Public Finance* (New York: McGraw-Hill, 1980).

8. William E. Donoghue and Thomas Tilling, *William E. Donoghue's Complete Money Market Guide* (New York: Harper & Row, 1981).The investor will find much useful and needed informationin 6, 7, and 8 for his bond (cash items) potfolio.

9. Sidney Homer, *A History of Interest Rates*, rev. ed.

(New Brunswick, N.J.: Rutgers University Press, 1977). Here the reader will be impressed with the extent to which interest rates fluctuate, convincing him that *short-term*, high-grade bonds will cause him the fewest problems.

10. W. B. Hickman, *Corporate Bond Quality and Investor Experience*, N.B.E.R. (Princeton, N.J.: Princeton University Press, 1958). This is a study of bond defaults for 1900 to 1943. The reader will see the merit in buying high-grade bonds and stocks of sound companies only.

11. Paul A. Samuelson, *Economics*, 11th ed. (New York: McGraw-Hill, 1980).

12. C. R. McConnell, *Economics*, 7th ed. (New York: McGraw-Hill, 1978). A study of these last two books will give the reader a sound grounding in economics.

13. Jean Gimpel, *The Medieval Machine* (New York: Holt, Rinehart and Winston, 1976).

14. Robert L. Heilbroner, *Business Civilization in Decline* (New York: W. W. Norton & Co., 1976).

15. Paul Johnson, *Enemies of Society* (New York: Atheneum, 1977).

16. Donella H. Meadows et al., *The Limits To Growth* (New York: Universe Books, 1972). These last four will give the reader an idea of long-term trends in the social, political, and economic climate as they might affect business and the stock market, convincing him of the need for conservatism in investing over the decades ahead.

17. Charles Mackay, *Extraordinary Popular Delusions and the Madness of Crowds* (Boston: L. C. Page & Company, reprinted 1932). Originally published as *Memoirs of Extraordinary Delusions* (London: Richard Bentley, 1841). Following the crowd may be a losing game for the investor, as so many of the stories here point out.

The investor will stay in touch with current events and their impact on business by reading the following publications regularly, since they contain many well-researched, in-depth articles pertinent to any investment program:

1. The *Wall Street Journal*—Read the lead articles and the articles on the editorial page for one or two years for an in-depth view of current events—tops.
2. *Forbes*
3. *Business Week*
4. *Fortune*
5. "The Week in Review," Section 4 of the Sunday *New York Times*
6. *Barron's*
7. *Financial World*

The investor will be aware of the tremendous amount of advice available on investing, the vast amount of it free. If he has not acquired a sound method of evaluating it but takes it anyway on the basis of how it sounds or the adviser's appearance, he is likely to end up in the 85% group of stock market investors who lose.

It is *not* a good idea to learn by doing. The tuition cost may be very high for such a learning method. So, study first before playing the market.

XVI
MOST IMPORTANT PREMISE—TO KEEP IT

We've stressed: To make it in stocks and bonds the investor must first be sure not to lose.

Should the investor miss one good deal, he will have his money intact for the next. If he gambles it for large prospective gains, he must remember with equal emphasis that where large potential gains are possible there are most of the time, also, large potential losses possible.

This system was developed around minimizing risk—minimizing rather than eliminating it since the only risk-free investments are short-term government bonds, Treasury bills, and almost certainly savings bank accounts up to $100,000—and we have kept in mind that 85% of those who play the market lose, and that those companies of weaker balance sheets are more prone to defaulting than are those of the stronger.

On these bases we have commented on several methods investors use in playing the market that we doubt will make it for the majority on a regular basis from here on:

1. Buy-hold
2. Buy because of inflation
3. Forecasting market level, earnings, economy, and interest rates for buy and sell signals
4. Buying new companies
5. Buying growth companies at any price

6. Buying and selling on the basis of technical analysis
7. Watching the tape for buy and sell signals
8. Acting on brokers' recommendations
9. Using advisory services
10. Investing in puts and calls
11. Buying based on industry analysis without regard for price
12. Buying blue chips at any time
13. Buying mutual funds
14. Playing the futures market
15. Short selling
16. Buying on margin

And we have been mindful of several impediments to economic growth that will affect profitability from the 1980s on:

1. Less productive capital investment
2. Raw materials vulnerability
3. Deteriorating balance sheets
4. Increasing household debt
5. Increasing transfer payments
6. Adverse attitude toward business
7. A weakened defense posture
8. An absence of resolve in international affairs

Then, over the longer term we have noted (p. 183) the convincing data that Western civilization, as we know it, is in its declining stage.

These economic, social, and political data point toward slower and declining profit growth over the longer term, emphasizing the importance of investing only in companies that have sound balance sheets and buying these only when their prices are at bargain levels for a diversified portfolio, with some money always in cash items ready for conversion to common stocks at better bargain prices, if the market continues to decline.

Our primary purpose in discussing the economic, social, and political climate in the United States is to emphasize the appropriateness of conservatism in investing.

But, in spite of this adverse economic forecast, should the economic climate become more favorable to free enterprise, how will that affect our security evaluation system? It won't.

We expect the market to continue to have its downs and ups, as it has over the past century, providing the investor with opportunities for buys and sales in the worst and best times.

By using a conservative security evaluation system, the investor should not only preserve his capital but also expect to beat the market averages over intermediate and long-term periods whether he has $10,000 or $1 billion to invest.

The investor who is too busy on other activities to make his own security evaluations should, nevertheless, become sufficiently familiar with security analysis so that he may be better able to evaluate the tremendous number of investment recommendations available, including those of his investment adviser.

Remember the 85% and good luck.

APPENDIXES

APPENDIX I
THE DECLINE OF WESTERN CIVILIZATION

Investors should be aware that economic, social, and political problems affect investment programs over the short term and over the long term, say, the next hundred years.

In our Western civilization each person participates in chosing his form of government and his legislators and also chooses his own form of intellectual and economic enhancement from which stems our free enterprise, capitalist economy.

To keep growing, the economy needs continued investment and still more investment for the productivity improvements that provide our improving standard of living.

That investment comes from savings. Most of it comes from the well-off; they have funds to invest. We need many more of the rich. That is, many more of those who save rather than spend all they make.

In previous chapters you've learned of the method to use for enhancing the bank account. The following commentary will further emphasize the appropriateness of a conservative investment policy.

Several analysts support the view that Western civilization is in its declining stage.

A. Economist Robert L. Heilbroner not only claims that

capitalism will eventually disappear since "no civilization, save only the most primitive, lasts 'forever,'" but also that the long-run termination of capitalism will occur within a century [2076].

Because "capitalist expansion is an *exponential* process . . . no social processes of an exponential character are capable of indefinite continuance. Sooner or later all such processes must overload their environment."

Here are some data from *The Limits to Growth* study that support that view.

For example, due to population growth and the desire for a continuously improved standard of living all over the world, the amount of land needed for agriculture will become greater than that available, while another limit to agricultural production will be the availability of fresh water.

"Opening new land, farming the sea, or expanding use of fertilizers and pesticides will require an increase of the capital stock devoted to food production," leaving less capital for other needs.

Then note the life estimates of our nonrenewable natural resources if we continue to use these at our present rate of annual increase (Table 1).

However vast these raw materials may be they are finite and will be "extremely costly 100 years from now [1972]."

Heilbroner can visualize "increasingly severe constraints on industrial growth . . . and the progressive elimination of profits," which could come sooner than later if our supplies of chrome, manganese, vanadium, and platinum from South Africa are cut off.

If Heilbroner is right in his estimate, the investor should not expect a continuously rising economy over the next 100 years.

B. Historian Arnold Toynbee doubts that democracy will be able to solve approaching economic problems and laments that totalitarianism will take its place.

We need but note that more people are beneficiaries of

TABLE 1

	FROM 1970 NUMBER OF YEARS KNOWN GLOBAL RESERVES WILL LAST GROWING AT GLOBAL CONSUMPTION GROWTH RATE	AND NUMBER OF YEARS AT 5 TIMES KNOWN GLOBAL RESERVES
Aluminum	31	55
Coal	111	150
Copper	21	48
Gold	9	29
Iron	93	173
Natural Gas	22	49
Petroleum	20	50
Silver	13	42
Tin	15	61

Source: *The Limits to Growth*, pp. 56–59.

federal government payments than there are taxpayers who carry the load.

Over the past, federal transfer benefits have been increasing at a real rate greater than that of the real gross national product. The reader can easily calculate that redistribution payments will equal GDP sometime in the next century.

Will the privately employed taxpayer, who pays for these benefits, be willing to continue working while greater amounts of his productive effort are passed on to a nonproductive population? If not, will we need a dictatorship to force people back to work?

C. Jean Gimpel in his study of the growth, maturity, and decline for the Medieval Age found many parallels to suggest that Western civilization is declining.

Let's take a closer look at those factors that Gimpel associated with growth on the one hand and decline on the other for both the Medieval and the present American periods.

TABLE 2

MEDIEVAL *AND* AMERICAN
FACTORS RELATED TO GROWTH VS. MATURITY

FACTORS IN AN ERA OF GROWTH	FACTORS IN AN ERA OF MATURITY
Rising Gross National Product (GNP)	*GNP Levels Off*. To 1981 we have not yet experienced a permanent leveling off in GNP, although there are many factors that portend a slower growth and decline in the future.
Growth of Population	*Growth of Population Levels Off*.

U.S. CENSUS DATA	ANNUAL POPULATION GROWTH
1790 to 1860 (70 yrs)	3.0%
1860 to 1890 (30 yrs)	2.3
1890 to 1930 (40 yrs)	1.7
1930 to 1970 (40 yrs)	1.3
1970 to 1980 (10 yrs)	1.1

Our rate of population growth has been declining steadily.

FACTORS IN AN ERA OF GROWTH	FACTORS IN AN ERA OF MATURITY
Free Enterprise	*Free Enterprise Limited*. One needs but recall that the corporate tax rate was zero in 1915 and that it was 46% in 1982, then note the proliferating regulation of U.S. industry, to believe this one.
Surplus of Wealth	*Tendency Toward Self-Interest*. Taxes and the distribution of earned wealth have supported consumption rather than saving, leaving less wealth for investment.

FACTORS IN AN ERA OF GROWTH	FACTORS IN AN ERA OF MATURITY
Aestheticism Undeveloped	*Greater Awareness of Aesthetics.* Note the billions being sepnt on pollution and environmental control, most of which spending is economically nonproductive. Would we have had the Industrial Revolution in the 18th century if England had an Environmental Protection Agency then?
Beginning of Inflation	*Inflation Increases.* A study of the wholesale price index from 1749 to 1980 revealed that we have had many inflationary periods, most of them during war periods. But in each instance after a war, except World War II, prices dropped considerably.

YEAR	WPI	COMPOUNDED RATE/YEAR
1910–1914 = 100		
1775	75	
1780	225	24.5% for 5 yrs War
1791	85	
1796	146	11.5% for 5 yrs
1812	131	
1814	182	18.0% for 2 yrs War
1861	89	
1864	193	29.2% for 3 yrs War
1926 = 100		
1915	69.5	
1918	131.3	23.5% for 3 yrs War

FACTORS IN AN ERA OF GROWTH	FACTORS IN AN ERA OF MATURITY

1945	105.8	
1948	165.1	16.0% for 3 yrs
1967 =	100	
1972	119.1	
1980	268.8	10.7% for 8 yrs

In the past two-and-a half centuries we have experienced higher inflation rates than those for the 1970s but none appear to have been as persistent as those of the 1970s.

Education

Higher Education Overextended. In liberal arts and social studies with those graduates figuring more ways and reasons to distribute the wealth produced on "wars" against poverty programs that worsen life rather than improve it, as the results of such programs already show.

For example, in the 1950s Denmark spent billions of Danish kroner to create a modern society for Greenlanders so that they would no longer need to live only as hunters. But the Danish government finds that money can't buy identity, that the former hunters-turned-shopkeepers-and-mechanics vent their frustration in alcohol and self-hatred. Greenland's suicide rate is four times Denmark's.

In the 1960s the Kennedy Administration started many social welfare programs in Micronesia to help or coopt the Islanders. With checks

FACTORS IN AN ERA OF GROWTH	FACTORS IN AN ERA OF MATURITY
	from the U.S. assured, hardly anyone works, and crime and alcoholism have taken the place of productive activity. Do we take credit for aiding the Islanders? Irving Kristol notes that we have abolished poverty in New York City through income redistribution. "It is largely a demoralized population, with higher rates of crime, juvenile delinquency, drug addiction, teenage pregnancy, alcoholism, etc., than when the welfare checks were less generous." People are entitled to what they earn and save themselves. Anyone getting more is living off someone else's productive efforts. The best thing anyone can do for poverty is to get himself out of it: Work, save, and study for the next step ahead. People should be given that chance to do so. Evidently, redistributing an excess of hard-earned dollars from the productive groups to the non-productive perpetuates dependency and poverty. Leo Tolstoy in a letter to a friend observed that the only true happiness is honest hard work and the overcoming of obstacles. Until our vociferous overeducated "intellectual class" reverses its

FACTORS IN AN ERA OF GROWTH	FACTORS IN AN ERA OF MATURITY
	views, in face of the evidence, on what eliminates poverty and promotes individual self respect, we should expect further deterioration in the moral fabric of the population.
Industrialization (Functional Technology)	*Survival of Obsolete Techniques (technical sclerosis).* We are experiencing a slower technical advance—fewer patents registered than 20 years ago. Many companies have given up basic research.
Exploitation of Inventions	*Resistance to Inventions Begins.* Note the recent environmental requirements for autos, and how long it takes to obtain a permit to build a nuclear plant or a chemical plant.
Psychological Drive	*Declining Psychological Drive.* After World War II we emerged as the strongest power in the world and were willing to use it. As a result we had a stable world until the 1970s. Since we lost our resolve to push out the communists in Vietnam, we've been losing our influence in the world. Beginning in the late 1970s the Soviets were calling the shots. In 1978 at the time of the Iranian uprisings against the Shah, Soviet Party Chairman Brezhnev warned the U.S. not to interfere. We heeded that warning in spite of our military alliance with Iran. How much is an alliance with us worth today?

FACTORS IN AN ERA OF GROWTH	FACTORS IN AN ERA OF MATURITY

During the 1970s seven countries joined the Soviet bloc: South Vietnam, Laos, Cambodia, Angola, Ethiopia, South Yeman, and Afghanistan.

Recall that in 1962 we pushed the Soviets out of Cuba. In the late 1970s they were back in Cuba with their arsenal, unchallenged by the U.S.

"The U.S. is no longer obsessed by a world-breaking spirit . . . no longer proclaiming we have the biggest, fastest, greatest of things," except probably in Texas.

And "the increase of the median age . . . is another factor in precipitating the decline of the psychological drive."

The U.S. median age for all races was 16.7 years in 1820. It rose to 22.9 years by 1900 and in another 80 years, 1980, it was 30.0 years.

Older people have less drive than the younger and the population average promises to become older, according to an estimate by the Bureau of the Census.

NUMBER OVER 65 YEARS OF AGE

$$1977 = 22 \times 10^6$$

$$2020 = 43 \times 10^6\text{E}$$

We might estimate that by the end of the century we will have less drive than we now have.

FACTORS IN AN ERA OF GROWTH	FACTORS IN AN ERA OF MATURITY
Community Spirit	*Private Living*. Too many workers don't care. Absenteeism is 20% on Fridays and Mondays in some auto plants. Workers take sick leave when not sick. And the civil service rules are such that it is almost impossible to fire an incompetent employee who stays incompetent. And recall that helicopter mission to rescue the hostages at the American Embassy in Iran when 3 of the helicopters developed maintenance problems. Was it inadequate supervision, inadequate training, or an attitude of do-the-least-for-my-pay attitude on the part of the maintenance crews? Growth of Permissiveness: Today the public has a greater "understanding" of why the depraved commit crimes on a regular schedule. Terrorists have rights, too, many claim, so we've constrained the FBI, the CIA, and our local police from doing their jobs to keep the peace. In contrast, Saudi Arabians credit their Sharia Law and "its sometimes harsh penalties for their nation's low crime rate. In Saudi Arabia one can walk the streets at night without worry. Mugging is almost unknown. Parked cars seldom are bothered, even when left unlocked with valuables inside."

FACTORS IN AN ERA OF GROWTH	FACTORS IN AN ERA OF MATURITY
	But, in the U.S. a power blackout in our cities is a signal for looting. Or note the care one must take in anchoring one's bicycle to inhibit pilferage; and that the libraries in Boston, Brookline, and Harvard College must now have check-out monitors to inhibit book stealing. We have lost our community spirit and in too many instances have replaced it with an every-man-for-himself attitude. The Dalai Lama during his visit to us in 1979 commented: "Material prosperity, all these goods, life is easy, it may spoil and soften people." And Pope John Paul II during his visit here, just before the Dalai Lama's, warned us that prosperity leads people to "assume they have a right to all that prosperity can bring," making them "more selfish in their demands." With a decline in personal responsibility, "the door is open for the justification of injustices, for the manipulation of the many by the few." The manipulation of the many by the few. The reader may be prompted to make his own list of how the legislators are listening to the few to promulgate laws that adversely affect the many.

The parallels Gimpel presents for the Medieval Age and the U.S. for growth periods and those of declines are strikingly similar. Many of those factors that contributed to the decline of the Medieval Age are observable right now in the U.S., suggesting that we are a declining civilization.

In another 10 years let's recheck.

D. In the meantime let us explore the causes of the decline of the Roman Empire and take note of any similarities occurring in the U.S. today.

Paul Johnson found that " . . . the elevation of the state is a very common feature . . . in civilizations in process of decay."

"To pay for an empire [the Roman] which had ceased to pay for itself, the regime had to raise money internally. This meant more and higher taxes, so in turn a bigger bureaucracy, more corruption, tighter central control." Hadrian even added a system of secret police and informers. About all of which ancient historian Lactantius said that "there were now more people involved in raising and spending taxes than in paying them."

In the U.S. we are not yet at this stage in every respect, but here are some past data for the analyst to add to over the years, for his once a decade evaluation of what stage of decline the U.S. is in or has just passed.

TABLE 3

	FEDERAL, STATE, AND LOCAL REVENUE AS A % OF GNP		CIVILIAN GOV'T LABOR FORCE, FEDERAL, LOCAL, AND STATE $\times 10^6$	TOTAL CIVILIAN LABOR FORCE—EMPLOYED ONLY $\times 10^6$	GOV'T TO TOTAL %
1929	6.9%				
1940	17.8	1940	4.474	47.520	9.4%
1960	30.4	1960	8.353	65.778	12.7
1970	34.8	1970	12.554	78.627	15.9
1980	35.4	1980	16.222	97.270	16.5

Although the federal payroll, according to one set of data, contains 2.1 million people on the direct payroll, the *National Journal* has found another 8 million "invisible workers" who get all or most of their income from the federal government.

These two sets of data in Table 3, though not including the 8 million, show that the government has been taking not only an absolutely but also a proportionately larger share of the GNP in taxes and has regularly increased the number of government employees absolutely and in proportion to the labor force.

It appears to us that some of the increases in the federal bureaucracy are pretty close to being a total waste of taxpayers' money, such as for these government departments: Agriculture, Corps of Engineers, the SBA, OSHA, DOE, LEAA, DOT, and Legal Services Corp. (Spending on nonproductive programs leaves less for productive ones.)

Rainer Esslen views the decline of the Roman empire from the viewpoint of a debased currency: "For most of its last 400 years until its demise in 475 A.D., Rome so inordinately debased its coinage and raised its taxes that its productive citizens found it less and less rewarding to produce."

"Byzantium, which became the successor to Rome in 324 A.D. under Constantine the Great, was one of the longest-lasting empires on the strength of a sound gold currency that retained its face value for 800 years. When debasement started in 1100 A.D. it was downhill until Constantinople, defended by another Constantine, was conquered by the Turks in 1452."

And John Maynard Keynes in 1920 in his *Economic Consequences of Peace* stressed that "there is no subtler, no surer, means of overturning the existing basis of society than to debauch the currency."

The U.S. has devalued the official currency rate, from

$20.67 per ounce of gold before 1934 to $42.22 in 1973, by 51.2%. Yet the real devaluation has been considerably greater, since a sale by the U.S. Treasury of 300,000 ounces of gold in May 1978 brought an average price of $180 per ounce, for an unofficial devaluation of 88.5% since 1933. And in 1980 at the market price of $600 per ounce the dollar was down 97% in terms of gold.

In terms of the wholesale price index of 34.0 in 1933 and 268.8 in 1980 the "devaluation" has been 87%, a more reliable figure to watch than the gold standard, probably.

Obviously we are getting there. What will the next 47 years bring us?

Edward Gibbon, in his analysis of why the Roman Army disintegrated, found that the army had a hard time finding recruits: ". . . the timid and luxurious inhabitants of a declining empire must be allured into the service by the hope of profit or compelled by the dread of punishment."

The U.S. Army has a hard time filling its requirements even though starting pay for a private at $551 a month in 1982 was 26 times what it was in 1940, $21 a month. The wholesale price index in this same period increased by about seven-and-a-half times.

And Gibbon noted that "the arts of luxury and literature were cultivated, and the elegant pleasures of society were enjoyed, by the inhabitants of a considerable portion of the globe."

People tend to relax when they've made it, when there is no longer the matter of economic survival to work for. Per capita disposable income in constant 1972 dollars rose from $1600 in 1930 to $4473 in 1980, 2.8 times. We don't believe this income is sufficient to induce people to relax and extend their good-time activity. But this per capita income figure is an average, meaning that many make more, and some quite a bit more, so that we may have a section of the population making enough to relax already, in addition to the larger segment of the population now nonproductive and collecting distribution payments.

We expect that with many more people relaxing, adding to the nonproductive group of the population, that economic growth will slow, then decline, diminishing the amount for consumption and investment, thus setting the stage for a further decline.

We are not at this GNP decline stage yet, but it is something for us to monitor as another signal for harder economic times ahead for the investor, business manager, and the population in general.

Then, from the point of view of perpetuating a continuous welfare class, Gibbon noted that "for the convenience of the lazy plebeians, the monthly distributions of corn were converted into a daily allowance of bread; a great number of ovens were constructed and maintained at the public expense."

As for present day similarities the reader will be aware by now of the increasing public expense for Social Security, welfare, unemployment compensation, medical care, food stamps, veterans' care, and rent subsidies.

Also, he noted that the Romans had become "an unwarlike populace enervated by luxury before they were emaciated by famine," just before Alaric ransomed Rome.

We were willing to fight World War I, World War II, and the Korean War but by the 1960s we had lost our drive to fight the Vietnamese War.

Recall those student demonstrations in the 1960s to protest the war in Vietnam to stop the killing. Since the communist takeover in Indochina, estimates of Cambodians killed have ranged from 1 to 3 million. Where were those demonstrators then?

When these students were protesting, were they truly protesting the killing or were they putting on an act to avoid the call to "national duty"?

E. Interest Rates. Do rising interest rates portend the decline of a civilization?

Note the interest rate history of 3 civilizations extracted from Sidney Homer's study:

Babylonia		
	3000 B.C.	20%
	550 B.C.	10%
	350 B.C.	40%
Greece		
	550 B.C.	16%
	50 B.C.	6%
	50 A.D.	8%
Rome		
	450 B.C.	8⅓%
	50 B.C.	4%
	350 A.D.	12%

He found for Babylonia, Greece, and Rome that "interest rates seemed to decline from earliest history until a period of late commercial development, and later to advance during the final centuries of political breakdown. Only Greek interest rate history ended with lower rates than it began, and this is probably an accident of economic reporting."

In this connection examine the history of interest rates and yields from near the time of settlement of the country to the present:

8%	Mass. fixed legal limit	1661
6%	Maryland fixed legal limit	1692
6%	Continental Congress	1776
7.56%	Fed. gov't bonds	1798
7.64%	Fed. gov't bonds	1814
5.32%	Long-term governments	1920
2.19%	Long-term governments	1946
4.01%	Long-term governments	1960
6.59%	Long-term governments	1970
11.39%	Long-term governments	1980
13.72%	Long-term governments	1981

Interest rates are higher now than they have been in the past 300 years of North American history, giving support to the view that the U.S. has entered its aging stage.

And an examination of interest rate history of the much older section of Western civilization, western Europe, appears to support the view that Western civilization is in its declining stage.

TABLE 4

INTEREST RATES
ON LONG-TERM LOANS TO GOVERNMENTS
PRESENT AND PAST

	GOVERNMENT BOND YIELDS 1981	HIGHEST PAST RATES	
England	14.74%	10%	17th cent.
France	15.66%	8⅓%	for *rentes* floated free of coercion—16th cent.
Italy	20.58%	5–10%	for *prestiti* voluntary loans—14th cent.
The Netherlands	11.55%	6⅙–12½%	for loans to Spanish Netherlands—16th cent.

The data in Table 4 show that interest rates in the early 1980s for 3 of the 4 countries are higher than they have been over a period of 300 to 600 years for similar type loans.

These data are for loans to governments. Yet, loans to princes during the Middle Ages and later were made at rates of from 15 to 100%. And some personal loans, commercial loans, and mortgages were recorded at rates of up to 100%.

If high interest rates are an indicator of a civilization in decline, the investor will have to observe the record of many more decades of future interest rates to be more certain of their significance.

F. *Conclusion*

We can correct our short-term problems but not all of the longer-term ones.

The business manager had best improve his balance sheet and reduce costs rather than expand at all costs. The investor should invest in conservatively financed companies and then only when priced at bargain levels. And the general public should plan on working harder for a lesser return and spend less in order to save more over the decades ahead.

APPENDIX II. CHAPTER II

STOCK PRICES VS. INFLATION—SHORT TERM

TABLE II–1

MARKET RISES VS. WHOLESALE PRICE INDEX

LOW		HIGH	TOTAL MARKET RISE %	YEARS FOR WPI	WPI ANNUAL RATE %
Cowles P-2 Industrials Index					
Jan.					
1871	–	1873	56.	1870–1873	– 0.5
1873	–	1874	24.	1873–1874	– 5.3
1877	–	1881	66.	1874–1881	– 2.8
1884	–	1889	83.	1881–1889	– 3.0
1890	–	1892	33.	1889–1892	– 2.0
1893	–	1895	31.	1892–1895	– 2.2
1896	–	1899	103.	1895–1899	+ 1.6
1900	–	1901	45.	1899–1901	+ 3.0
1903	–	1906	101.	1901–1906	+ 2.4
1907	–	1909	109.	1906–1909	+ 2.9
1911	–	1912	30.	1909–1912	+ 0.7
1915	–	1916	98.	1912–1916	+ 5.5
1917	–	1919	67.	1916–1919	+17.3
1921	–	1929	365.	1919–1929	– 3.7
DJIA					
1932	–	1937	373.	1929–1937	– 1.2
1938	–	1939	58.	1937–1939	– 5.5
1942	–	1946	129.	1939–1946	+ 6.6
1949	–	1952	81.	1946–1952	+ 6.0
1953	–	1956	104.	1952–1956	+ 0.6
1957	–	1961	75.	1956–1961	+ 0.8
1962	–	1966	85.	1961–1966	+ 1.0
1966	–	1968	32.	1966–1968	+ 1.3
1970	–	1971	51.	1968–1971	+ 3.6
1971	–	1973	32.	1971–1973	+ 8.8
1974	–	1976	76.	1973–1976	+10.8
1978	–	1980	35.	1976–1980	+10.1

TABLE II–2

MARKET DROPS VS. WHOLESALE PRICE INDEX

HIGH		LOW	TOTAL DECLINE %	YEARS FOR WPI	WPI ANNUAL RATE %
Cowles P-2 Industrials Index					
1873	–	1873	−19.	1872–1873	− 2.2
1874	–	1877	−38.	1873–1877	− 5.5
1881	–	1884	−24.	1877–1884	− 1.8
1889	–	1890	−27.	1884–1890	− 2.1
1892	–	1893	−40.	1890–1893	− 1.6
1895	–	1896	−30.	1893–1896	− 4.5
1899	–	1900	−21.	1896–1900	+ 4.9
1901	–	1903	−44.	1900–1903	+ 2.0
1906	–	1907	−45.	1903–1907	+ 2.3
1909	–	1911	−25.	1907–1911	0
1912	–	1915	−28.	1911–1915	+ 1.7
1916	–	1917	−36.	1915–1917	+30.0
1919	–	1921	−44.	1917–1921	− 4.6
DJIA					
1929	–	1932	−89.	1921–1932	− 3.6
1937	–	1938	−49.	1932–1938	+ 3.2
1939	–	1942	−40.	1938–1942	+ 5.9
1946	–	1949	−24.	1942–1949	+ 6.4
1952	–	1953	−12.	1949–1953	+ 2.7
1956	–	1957	−19.	1953–1957	+ 1.7
1961	–	1962	−27.	1957–1962	+ 0.3
1966	–	1966	−25.	1962–1966	+ 1.2
1968	–	1970	−36.	1966–1970	+ 2.5
1971	–	1971	−16.	1970–1971	+ 3.2
1973	–	1974	−45.	1971–1974	+12.1
1976	–	1978	−27.	1974–1978	+ 6.9
1981	–			1978–	

STOCK PRICES INCLUDING DIVIDENDS VS. WPI—SHORT TERM

TABLE II–3

RETURNS ON INDUSTRIALS, DIVIDENDS INCLUDED, AND HIGH-GRADE BONDS VS. WHOLESALE PRICE INDEX

YEAR-END	NO. YRS.	RETURN PER YEAR ON STOCKS %	HIGH-GRADE BONDS AVG. YIELD %	WPI RATE PER YEAR %
Cowles C-2 Industrials Index—Dividends Included				
1870–1880	10	8.9	5.47	−3.0
1880–1890	10	7.0	3.92	−2.0
1890–1900	10	9.1	3.48	0
1900–1910	10	7.8	3.53	2.3
1910–1920	10	7.4	4.37	8.2
1920–1930	10	12.3	4.46	−5.6
DJIA—Dividends Reinvested Quarterly				
1930–1940	10	3.0	3.48	−1.0
1940–1950	10	11.9	2.60	7.3
1950–1960	10	15.4	3.51	1.5
1960–1970	10	6.9	5.37	1.5
1970–1980	10	6.3	8.62	9.3
1870–1980	110	8.7	4.44	1.6

Notes: 1870–1900 high-grade RR bond yields and 1900–1960 high grade corporate bond yields from Sidney Homer, *A History of Interest Rates*, 2nd ed. (New Brunswick, N. J.: Rutgers University Press, 1977).

1960–1980 high grade corporate bond yields from Moody's Investor's Service, *Moody's Industrial Manual* (New York: blue pages, annual). Year-end 1930–1937 dividends reinvested annually rather than quarterly.

APPENDIX II. CHAPTER VI

TABLE VI–2

PERFORMANCE OF
39 OPEN-END NO-LOAD MUTUAL FUNDS FOR
TWO CONSECUTIVE 5-YEAR PERIODS

	FUND PERFORMANCE	
FUND	1ST 5 YEARS 1966–1971 %	2ND 5 YEARS 1971–1976 %
American Investors	−8.3	3.6
D. L. Babson Income	16.3	106.
D. L. Babson Invest.	64.5	11.3
DeVegh Mutual	53.7	0.6
Dodge & Cox Balanced	35.8	24.5
Dodge & Cox Stock	49.2	22.2
Elfun Trusts	50.5	−4.2
Energy Fund	31.5	41.8
Fidelity Equity Inc.	69.2	39.2
Financial Industrial Inc.	67.0	64.2
Financial Industrial F.	22.5	34.0
Growth Industry S.	41.5	1.0
Guardian Mutual	47.5	45.3
Ivy Fund	103.0	−10.8
The Johnston Mutual	62.5	3.6
Loomis-Sayles Cap. D	53.5	−5.0
Loomis-Sayles M.F.	41.0	9.9
Mathers	166.0	10.7
Neuwirth	47.6	−29.4
Newton	84.4	−21.5

(cont'd)

N'West Invest. Tr.	33.8	33.9
One William St. F.	40.7	13.8
Penn Square M.	27.5	43.5
Pine St.	49.0	26.0
T-Rowe Price Gr.	68.0	−11.0
Rowe Price N.H.	175.0	−29.6
Scudder Int'l	51.5	24.5
Scudder Spec'l	90.5	−21.7
Scuder, Stevens & C.	22.2	14.0
Scudder, Stevens & Co.	18.5	7.3
Selected Amer.	33.4	−9.0
State St. Invest.	46.0	15.4
Steadman Amer I	17.6	−42.3
Steadman Assoc.	39.0	14.5
Steadman Invest.	37.0	11.0
Stein Roe & Far. Bal.	42.5	8.2
Stein Roe & Far. Cap.	65.0	0
Stein Roe Far. Stk	48.5	4.6
Twent. Cent. I. Gr.	7.8	65.0
DJIA, Dividends added	33.3	33.5

TABLE VI–3

PERFORMANCE OF 39 OPEN-END NO-LOAD MUTUAL FUNDS FOR TWO FIVE-YEAR PERIODS

FIRST 5-YEAR PERIOD IN DESCENDING ORDER OF PROFITABILITY DATA FROM TABLE VI–2

	5 YEARS 1966–1971 %	5 YEARS 1971–1976 %
	175.0	−29.6
	166.0	10.7
	103.0	−10.8
	90.5	−21.7
5 To here	84.4	−21.5
	69.2	39.2
	68.0	−11.0
	67.0	64.2
	65.0	0
	64.5	11.3
	62.5	3.6
	53.7	0.6
	53.5	− 5.0
	51.5	24.5
	50.5	− 4.2
	49.2	22.2
	49.0	26.0
	48.5	4.6
	47.6	−29.4
	47.5	45.3
	46.0	15.4
	42.5	8.2
	41.5	1.0
	41.0	9.9
	40.7	13.8
	39.0	14.5
	37.0	11.0

(cont'd)

	35.8	24.5
	33.8	24.5
	33.8	33.9
30 To here	33.4	− 9.0
	31.5	41.8
	27.5	43.5
	22.5	34.0
	22.2	14.0
	18.5	7.3
	17.6	−42.3
	16.3	106.0
	7.8	65.0
39 To here	−8.3	3.6
DJIA, Dividends added	33.3	33.5
	5.9%/yr	5.9%/yr

APPENDIX II. CHAPTER VII

HOUSAILLE INDUSTRIES, INC.
STATEMENT OF CONSOLIDATED INCOME

FOR THE YEAR ENDED DECEMBER 31, 1976

	1976
Net Sales	$332,844,654
Cost of Sales (Note E)	245,324,441
Gross Margin	87,520,213
Selling, Administrative, and General Expenses	45,501,708
Income from Operations	42,018,505
Other Income Net of Other Expense:	
Interest received	2,577,251
Gain on assets retired—less losses	1,996,968
Sundry income—less other income deductions	246,739
Total	4,820,958
Less interest expense, principally on long-term debt	1,638,072
Other Income—net	3,182,886
Income Before Provision for United States and Canadian Taxes on Income	45,201,391
Provision for Taxes on Income (Notes A and M):	
Current year	19,359,617
Deferred to future periods	1,020,383
Total	20,380,000
Net Income	$ 24,821,391
Earnings per share of common stock and common stock equivalents outstanding at the end of each year (Note A)	$2.88

HOUDAILLE INDUSTRIES, INC.

ASSETS	*1976*
Current Assets:	
Cash	$ 7,610,022
Certificates of deposit and treasury bills (including accrued interest)	20,946,267
Receivables—net (Note D)	42,252,440
Inventories—net (Notes A and E)	62,932,007
Prepaid expenses	606,482
Total current assets	134,347,218
Property, Plant, and Equipment—at cost (Notes A and F):	
Land and land improvements	9,753,350
Land—aggregate reserves	2,373,998
Buildings	31,772,498
Machinery and equipment	100,486,745
Office furniture and fixtures	3,081,176
Mobile equipment and motor vehicles	24,636,681
Construction in progress	1,352,425
Total	173,456,873
Less accumulated depreciation, depletion, and amortization	106,667,138
Property, plant, and equipment—net	66,789,735
Other Assets:	
Excess of investment over net assets acquired (net of amortization) (Notes A and B)	10,979,626
Patents (Note A)	1
Other	990,419
Total other assets	11,970,046
Total	$213,106,999

LIABILITIES	*1976*
Current Liabilities:	
Accounts payable	$ 16,709,590
Current maturities of long-term debt (Note J)	1,315,000
United States and Canadian taxes on income (Note M)	6,118,752
Other taxes	1,991,824
Accrued payrolls, compensation and related items (Note G)	5,163,762
Sundry accrued liabilities	5,715,184
Total current liabilities	37,014,112
Other Liabilities (current portion included in current liabilities):	
Long-term debt (Note J)	23,985,000
Long-term lease obligation—net (Note N)	195,367
Deferred compensation plans (Note G)	2,961,667
Taxes on income deferred to future periods (Notes A and M)	5,688,680
Total other liabilities	32,830,714
Stockholders' Interest:	
Capital stock (Note H):	
$2.25 prior cumulative preferred; authorized and outstanding—190,000 shares of $50 par value each	9,500,000
Convertible voting cumulative preferred; authorized—426,000 shares of $25 par value each; issued and outstanding: —0—shares	—0—
Common; authorized 20,000,000 shares of $.75 par value each; issued 1976, 8,862,001 shares; 1975, 8,846,501 shares	6,639,001
Paid-in capital	14,090,404
Retained earnings (Note J)	115,171,198
Total	145,400,603

(cont'd)

Less cost of common stock in treasury—	
476,360 shares	$ 2,138,430
Total stockholders' interest	143,262,173
Total	$213,106,999

APPENDIX II. CHAPTER VIII

BASIS FOR THE SYSTEM

1. *Company Size*

Pay less for a small company than for a large one. There's a very good reason for this. Note in Table VIII-3 the defaults on bond issues vs. company size as compiled by W. B. Hickman.[1]

TABLE VIII–3

INDUSTRIALS

COMPANY SIZE VS. DEFAULTS 1900–1943

ASSET SIZE OF OBLIGOR × 10^6	PROPORTION OF BOND OFFERINGS, 1900–1943, THAT WENT INTO DEFAULT BEFORE 1944
under $5	38.0%
5–99	25.3
100–199	17.2
200–over	3.4

Perusing Table VIII-3, the reader will find that smaller companies had more bond defaults than the larger companies. These data are sufficient reason to eliminate investments in small companies or to pay a good deal less for samll ones, in our general conservative investment policy.

But to investigate the cut-off points between small and large companies, we studied the first 500 or so companies, in alphabetical order, listed in the Standard & Poor's *Stock*

Guide[2] for year-end 1974, and to this group we added the 30 stocks in the Dow Jones industrial average for our study totaling 516 companies.

We noted the high price in 1973 for each security and the percent drop from there to its low of 1974 and related these data to working capital as a determinant of company size.

We note a summary of that effort in Table VIII-4, columns 1 to 3, which shows that the smaller the company the greater the price drop, on the average.

These data were insufficient for us to delineate between small and large companies, so we took the additional step of determining what percentage of companies by company size declined 40%, 50%, 60%, 70%, 80%, and 90% in price. See columns 4 through 9.

These data gave us better cut-offs related to company size, but we then compiled data on P/E ratios of companies at their lows of 1974 and included them in column 10.

We note that the smaller companies in the 1974 lows sold at lower P/Es than did the larger ones, again indicating a greater price drop for the smaller companies.

As another aid in determining company size cut-off, we took Hickman's data on percent defaults vs. assets and drew a curve relating default rate to assets, stretching the last point asymptotically. Then, from our own data for 1973 through 1974, we plotted asset size vs. working capital and found that 4 times working capital = assets, on the average. From these data we related Hickman's data on default rates to working capital in column 11 of Table VIII-4.

After examining all of the data in Table VIII-4 we made our divisions between small and medium, and medium and large companies in column 12 of Table VIII-4: a small company has working capital of up to $\$25 \times 10^6$, a medium-sized company has working capital of $\$25 \times 10^6$ to $\$200 \times 10^6$, and a large one has $\$200 \times 10^6$ and over.

TABLE VIII–4

COMPANY SIZE VS. STOCK PRICE DROPS, PRICE-EARNINGS RATIOS IN THE 1973–1974 MARKET DROP, AND DEFAULT RATES OF 1900–1943

1	2	3	4	5	6	7	8	9	10	11	12
COMPANY SIZE BY WORKING CAPITAL $\times 10^6$	NO. COS. IN THIS STUDY	AVERAGE PRICE DROP 1973 HIGH TO 1974 LOW %	WHAT % OF COMPANIES HAD PRICE DROPS OF 40% OR MORE, ETC., FROM THEIR 1973 HIGHS VS. COMPANY SIZE?						MEDIAN P/E RATIO AT MARKET LOW	ESTIMATED DEFAULT RATES VS. COMPANY SIZE %	CO. SIZE
			40% OR MORE	50% OR MORE	60% OR MORE	70% OR MORE	80% OR MORE	90% OR MORE			
Deficit	27	62.5%							5.4		
0–5	108	72.8	97.3%	88.0%	78.6%	60.2%	39.8%	12.0%	4.2	38–32%	S
5–10	84	69.2	91.7	87.0	72.5	51.2	34.5	10.7	3.6	32–27	S
10–25	97	69.1	88.7	80.5	67.0	53.7	32.0	11.3	3.8	27–21	S
25–50	71	63.6	89.5	79.0	59.2	40.9	21.1	4.2	5.1	21–12	M
50–100	42	62.4	85.7	76.2	59.5	38.1	23.8	9.5	4.6	12–5	M
100–200	32	59.2	97.0	81.2	50.0	21.9	3.1	3.1	4.8	5–0	M
200–500	28	57.6	82.3	71.5	42.8	21.4	10.7	0	6.1	0	L
500– +	27	53.2	81.5	66.7	33.3	11.1	7.4	0	5.7	0	L
Total	516										

The dotted lines represent our temporary division between small and medium; and medium and large companies.

We prefer working capital as a determinant of company size rather than assets for our analytic purposes since working capital is a more significant resource in helping a company out of a problem, should one come up.

As we have indicated, we pay less for smaller than larger companies and only bargain prices at that.

2. *Buy Price*

What is a bargain price?

First, something is worth what people will pay. We have heard that often enough. But recall that some companies at one time sold at a price-earnings ratio of 60 and at another time at 10. Also run over the 100-year list of price-earnings ratios for any series and note the fluctuation in what "investors will pay."

But, although many investors try, many also find it hard to work with establishing a price that others will pay.

Consequently, we have developed something definite that an investor may use mechanically and continuously.

Then we added to the requirement, very significant to us, of conservatism. We strive to improve the investor's net worth, but not by taking undue risk.

On this basis the investor will notice that our security evaluation system is conservative: balance sheet must be adequate, average of *past* earnings as a determinant of what a company can do (rather than a projection), and a conservative price-earnings ratio.

We have given an example of how to compute investment value: average earnings for the past 10 years times a price-earnings ratio dependent on average earnings growth.

It is from this point, investment value, that we compute a buy price.

In Table VIII-1, p. 79, we show that we would buy a large company if it sold at a third off investment value, medium and sold at a half off I.V., or small if it sold at two-thirds off I.V. We would pay still less for each of these if company earnings fluctuated widely—more on this shortly.

How did we select a buy price of a third, a half, and two-thirds off I.V. as constituting a bargain price for large, medium, and small companies, respectively?

We started with a third off investment value as a buy price for large companies on the basis of Ben Graham's commentary in his *The Intelligent Investor*,[3] but developed our own system.

We have a somewhat unrigorous back-up for this portion of the system but it will help the investor see the picture better.

First, since we compute our buys from investment value, we noted in the 25-Sample Study, 1973–1977, Table VIII-8, that the median price-earnings ratio of our sales prices (investment values) was 9.9 (call it 10.0). (It is from this point, I.V., that the price has to drop a third, a half, or two-thirds, to become a buy, keep in mind.)

Next, from that same study, we noted the P/E ratios at their lows of 1974, then determined how far these had dropped, but from P/E = 10. That turned out to be 61%, 52%, and 41% for small, medium, and large companies, respectively.

We compared these actual market drops in P/E ratios with our percent off investment value criteria for each size company, and noted these data in Table VIII-5.

Note that the average price drop, using this method, column 3 of Table VIII-5, was 61% for a small company, whereas we require that a small company sell at 66⅔% off investment value before we consider it a buy for our portfolio.

On the average, small companies did not drop enough in price to meet our buy criteria. As it turned out we found but 3 small companies in the sample study depicted in Table VIII-10 that fitted our criteria.

We had an easier time finding medium and large companies. Obviously, we favor the larger companies.

We should stress that these data in column 3 are *aver-*

TABLE VIII–5

BUY PRICE DETERMINATION

1 COMPANY SIZE	2 AVERAGE OF MEDIAN P/E RATIOS AT LOW OF 1974 FROM TABLE VIII–4	3 AVERAGE % DROP FROM P/E RATIO OF 10	4 BUY PRICE—% OFF INVESTMENT VALUE TO PAY FOR A COMMON STOCK
S	3.9	61%	66⅔% or ⅔ off I.V.
M	4.8	52	50 or ½ off I.V.
L	5.9	41	33⅓ or ⅓ off I.V.

age, consequently, the investor will find securities that drop more in price, making available bargains from time to time for investing in stocks in a conservative manner.

Now for another aspect of our system.

3. *Widely Fluctuating Earnings (WFE)*

Some companies' earnings increase regularly with no retreat, while others' earnings fluctuate slightly, and still others' earnings move up and down considerably. We pay less than standard for this last type, as note the schedule in Table VIII-1, last column, p. 79, which allows for twice the theoretical profit as for the standard buy price for each company-size category.

As an example of how widely fluctuating earnings affect investment value, buy price, and transaction profits, we discuss The Anaconda Company (acquired by Atlantic Richfield Company in 1977), a company in our criteria that had widely fluctuating earnings (WFE): at least one cycle of earnings of up 100% and down 50% in a 15-year period.

Note how the adjusted earnings fluctuated for this company. Drastic year to year earnings fluctuation may result in just as drastic changes in investment value and buy price. To show that, we computed the I.V. for 10 successive years and condensed the results in Table VIII-6.

THE ANACONDA COMPANY (LARGE COMPANY)

COMMON OUT. × 10^6	YR	PER SHARE EARN. AFTER EXTRAOR-DINARY ITEMS	STOCK SPLITS OR STOCK DIV.	EARN-INGS DIVISOR	ADJUSTED EARN-INGS PER SHARE	EARNINGS FLUCTUATION
22.090	1975	d1.80		1.00	d1.80	Down 50% or more
	4	11.19			11.19	Up
	3	3.93			3.93	
	2	5.97			5.97	Up 100% +
	1	d16.17			d16.17	Down
	1970	2.91			2.91	Down 50% or more
	9	4.54			4.54	
	8	4.06			4.06	
21,891	7	4.31	2 for 1	1.00	4.31	
10.891	6	12.10		2.00	6.05	Up
	5	7.27			3.64	Up 100% +
	4	5.26			2.63	
	3	4.14			2.07	
	2	4.56			2.28	
	1	3.93			1.97	
	1960	4.30			2.15	
	9	5.53			2.77	
	8	3.16			1.58	Down
10.409	7	4.23			2.12	Down 50% or more
8.674	6	12.85			6.43	Up
	5	7.52			3.76	Up 100% +
	4	3.07			1.54	
8.674	1953	3.52		2.00	1.76	

Keep in mind that each I.V. determination required 10 years of earnings: 1970, for example, required earnings from 1970 through 1961, from which we determined an investment value of $68.80 per share and, being a large company with widely fluctuating earnings, a buy price of half off I.V. or $34.40 per share.

Since companies issue their annual reports about 3 months after fiscal year-end, our investment value and buy price for year-end 1970 would be ready for buying the company's stock from April 1971 to March 1972, by which time another annual report would provide the data for still another I.V. and buy price.

TABLE VIII–6

THE ANACONDA COMPANY—
BUY PRICE AND SELL PRICE

YR. END DEC. 31	INVEST-MENT VALUE (I.V.)	(WFE) BUY PRICE	PRICE RANGE	BUY-SELL DATA
1975	20.00	10.00	20¾–13½	
1974	24.32	12.16	30 –13⅛	
1973	17.52	8.76	29½–17⅜	
1972	16.08	8.04	21⅞–15⅜	Sell 2dQ 1972 @ 20.
1971	13.04	6.52	23¾–11⅛	Buy 2dQ 1971 @ 23.
1970	68.80	34.40	32¾–19⅛	Buy 2dQ 1970 @ 30.
1969	67.40	33.70	66 –26⅞	Buy 3dQ 1969 @ 32.
1968	64.00	32.00	66¼–39	
1967	59.00	29.50	53½–39⅛	
1966	43.70	21.85		

The buy price for 1970 was $34.40 per share but around the first of April 1971 the price was lower than that or $23; consequently, we bought at $23.

Note, also, the considerable dip of I.V. in 1971 from 1970, due to the reported loss of $16.17 per share in 1971. So, in spite of our conservatively put together security evaluation system, it will not eliminate individual security losses from time to time.

For example, if we had bought Anaconda in 1969 @ 32, we would have sold in 1972 @ 20 for a 38% loss in 3 years, according to our system.

Consequently, because of the added risk, we pay less for a company whose earnings fluctuate widely.

As for those companies whose earnings fluctuate little or whose earnings growth from year to year is erratic, we suggest an alternate method of computing I.V.

By way of example note the earnings for National Distillers and Chemical Corporation:

EARNINGS/SHARE DILUTED, INCLUDING EXTRAORDINARY ITEMS	
12/31/1980	$2.96
9	3.96
8	3.21
7	3.15
6	3.38
5	2.31
4	3.35
3	2.59
2	1.21
1	1.05

This company grew 200% from 1971 to 1974 but experienced flat growth from 1974 to 1980. We have computed investment value and buy price for periods using the latest 10, 7, and 5 years of earnings data:

	PER SHARE	
	INVESTMENT VALUE	BUY PRICE
10-year period—our method	$43.50	$29.00
10-year period—least squares method	43.52	29.00
7-year period (up to 1980)	31.90	21.27
5-year period (up to 1980)	29.97	19.98

In this instance we would buy the company at $20.00, but hang on expecting to sell the company at $43.50 or at whatever subsequent I.V. computed for the latest 10-year period.

Now let's discuss the back-up for the final part of our security evaluation system, price-earnings ratios.

4. *Price-Earnings Ratios*

In setting up our range of price-earnings ratios vs. earnings growth, we examined 110 years, 1872–1981, of P/E ratios using the Cowles P-2 industrials index [4] and the DJIA,[5] Table VIII-7. We found that the median P/E ratio for year-end price and year-end earnings was 11.9 for an approximate 3.6% growth, compounded, in stock-index prices in this period, Part A of Table VIII-7.

We next determined the low (price) months for each year for the Cowles P-2 industrials index, compared this price to the year-end earnings and for the DJIA, from 1933 on, we determined the actual low for the year and compared that with the 4 most recent quarters of earnings for a price-earnings ratio. From these data we found the median P/E ratio to be 10.3 for the same 3.6% price growth over this 110-year period, Table VIII-7, Part B.

Using these data as back-up, for this part of our system, we established that 3% in earnings growth per year was worth a 10 times price-earnings ratio.

Then, we established for a second point that a 10% earnings growth rate would call for a P/E ratio of 15.

We determined this second point on the basis that in 5 years the 10% growth rate, simple basis, earnings would increase by 50% which, when divided into the initial I.V., would produce a P/E ratio of 10.

For example, company ABC had average earnings of $2.00 per share over the past 10 years and a growth rate of 10% in earnings, which produced an investment value of $30 per share ($2.00 × P/E ratio of 15). In 5 years we would expect earnings to grow 50%, to $3.00 per share. That $3.00 divided into the initial investment value of $30 would produce the P/E ratio of 10.

From these 2 points, 3% and 10% growth rates, we worked up the remainder of our growth vs. P/E ratios that appear in Table VIII-2 (see Chapter VIII of text).

Obviously, we do not have what one would call a clear-cut, scientifically based system on P/E ratios.

However, what we are able to affirm is that our overall system, including the P/E ratio part of it, did a good job for

TABLE VIII–7

P/E RATIOS

COWLES INDUSTRIALS AND THE DJIA

PART A						PART B					
	YEAR-END P/E RATIO		YEAR-END P/E RATIO		YEAR-END P/E RATIO		YEAR LOW P/E RATIO		YEAR LOW P/E RATIO		YEAR LOW P/E RATIO
1871		1908	15.0	1945	18.3	1871		1908	10.1	1945	15.1
2	5.1*	9	11.5	6	13.0	2	4.5*	9	8.4*	6	14.1
3	9.9*	1910	9.4*	7	9.6*	3	8.9*	1910	8.8*	7	9.8*
4	4.4*	1	12.5	8	7.7*	4	4.3*	1	11.5	8	8.8*
5	12.5	2	11.8	9	8.5*	5	12.0	2	10.6	9	6.8*
6	17.2	3	8.6*	1950	7.7*	6	17.1	3	8.5*	1950	8.4*
7	–	4	11.9	1	10.1*	7	–	4	11.9	1	7.8*
8	9.8*	5	9.3*	2	11.8	8	9.7*	5	5.6*	2	10.2
9	7.0*	6	4.2*	3	10.3*	9	5.7*	6	3.8*	3	9.5*
1880	6.7*	7	3.5*	4	14.4	1880	6.4*	7	3.5*	4	10.2
1	10.1*	8	6.6*	5	13.7	1	9.4*	8	5.9*	5	13.8
2	9.8*	9	9.5*	6	15.0	2	9.8*	9	7.3*	6	12.9
3	8.3*	1920	6.5*	7	12.1	3	8.3*	1920	6.5*	7	11.4
4	9.8*	1	–	8	20.9	4	9.4*	1	–	8	12.1
5	13.3	2	14.5	9	19.8	5	11.2	2	11.8	9	20.5
6	11.4	3	9.4*	1960	19.1	6	10.4	3	8.5*	1960	17.9
7	16.2	4	12.0	1	22.9	7	16.0	4	9.9*	1	18.9
8	23.8	5	10.1*	2	17.9	8	20.1	5	8.1*	2	15.7
9	17.2	6	11.0*	3	18.5	9	17.2	6	9.7*	3	17.7
1890	14.5	7	15.8	4	18.8	1890	14.5	7	12.4	4	18.5
1	9.7*	8	16.4	5	18.1	1	8.9*	8	12.4	5	17.4
2	8.9*	9	12.3	6	13.6	2	7.9*	9	12.3	6	13.0
3	6.9*	1930	16.1	7	16.8	3	6.1*	1930	16.1	7	13.6
4	10.3*	1	29.2	8	16.3	4	10.3	1	29.2	8	15.3
5	8.5*	2	–	9	14.0	5	8.4*	2	–	9	12.9
6	15.2	3	47.3	1970	16.4	6	13.1	3	–	1970	11.6
7	14.1	4	26.6	1	16.2	7	12.2	4	22.1	1	15.0
8	15.2	5	22.7	2	15.2	8	11.2	5	24.7	2	16.1
9	7.4*	6	17.9	3	9.9*	9	7.4*	6	22.6	3	9.6*
1900	11.9*	7	10.5*	4	6.2*	1900	9.8*	7	9.3*	4	5.8*
1	11.9*	8	25.8	5	11.3	1	11.9	8	10.1	5	6.4*
2	5.9*	9	16.5	6	10.4*	2	5.9*	9	18.7	6	11.4
3	7.8*	1940	12.0	7	9.2*	3	7.4*	1940	11.0	7	9.0*
4	15.7	1	9.5*	8	7.1*	4	11.0	1	9.1*	8	8.4*
5	10.2*	2	13.0	9	6.7*	5	8.2*	2	8.5*	9	5.9*
6	7.4*	3	14.0	1980	7.9*	6	6.6*	3	13.0	1980	6.3*
7	4.8*	4	15.1	1	7.7*	7	4.6*	4	13.8	1	6.9*

Part A = * = P/E Ratio = 11.0 or under

Part B = * = P/E Ratio = 10.0 or under

P/E Ratio Part B—From 1933 on, actual low compared to prior 4 quarters of earnings; prior to that, the low compared to year-end earnings.

the investor in 20% to 45% market drops and, also, from our view, even more important, the overall system did an exemplary job for us during one of the worst investment periods in the past 110 years, the Depression (we show the specifics on this later).

Note that in the Depression Portfolio, Table VIII-13, we had some losers in spite of our conservative security evaluation system. American Type founders, which we bought at 80% off investment value, our lowest deduction, lost us 75% in 2.0 years. But making the system any more conservative in an attempt to eliminate losers in a portfolio probably would not work, since greater conservatism would eliminate many profitable buys. But we expect some losers. Consequently, we usually talk of aggregate results of a *portfolio* rather than individual results of specific securities.

Now for something more significant. Checking over the past 110 years of P/E ratios, Table VIII-7, Part A, ending in 1981, we found that year-end prices vs. year-end earnings showed that 44% of the P/E ratios were 11.0 or less and that 35% were 10.0 or less. Then, taking the low monthly price of the Cowles P-2 industrials index vs. the year-end earnings for a P/E ratio to 1932, and the DJIA low for the year from 1933 on vs. the nearest, prior 4 quarters of earnings for a P/E ratio up to 1981, we found that 46% of these P/E ratios were 10.0 or less, depicted in Part B, Table VIII-7.

There were many times when the *averages* sold at a P/E of 10.0 or less. And if the *averages* sold at 10.0 or less there were many securities that sold at a good deal less, providing opportunities for investment, according to our criteria, often.

As a further commentary on P/E = 10, if we go to Table VIII-8, depicting our 1973–74 buys and investment values, and compute the individual P/E ratios for those 25 of the portfolio that we "sold," we find that our median invest-

TABLE VIII–8

25-SAMPLE STUDY 1973–1974

PRICE-EARNINGS RATIOS OF BUY AND SALES

	BUYS			SALES		
	BUY PRICE	EARN-INGS FOR YEAR BOUGHT	P/E RATIO	PRICE (I.V.)	EARN-INGS FOR YEAR SOLD	P/E RATIO
Johns Manville	16.	3.04	5.3	24.00	3.04	7.9
Std Oil of Calif.	24.75	4.97	5.0			
Texaco	24.13	4.75	5.1			
Akzona	11.63	2.87	4.0	20.00	2.68	7.5
Alberto Culver	8.13	1.12	7.3	8.38	0.37	22.7
Altamil	1.25	1.10	1.1			
Amer. Broadcast	15.25	2.77	5.5	22.75	2.77	8.2
Amer. Greetings	6.88	1.20	5.7	13.75	1.20	11.5
Amer. Rubber & Plast.	3.38	.01	338.	9.13	.34	26.8
Amer. Smelt. & Ref.	15.	4.25	3.5	20.50	.95	21.6
Anchor Hocking	19.38	2.38	8.1	26.38	2.38	11.1
Anderson Clayton	10.	1.97	5.1	24.00	2.67	9.0
Angelica Corp.	5.13	.90	5.7			
Assoc. Coca Cola Bot.	5.50	.95	5.8	11.00	.92	12.0
Avon Prod.	19.25	2.34	8.2	28.88	2.34	12.3
Ball Corp.	10.50	1.55	6.8	19.25	2.05	9.4
Basset Furn.	11.88	1.97	6.0	20.00	1.97	10.2
Binks Mfg.	9.00	2.25	4.0			
Borg Warner	17.38	3.70	4.7	23.75	2.66	8.9
Bowne & Co.	5.25	.82	6.4	10.88	1.08	10.1
British Petroleum	6.00	1.96	3.1			
Brockway Glass	12.00	2.12	5.7	32.75	3.72	8.8
Brown Forman Dist.	7.50	1.39	5.4	14.25	1.46	9.7
Brush Wellman	7.63	2.83	2.7			
Bundy Corp	6.38	1.94	3.3	10.25	1.07	9.6
Median P/E Ratio			5.4			9.9

Note: By the end of 1977 the prices of 7 securities had not reached their I.V. so we did not "sell" them.

ment value (same as selling price) vs. the latest earnings at the time of sale was 9.9 times (at the time of buy, the median P/E ratio was 5.4 times).

Obviously, we buy bargains only and just as obviously it is apparent that there have been many years in the past 100 or so when they were available.

Now that we have commented about bargains, how about those times when there were few bargains available? This is a good thing to know, is it not? In other words, were there long periods when the investor might have had trouble finding values? There were. Note Part A of Table VIII-7 again. We have marked the periods of P/E ratios of 11.0 or less, indicating the favorable investment periods, according to our system. There are many of them, but there are also many of the others.

Note in Part B of Table VIII-7 (where we have marked those years of P/E ratios of 10.0 or less) that P/E ratios were 15.0 or over for the 7-year period from 1959 to 1965. We had another period of high P/E ratios of 7 years, from 1930 to 1936, but that was because of extremely low or nonexistent earnings. In the 1959–1965 period we had a hard time finding security values, although they almost always exist no matter how high the *average* P/E ratio. We should view that 1959–1965 period as part of the period of predominant growth of the U.S. economy. The conservative investor should not base his investment policy on another subsequent period like it. But even if we have another one, our system will keep the major portion of the investor's portfolio out of common stocks in such times, which were not always favorable for investors. Over the long pull, on the average, the investor should end up better off than the majority of investors by playing it conservatively.

The predominant position of the U.S. in the world economy may be over, therefore we may not see increasing stock prices for several years in a row from here on. But whatever the case, this conservative system will keep the investor out of the market when prices are too high.

To further support our views on our investment requirement for low P/E ratios, note in Table VIII-9 on utility P/E ratios over the past 109 years, 1872 to 1980, that there have

TABLE VIII–9

PRICE-EARNINGS RATIOS, 1872–1980—UTILITIES

	P/E RATIO			P/E RATIO		P/E RATIO
1981	*		1944	11.9*	1907	15.1
0	6.1*		3	12.2*	6	18.5***
9	6.8*		2	9.2*	5	15.3
8	7.4*		1	11.4*	4	17.3***
7	7.8*		1940	14.2	3	17.1***
6	7.4*		9	15.4	2	21.8***
5	6.6*	Low	8	17.1***	1	25.3***
4	6.3*		7	16.1	1900	17.7***
3	9.4*		6	20.0***	9	18.9***
2	10.4*		5	17.7***	8	13.9
1	11.8*		4	22.8***	7	14.0
1970	11.5*		3	22.0***	6	13.8
9	13.7		2	15.8	5	14.2
8	14.8		1	18.4***	4	12.7*
7	15.3		1930	23.5***	3	12.6*
6	16.3		9	26.3***	2	11.1*
5	19.8***		8	14.0	1	11.4*
4	20.1***		7	12.2*	1890	35.5***
3	20.6***		6	10.0*	9	34.2***
2	19.3***	High	5	10.4*	8	22.4***
1	20.9***		4	9.2*	7	35.8***
1960	17.0***		3	8.7*	6	20.4***
9	17.4***		2	8.1*	5	13.6
8	16.0		1	8.2*	4	11.1*
7	14.5		1920	9.4*	3	10.5*
6	14.8		9	11.7*	2	9.9*
5	15.3		8	11.8*	1	9.3*
4	15.1		7	11.2*	1880	8.6*
3	13.6		6	10.2*	9	10.4*
2	13.5		5	10.7*	8	10.1*
1	13.3		4	11.9*	7	9.4*
1950	11.9*		3	12.1*	6	27.1***
9	12.0*		2	12.5*	5	12.1
8	12.3*		1	12.4*	4	7.7*
7	13.6		1910	11.4*	3	11.5*
6	15.6		9	14.7	1872	7.4*
5	15.3		8	13.9		

Notes to table are on next page.

Notes to Table VIII–9:
*Low P/E ratios = 13.0 or less
***High P/E ratios = 17.0 or more
P/E ratios 1872–1928:
Cowles R-4 utilities earning-price ratios converted to P/E ratios *from* Alfred Cowles III and Associates, *Common Stock Indexes, 1871–1937*, Cowles Commission for Research in Economics (Bloomington, Ind.: Principia Press, 1938).
P/E ratios 1929–1980:
Moody's utility stock P/E ratios *from* Moody's Investors Service, *Moody's Public Utility Manual* (New York: 1981), annual.

been long periods of high P/E ratios and others of low ones.

Should the investor have studied a shorter cycle of these data, say, from 1948 to 1965, 18 years, noting steadily rising P/E ratios, he might easily enough have concluded in 1964 that high P/Es are now customary for utilities. If he'd based his investment policy on such a conclusion, he would have been disappointed; from 1964 to 1980 they declined to 6.1. It was easy to be fooled by these data.

Even Ben Graham[6] noted that historically a P/E of 14 to 15 times has been associated with a 5% growth for electric utility common stocks. After 1961 a P/E of 18 appears to be a reasonable multiplier for a 5% growth utility, he thought, with some caveats, after which they declined to 6.1, as we've noted.

So, the best bet for the investor is don't pay too much, whatever the long history of P/E ratios. There could be a long history of lower P/Es. Of course any investor who could have predicted higher P/Es for utilities after 1948 and hung on to the early 1960s would have shown excellent portfolio results. We, however, are not able to predict anything of the sort and have a strong feeling that an investor with such predictive potentials is mythical.

Note also that IBM, one of the best managed companies anywhere, sold at a P/E of 50 and over, then in 1978 sold at a P/E = 11, while recording rising earnings. A well-managed company is one thing, but the price to pay for it is quite another. It should be obvious by now that we stress price.

So far we have elaborated on the back-up for our system for computing investment value and buy price, widely fluctuating earnings, and price-earnings ratios.

SECURITY EVALUATION SYSTEM TRYOUT

The investor will be interested to know how our system might have worked during various periods.

Of the 516 securities investigated, we found 25 that fitted our balance sheet and buy price criteria (see Table VIII-10).

In summary, assuming we sold all by year-end 1977, our gain in the 2.02 years average hold would have been 40.% per year, a fairly respectable one. Yet these results came from a market drop of 45%, from 1973 to 1974, and a rise back to over 1000 on DJIA.

In a steep market drop the investor should have no trouble finding bargains and then making fairly good gains on the market rise as occurred in the story. But how would the investor have fared with this system if the market had taken a lesser drop than the 45 percenter? Is the system for 45% market drops only?

To answer that, we examined the potential investment probabilities for market price drops from the 1973 high of 10%, 20%, 25%, 30%, 35%, 40%, and 45% and pinpointed the dates for these when they occurred.

We then checked out the prices of the 25, listed in our Table VIII-10 for these dates, and if they met our buy price criteria, we checked the appropriate block in Table VIII-11 (we computed the investment value and buy price when necessary for the periods).

In other words, could we have bought any of the 25 stocks that we bought during the 45% market drop, at

TABLE VIII–10

25-SAMPLE STUDY 1973–1974

STUDY RESULTS OF 516 STOCKS

1	2	3	4	5	6	7	8	9	10	11
	CO. SIZE L M S	IF WFE	BOUGHT AT ⅓, ½, ⅔ OR ⅘ OFF I.V.	BUY PRICE $	BUY DATE YR-Q	SELL PRICE $	SELL DATE YR-Q	GAIN %	LOW PRICE AFTER BUY $	DROP FROM BUY TO LOW %
Johns Manville	L	—	⅓	16.	74-3	24.	75-1	50.0	14.38	10.2
Std Oil of Calif.	L	—	⅓	24.75	74-3	38.88		(57.0)	20.13	18.7
Texaco	L	—	⅓	24.13	74-3	27.75		(15.0)	20.	16.4
Akzona	M	—	½	11.63	74-4	20.	75-4	72.0	8.75	24.7
Alberto Culver	M	—	½	8.13	74-2	8.25	76-4	1.5	4.	51.0
Altamil	S	WFE	⅘	1.25	74-4	7.63		(510.0)	1.13	10.0
Amer. Broadcast.	L	—	⅓	14.50	74-4	21.75	75-1	50.0	11.50	20.7
Amer. Greetings	M	—	½	6.88	75-1	13.75	75-2	100.0	6.38	5.5
Amer. Rubber & Plast.	S	—	⅔	3.38	73-4	9.13	76-1	170.0	2.50	26.2
Amer. Smelt. & Ref.	La	WFE	½	15.	74-4	20.50	77-1	36.5	12.	20.0
Anchor Hocking	M	—	½	19.38	74-2	26.38	75-4	36.2	12.	38.1
Anderson Clayton	M	—	½	10.25	74-4	24.	76-4	137.5	7.75	24.4
Angelica Corp.	M	—	½	5.00	74-3	6.13		(22.5)	4.	20.0

Assoc. Coca Cola Bot.	Ma	—	½	5.50	74-3	11.	75-1	100.0	4.75	13.6
Avon Prod.	L	—	⅓	19.25	74-4	28.88	74-4	50.0	18.63	3.3
Ball Corp.	M	—	½	10.50	74-2	19.25	75-2	83.0	8.25	21.4
Basset Furn.	M	—	½	11.88	74-4	20.	75-2	68.5	9.50	20.0
Binks Mfg.	Ma	—	½	9.	74-3	18.		(100.0)	8.13	9.7
Borg Warner	L	—	⅓	17.38	74-3	23.75	76-1	36.5	12.50	27.1
Brown & Co.	S	—	⅔	5.50	74-1	10.88	75-2	98.0	3.50	36.4
British Petroleum	L	WFE	½	6.	74-3	16.50		(175.0)	4.50	25.0
Brockway Glass	M	—	½	12.	74-1	32.75	76-2	173.0	10.	16.7
Brown Forman D.	M	—	½	7.50	74-3	14.25	75-3	90.0	7.13	5.0
Brush Wellman	M	WFE	⅔	7.63	74-4	18.25		(140.0)	6.38	16.4
Bundy Corp.	Ma	—	½	6.38	74-3	10.25	76-1	60.5	4.25	33.4
										20.6% AVG.*

Notes:
Of the first 500 or so stocks listed in the Standard & Poor's *Stock Guide* plus the 30 stocks in the DJIA, for a total of 516, these 25 fitted our balance sheet, buy price, and current price criteria.
*Based on a uniform dollar amount invested in each stock.
WFE = Widely fluctuating earnings, one earnings cycle of up 100% and down 50% in 10–15 yrs.
YR-Q = Year-Quarter
( ) = % gain from buy price to 1977 close price. In these instances the price had not yet reached investment value.
I.V. = Investment value (also selling price).
La, Ma = Working capital increased to push company into next size category if that extra "debt" did not push the "new debt" beyond ⅓ of total capital.

TABLE VIII–11

BUYS AT LESSER MARKET DECLINES, 1973–1974

BUYS IN THE 45% MARKET DROP OF 1973–74 25-SAMPLE STUDY.		HOW MANY OF THE 25 COULD WE HAVE BOUGHT IF THE MARKET DROPPED (FROM THE 1973 HIGH): 0% ON 1–11–73	10% ON 5–9–73	20% ON 11–26–73	25% ON 12–5–73	30% ON 8–16–74	35% ON 8–27–74	40% ON 9–13–74	45% ON 12–6–74
Johns Manville	L				√		√	√	
Std. Oil of Calif.	L						√	√	√
Texaco	L						√	√	√
Akzona	M								
Alberto Culver	M			√	√	√	√	√	√
Altamil	S								
Amer. Broadcast.	L								√
Amer. Greetings	M								
Amer. Rubber & Plast.	S								
Amer. Smelt. & Ref.	L								
Anchor Hocking	M			√	√	√	√	√	√
Anderson Clayton	M								

Angelica Corp.	M						√		√
Assoc. Coca Cola Bot.	M						√	√	√
Avon Prod.	L								
Ball Corp.	M			*	*	√	√	√	√
Basset Furn.	M								√
Binks Mfg.	M							√	√
Borg Warner	L					√	√	√	√
Bowne & Co.	S					√	√	√	√
British Petroleum	L								√
Brockway Glass	M			√	√	√	√	√	√
Brown Forman Dist.	M								
Brush Wellman	M								√
Bundy Corp.	M							√	√
Totals	25	0	0	3	4	6	11	12	17

*The prices on these dates for Ball Corp. appeared low enough to buy but we were not able to obtain 1963 earnings for our 10-year-average computation to ascertain this.

See note, Table VIII–12, on 25 stocks in portfolio vs. but 17 on 12/6/74.

lesser market drops? We could have and we show the results in Table VIII-11.

See Table VIII-12 for a summary of these results.

Note that we did not find any buys at the top of the market or when it had declined 10%. But from a decline of 20% on we found an increasing number. Recall that we merely determined whether our 25 fitted the criteria on specific dates between the high and the low. Such a restriction, a specific date, cuts down on the number of bargains one may find, as note that we found 25 without the restriction but only 17 with it at the low of the DJIA as we show in Table VIII-11, last column.

The principal point, though, that we want to stress in this exercise is that even less drastic drops than the 45 percenter produced bargains.

Projecting the study further, to the point of having examined all of the securities listed in that *Stock Guide*, we theoretically could have produced 7.1 times the number represented by our actual study, as shown in column 8 of Table VIII-12.

We suspect that a more intensive search, that is, a greater sample than our 516, would have produced some bargains even at the average high.

We've pointed out that the system works for less drastic market drops than those of 45%. There were no losses in the individual selections. Yet, we expected some. The investor *should* expect some. But his evaluation should be based on *overall* portfolio results, since we work the system mostly on a *statistical* basis, seldom taking into account any impending adverse earnings results that we might read about. The price will have reflected the adverse data before we've read of it.

In our section on widely fluctuating earnings we gave the example of the Anaconda Company producing a loss from buy to sell. Who might have detected ahead of time that the company would have a write-off of $16.17 per share in

TABLE VIII–12

INVESTMENT POTENTIAL FOR THE MARKET DECLINE OF 1973–1974
AT VARIOUS STAGES OF DECLINE

1	2	3	4	5	6	7	8
DJIA DECLINE FROM HIGH OF 1973 %	DJIA	DATE	OF THE 25 STOCKS IN TABLE VIII-11, THIS NO. MET THE BUY CRITERIA ON THE SPECIFIC DATE	DJIA EARNINGS PER SHARE* $	DJIA P/E RATIO 2 ÷ 5	NO. BOUGHT OF TOTAL INVESTI-GATED %	NO. WE COULD EXPECT TO FIND IF WE CHECKED ALL STOCKS AS AGAINST THE 516 COL. 4 × 7.1
0%	1052	1/11/73	0	$67.11	15.6	0%	0
10	947	5/ 9/73	0	71.98	13.1	0	0
20	842	11/26/73	3	82.09	10.3	0.6	21
25	790	12/ 5/73	4	82.09	9.6	0.8	28
30	736	8/16/74	6	93.26	7.8	1.2	43
35	684	8/27/74	11	93.26	7.3	2.1	78
40	632	9/13/74	12	93.26	6.8	2.3	85
45	578	12/ 6/74	17	99.73	5.8	3.3	121
		1973–1stQ 1975	25			4.9	178

Note that on 12/6/74, the low point of the DJIA in 1974, only 17 of the 25 "portfolio" were at our buy price. How do we explain that we had 25 securities that fitted our criteria for the overall market drop, 1973–1974, but at the low point date, 12/6/74, we could find but 17 that fitted the criteria?

The DJIA had a low of 578 on that day but many securities made their lows before or after that date.

*Earnings per share are the total of nearest 4 quarters of earnings prior to the date in column 3.

1971? We don't try too hard to find and eliminate these in our system of security evaluation.

Another question is: Should the market continue to drop after buying, how might the investor fare? We compute a new I.V. each year a company publishes new earnings. If we pick up a bargain based on one I.V. and if successive I.V.s and buy prices are lower, it might mean buying at one price and selling at a *lower* price, as successive I.V. computations, according to our criteria, produce a selling price (I.V.) lower than the initial buy price.

During the stock market decline of the Depression, from 1929 to 1932, company earnings *were* successively lower and produced a lower selling price, regularly.

So, how might the investor make out in another such drastic write down of stock and earnings values? To help answer that question we made a retrospective study, evaluating securities according to our system for the Depression.

We listed securities in alphabetical order from the Jan. 1, 1929 *New York Times*, about 75 each from the NYSE, the Curb, and the OTC market for a total of 227, and evaluated these.

Of the 227 companies studied, we found 26 that met our criteria and these showed an overall gain of 73.5% in 2.40 years for a 25.8% per year compounded gain, Table VIII-13.

We had some individual losers, as note the American Ice Co. That lost us 70.5% and took 8.50 years to do it.

Ben Graham preferred to dump his securities in 2 to 3 years, according to our correspondence with him back in 1975, loss or gain. But we have had some gainers in a 4-year hold so we adhere to the policy of selling at I.V. whatever the time hold period.

The more significant point is that we made a gain "playing the market" during the Depression. We conclude that we should be able to repeat this performance if we experience another 89% market drop because we knock so much off the investment value before buying that we have a comfortable margin of safety in our evaluation system.

So overall we find that we not only preserve our capital with our conservative investment policy but that we make money with it also. As a corollary we must stress, though, that there have been times and probably will continue to be times when the investor using this conservative security evaluation system, will be *out* of the market, and consequently, missing gains if the market not only is high, but continues to rise. We purposely designed our system to miss these. Buying at too high a price is not conservative investing.

* * *

Footnote: Comment on the Depression Portfolio

We used the identical system for determining company size for the 1973–1974 portfolio and for the Depression portfolio. Yet, a company of $\$25 \times 10^6$ in working capital in the Depression was relatively larger than our present-day company of $\$25 \times 10^6$ in working capital.

Back in 1930 would we have made our divisions between small, medium, and large companies in the same place as for 1973? Probably not.

Note that the Depression portfolio contains no large companies, only medium and small. So for the 1930s we feel fairly certain that any system we would have developed *then* would have designated some of the medium-sized companies as large and some of the small as medium. What difference would that have made in the study?

We buy large companies at smaller price drops than we do the medium and small companies.

Consequently, for a system we would have set up then, some of the medium-sized companies would have been redesignated as large and bought at higher prices than we paid, and the same for the redesignated small to medium-

TABLE VIII–13

DEPRESSION PORTFOLIO

NYSE	CO. SIZE	WFE OR NOT	DATE BUY MO-YR	DATE SELL MO-YR	ELAPSED TIME IN YRS BUY TO SELL	PRICE/SHARE BUY $	PRICE/SHARE SELL $	GAIN OR LOSS %	LOW BETWEEN BUY & SELL $	PRICE DECLINE AFTER BUY %
Allis Chalmers Mfg.	Ma	WFE	8–31	5–33	1.75	14¾	14⅞	0.8	4⅛	72.2
Amer. Bank Note	S	—	12–31	5–33	1.42	16⅛	18½	14.7	5	69.0
Amer. Bosch Magneto	S	WFE	9–31	9–32	1.00	6⅛	9⅜	53.1	3½	43.0
Amer. Can	M	—	6–32	4–33	.83	31	76¼	146.0	29⅝	4.4
Amer. Car & Fdry	M	—	12–30	6–33	2.50	25	25⅜	1.5	3⅛	87.5
Amer. Ice	S	—	10–31	4–40	8.50	10⅝	3⅛	−70.5	1⅛	89.5
Amer. Locomotive	M	WFE	6–31	6–33	2.00	14	23¼	66.2	3⅝	74.0
Amer. Metal	S	WFE	9–31	5–33	1.67	5¾	21¼	270.0	1½	74.0
Amer. Safety Razor	S	WFE	6–32	4–34	1.83	13¾	48	249.0	13¾	2.7
Amer. Smelt & Ref.	M	WFE	5–31	6–33	2.08	32½	33¾	3.8	5⅛	84.0
Amer. Steel Fdries.	Ma	WFE	9–31	4–34	2.58	10¾	18¾	75.0	3	72.0
Amer. Sugar Ref.	M	WFE	4–32	4–33	1.00	18	47¼	157.0	13	33.3
Amer. Tobacco	M	—	5–32	6–33	1.08	43	85⅝	99.0	40½	5.8
Amer. Type Founders	S	WFE	12–31	12–33	2.00	20	5	−75.0	4	80.0
Asso. Dry Goods	Ma	WFE	9–31	7–35	3.83	10¼	11½	12.2	3	70.6

Asso. Oil	Ma	WFE	12–31	6–33	1.50	8⅞	21¼	139.0	6½	26.7
Atch. Top. & S. Fe	M	WFE	4–32	7–36	4.25	43½	83¼	91.5	17¾	58.8
CURB										
Acme Steel Co.	S	WFE	2Q–32	1Q–34	2.00	13¼	38¼	189.0	8¼	37.7
Alabama Grt. So. RR	S	WFE	4Q–31	3Q–36	5.00	41¾	64¾	55.0	7	83.2
Alpha. Port. Cement	S	WFE	2Q–32	2Q–33	1.25	5¼	22	320.0	4½	14.3
Amer. Chain	S	WFE	3Q–31	2Q–34	3.00	14⅜	4⅛	−71.5	1⅝	88.8
Amer. Cigar	Ma	—	6–30	4–31	.83	75¾	65	−14.3	46	39.3
Amer. Laundry Mach.	Ma	WFE	3–32	4–36	4.08	15⅜	27⅛	76.5	6¾	56.2
Amer. Pneumatic	S	WFE	4Q–31	2Q–31	1.75	⅞	1.00	14.3	¼	71.5
OTC										
Babcock & Wilcox	Ma	WFE	6–32	7–34	2.08	25⅛	47½	89.0	18½	26.4
Clinchfield Coal	S	WFE	7–30	7–33	3.00	4⅝	5½	18.9	3	35.1
Avg. of 26					2.40	yrs		73.5%		53.8%

WFE = Widely fluctuating earnings in the past 10–15 years.
Ma = Working capital increased to push company from small to medium category provided this adjustment did not push the "new debt" beyond ⅓ of total capital.
2Q, 3Q, 4Q = 2nd, 3rd, 4th quarter

sized companies. Therefore, we expect that we would have had more losers in the portfolio than the four, with a less prominent overall portfolio result.

Less prominent to what extent?

Another Depression portfolio, put together for an article,[7] recorded a *loss* of 16.8% in 2.3 years for a portfolio of 15. Here, I eliminated investing in companies of less than 1 million shares in a quick attempt to eliminate small companies, and used one criteria (rather than 3) for determining buy price, a third off I.V. (or half off I.V. for companies of widely fluctuating earnings).

The 16.8% loss for that portfolio compares with a 73.5% *increase* in 2.40 years for the Depression portfolio, Table VIII-13, where we used 3 company sizes and bought stocks at from one-half to four-fifths off I.V.

We expect that for the Depression portfolio, had we made 3 divisions in company size, wherever we might have based our company-size divisions of small, medium, and large in the 1930s, that we would have bought some of those stocks at higher prices and experienced an overall portfolio result of between −16.8% to +73.5% in about 2.4 years, still not bad in a period of an 89% market drop.

Using the above commentary as a reminder, we made a note to ourselves to reevaluate our system in 25 years to determine the new cut-offs for company size.

* * *

APPENDIX II. CHAPTER XII

BASIS FOR FUNDS DISTRIBUTION SYSTEM

We have settled on a funds distribution policy of 25% bonds (cash items)—75% stocks for the first buy round.

Let's discuss why we picked that system over these 5 plans: 0% bonds—100%stocks, (25–75), 50–50, 75–25, and 100% bonds—0% stocks, in the following order:

1. Potential results of each of the 5 funds-distribution plans for 4 buy rounds in one market cycle.
2. The number of buy rounds for the 1973–1974 portfolio and for the Depression protfolio.
3. The 25 general market declines, 1870–1978.
4. The number of buy rounds for each of the 25 market declines.
5. The back-up in method used to determine the number of buy rounds for each of the 25 market declines.
6. The results of investing $1,000 circa 1870 in a portfolio of bargain-priced securities for each of the 5 plans, selling these at investment value, then repeating the process, compounding the gains for 19 of the 25 market declines, and comparing these results with a buy-hold policy for 1870 through 1978.

Let's elaborate on these 6 points in the same order.

1. Here's how these various funds distribution plans would have worked for 4 rounds of buys assuming that we expect to make 100% on the first buy round as we did for the 1973–1974 portfolio (102.6% in 2.02 years), which contained a mixture of large, medium, and small companies.

TABLE XII–3

POTENTIAL RESULTS OF USING VARIOUS FUNDS DISTRIBUTION PLANS PER MARKET CYCLE, AS MARKET DECLINES

BUY ROUND	OF ORIGINAL $100,000 IN FUNDS AMOUNT ALLOCATED TO: CASH ITEMS	COMMON	CASH ITEMS	COMMON	AS MARKET DECLINES, ADDITIONAL AMMOUNT INTO COMMON $	EXPECTED GAIN ON COMMON EACH BUY ROUND %	$	INTEREST ON CASH ITEMS @ 8% FOR 2 YEARS	TOTAL PORTFOLIO GAIN AFTER EACH BUY ROUND $	%
PLAN A.	Start with 0% in Bonds (cash items)—100% Common									
1st	0	$100,000	0%	100%		100%	$100,000	0	$100,000	100.0%
2nd					0					
3rd					0					
4th					0					
PLAN B.	Start with 25% in Bonds—75% in Common									
1st	$25,000	75,000	25	75		100	75,000	$ 4,160	79,160	79.2
2nd	12,500	87,500	12½	87½	12,500	200	25,000	2,080	102,080	102.1
3rd	6,250	93,750	6¼	93¾	6,250	400	25,000	1,040	126,040	126.0
4th	3,125	96,875	3⅛	96⅞	3,125	800	25,000	520	150,520	150.5
PLAN C.	Start with 50% in Bonds—50% in Common									
1st	50,000	50,000	50	50		100	50,000	8,320	58,320	58.3
2nd	25,000	75,000	25	75	25,000	200	50,000	4,160	104,160	104.2
3rd	12,500	87,500	12½	87½	12,500	400	50,000	2,080	152,080	152.1
4th	6,250	93,750	6¼	93¾	6,250	800	50,000	1,040	201,040	201.0
PLAN D.	Start with 75% in Bonds—25% in Common									
1st	75,000	25,000	75	25		100	25,000	12,480	37,480	37.5
2nd	37,500	62,500	37½	62½	37,500	200	75,000	6,240	106,240	106.2
3rd	18,750	81,250	18¾	81¼	18,750	400	75,000	3,120	178,120	178.1
4th	9,375	90,625	9⅜	90⅝	9,375	800	75,000	1,560	251,560	251.6
PLAN E.	Start with 100% in Bonds—0% in Common									
1st	100,000	0	100	0	0	100	0	16,640	16,640	16.6
2nd	50,000	50,000	50	50	50,000	200	100,000	8,320	108,320	108.3
3rd	25,000	75,000	25	75	25,000	400	100,000	4,160	204,160	204.2
4th	12,500	87,500	12½	87½	12,500	800	100,000	2,080	302,080	302.1

Keep in mind that before we commit funds for buying another round of common stocks, the market will have had to drop enough so that we might, theoretically, make twice what we might expect to make on the previous buy round.

Taking note of the last column of Table XII-3, the investor will observe that portfolio results differ considerably, depending on the funds distribution plan and the depth of the market drop.

For minor market drops, the most profitable plan is the 100% investment in common stocks, that is, with no funds set aside for bonds.

And for somewhat greater market declines, those that permit a second buy round, any of the 5 plans would produce about uniform portfolio results: 100.0%, 102.1%, 104.2%, 106.2%, and 108.3%.

But for the steeper drops, those that permit a third and fourth buy round, Plan E would produce the best overall portfolio results.

2. Before we determine how steep the past 25 market drops were, let's look at those 2 portfolios of Chapter VIII relative to buy rounds possible.

Of the 23 securities in the 1973–1974 portfolio, prices dropped enough so that we were able to buy 3 in the second buy round: Borg Warner Corp., Alberto Culver Company, and Anchor Hocking Corp.

Extending that number by 7.1 times, representing what we probably could have found had we examined all of the securities in Standard & Poor's *Stock Guide* rather than the 516, we might have found a total of 21 for the second buy round vs. the 23 in the first buy round.

Prices had not declined enough for a third buy round. And keep in mind that this result is for a 45% market decline.

Our Depression portfolio of 26, constructed during an 89% market decline, could have contained 3 buy rounds. Here, also, we checked out only the original 26 in the portfolio for the other 2 buy rounds, recomputing invest-

TABLE XII–4

DEPRESSION PORTFOLIO
2ND BUY ROUND & 3RD BUY ROUND

	BUY PRICE 2ND ROUND $	SELL PRICE $	GAIN OR (LOSS) %	BUY PRICE 3RD ROUND $	SELL PRICE $	GAIN OR (LOSS) %
Allis Chalmers	5¾	14⅞	158.5			
Amer. Car Found.	9¾	25⅜	160.0	4⅛	25⅜	514.
Amer. Ice Co	6⅛	3⅛	(49.0)	2½	3⅛	25.
Amer. Locomotive	5¾	23¼	304.0			
Amer. Metal	2⅞	21¼	640.0	1½	21¼	1,317.
Amer. Smelt & Ref	19½	33¾	73.0	10⅞	33¾	211.
Amer. Steel Fdry	6½	18¾	189.0	3⅝	18¾	417.
Amer. Type Found.	12⅞	5	(61.3)	6	5	(17.)
Asso. Dry Goods	4	11½	187.5			
Atch. Top. & S. Fe	26	82¼	216.0			
Ala. Grt So. RR	11½	64¾	462.0			
Amer. Chain	3¼	5⅜	65.0			
Amer. Laundry M.	9¼	27⅛	193.0			
Amer. Pneumatic	½	1	100.0			
	AVG. GAIN =		188.4	AVG. GAIN =		411.2

1st Round gain = 73.5% (Table VIII-13, p. 238)
2nd Round gain = 188.4%
3rd Round gain = 411.2%

ment value where we had to, and "bought" 14 out of the 26 in the second buy round and 6 of the 26 in the third buy round. In this instance 10.8 was the ratio of those securities investigated in the *New York Times* vs. the total listed, so we could easily have ended up with 26 securities for each of the 3 buy rounds (see Table XII-4).

We did one more computation with the Depression portfolio, which was to assume that the 89% market drop occurred within one year so that we could use the same I.V.

as for the first buy round to determine the number of subsequent buy rounds.

Our computations showed that we could have bought 4 rounds in such an instance, but not 5.

3. Now let's set up the 25 market declines of the past century in such a manner that will permit us to determine whether the market declines were steep enough to permit us to buy one or more rounds of common stocks.

Column 5 of Table XII-5 lists the market drops from high to low in percent. Also, notice that these declines began at P/E ratios of 23.0 to 4.6. A market decline of 20%, say, from a P/E ratio of 25 will not produce as many buys, if any, as will a 20% market decline beginning at a P/E ratio of 10, obviously.

So, we want to find a uniform method of appraising the data on market declines. The way we've done that is to determine the market declines from a P/E ratio of 10. For example, from 1929 to 1932 the market declined 89%. The P/E ratio in 1929 was 19.1, using year-end 1929 earnings. That 89% decline, therefore, brought the P/E ratio down to 2.1, column 6, based on the 1929 earnings (not earnings for 1932, when the market hit its low). And from P/E = 10 to P/E = 2.1, the decline was 79% for 1929, $\frac{10.0 - 2.1}{10.0} = 79\%$, column 7 of Table XII-5).

We picked P/E = 10 as our base since it was from this (DJIA) market average level of P/E = 10, that we started to pick up securities that met our investment criteria (see Table VIII-12, p. 235.

Keep in mind also that while the DJIA registered a P/E ratio of about 10, the individual securities we bought had a lower P/E ratio (see Table VIII-8, p. 225).

Now that we have our buy signal from the DJIA as a P/E ratio of 10 plus, we need one for a sell signal for our analysis of the 25 market drops.

We find that our sell signal on the DJIA is also a P/E

TABLE XII–5

PRICE-EARNINGS RATIO OF HIGH VS. % MARKET DROP FROM HIGH TO LOW AND

PRICE DROPS FROM P/E RATIO = 10

COWLES P-2 INDUSTRIALS INDEX							DJIA						
1	2	3	4	5	6	7	1	2	3	4	5	6	7
YEAR	MONTH-END HIGH FOR YEAR	YEAR-END EARN. $	P/E RATIO	MKT DROP HIGH TO LOW %	P/E AT END OF DROP	DROP FROM P/E = 10 %	YEAR	HIGH FOR YEAR	YEAR-END EARN. $	P/E RATIO	MKT DROP HIGH TO LOW %	P/E AT END OF DROP	DROP FROM P/E = 10 %
1873	23.7	2.17	10.9	19	8.8	12	1929	381	19.94	19.1	89	2.1	79
1874	24.0	5.17	4.5	38	2.8	72	1937	194	11.49	17.1	49	8.7	13
1881–2	24.7	2.32	10.4	24	7.9	21	1939	156	9.11	17.3	40	10.4	—
1889	34.2	1.67	20.5	27	15.0	—	1946	213	13.63	15.6	24	11.9	—
1892	33.4	3.69	9.1	40	5.5	45	1952	292	24.78	11.8	12	10.4	—
1895	26.4	2.57	10.1	30	7.1	29	1956	521	33.34	15.7	19	12.9	—
1899	37.8	4.55	8.3	21	6.6	34	1961	735	31.91	23.0	27	16.8	—
1901	43.3	3.07	13.6	44	7.6	24	1966	995	57.68	17.3	25	13.0	—
1906	48.9	6.54	7.5	45	4.1	59	1968	985	57.89	17.0	36	10.9	—
1909	55.8	4.87	11.5	25	8.6	14	1971	951	55.09	17.3	16	14.5	—
1912	54.1	4.23	12.8	28	9.2	8	1973	1052	86.17	12.2	45	6.7	33
1916	77.3	16.95	4.6	36	2.9	71	1976	1015	96.72	10.5	27	7.7	23
1919	82.5	8.20	10.1	44	5.6	44	1981	1024	113.71	9.9			

Notes: High and percent market drop extracted from Table XII–1.
Year-end earnings to 1919 from *Common Stock Indexes 1871–1937*, Cowles Commission for Research in Economics.
Column 6: For 1873, 10.9 minus 19% = P/E of 8.8 and
Column 7: $\frac{10.0–8.8}{10.0} = 12\%$

ratio of 10 plus. We determined that by listing the sales dates of those securities we sold from our 25-Sample Study 1973–1974, Table VIII-10, p. 230 then by finding the P/E ratio of the DJIA for each date. The median DJIA P/E ratio turned out to be 10.5.

So, we have our DJIA buy signal at P/E = 10 and DJIA sell signal at P/E = 10. We explain the feasibility of this by recalling that even though the DJIA P/E ratio was 10 when we found stocks that fitted our criteria, we bought those stocks for our 1973–1974 portfolio at a median P/E ratio of 5.4. Then when we sold these, the median P/E ratio of those we sold rose to 9.9 while the DJIA P/E ratio was 10.5.

Obviously, according to our security evaluation system, we buy those securities that drop in price more than the average. Later, the prices of these rise more than the average.

4. From these market declines, beginning from P/E = 10, we tried to determine the number of buy rounds we might have been able to make for each of the 25 market declines as an aid in selecting a funds distribution system that we will use in the future instead of in retrospect.

According to the data in Table XII-6, column 5, we probably could have bought one round, at least most of the time, for 44% of the market declines, two buy rounds for an additional 16%, and three buy rounds for another 16% of the 25 market declines that occurred in the past century.

5. What we want to do next is show how we arrived at our divisions between one and two buy rounds, and two and three buy rounds as depicted in Table XII-6, in several steps.

Ready?

Column 7

Table VIII-12, p. 235, shows that we were not able to make any buys when the DJIA P/E ratio was higher than

TABLE XII–6

PROBABLE BUY ROUND 1873–1978 VS. MARKET DECLINES

1	2	3	4	5	6	7	8	9	10
P/E RATIO INDUSTRIALS AT END OF MARKET DECLINE	DECLINE FROM P/E = 10 %	NUMBER OF MARKET DECLINES DURING 1873–1978	PROBABLE BUY ROUNDS FOR THE 25 MARKET DECLINES						
16.0–over	–	1	Zero		A	x			
15.0–15.9	–	1	Full		B	x			
14.0–14.9	–	1	Buy		C	x			
13.0–13.9	–	1	Rounds 0	24%	D	x			
12.0–12.9	–	1			E	x			
11.0–11.9	–	1			F	x			
10.0–10.9	–	3	One		G	x			
9.0– 9.9	1–10	1	Buy		H				x
8.0– 8.9	11–20	3	Round 11	44%	I				x
7.0– 7.9	21–30	4			J				x

6.0– 6.9	31–40	2	Two			K			x
5.0– 5.9	41–50	2	Buy			L		x	
			Rounds	4	16%				
4.0– 4.9	51–60	1	Three			M			x
3.0– 3.9	61–70	0	Buy			N		x	
2.0– 2.9	71–80	3	Rounds	4	16%				
Total		25	3–4 Buy Rounds	19		P	x		

NOTE: Data for columns 1, 2 & 3 from Table XII–5.

FOOTNOTE ON TABLE XII–6:

Before we put these data together we considered adopting a funds distribution plan of 50% bonds—50% common for the initial buy round. But, we decided to determine, as well as we could, the number of times in the past century that we, using our security evaluation system for the past 25 market declines, would have been limited to one, two, or three buy rounds.

The data for this determination are in this table and are on the rough side. Yet, we found these data useful as a basis for selecting the 25% bonds–75% stocks plan over the 50-50 plan.

The 50% bonds–50% stocks plan we think would prove to be too conservative, thus making less money for the investor over the long pull.

10.3, but at 10.3 we began to find a few that fitted our criteria, therefore *check off* A, B, C, D, E, F, for zero buys and G for one buy. From Table XII-4 note that we were able to buy 3 rounds of common stocks for our Depression portfolio during the time the market declined in this period by 79% from a P/E ratio of 10.

And, when we assumed that this decline occurred within one year, rather than the actual 3 years, so that we could use the same investment value for all buy rounds, we found that we could have bought 4 rounds, expecting to gain twice what we expected to make on the previous buy round, therefore *check off* P.

Column 8

We need the next table to show our next step.

LARGE COMPANY, INVESTMENT VALUE (SELLING PRICE) = $30

P/E RATIO AT SELL PRICE = 10

BUY ROUND	BUY PRICE $	EXPECTED GAIN %	P/E AT BUY	DROP FROM P/E = 10 %
1st @ ⅓ off I.V.	$20	50%	6.7	33%
2nd @ ½ off I.V.	15	100	5.0	50
3rd @ ⅔ off I.V.	10	200	3.3	67
4th @ ⅘ off I.V.	6	400	2.0	80

(Buy @ $20 and Sell @ I.V. of $30 for a 50% gain in the 1st Buy Round)

From Table VIII-8, p. 225, recall that those 18 securities we sold at I.V. had a median P/E ratio of about 10. Consequently, we'll assume that same P/E ratio for our large company at its I.V. (selling price) in this exercise. Therefore, on the first buy round we'd buy that company at a third off I.V., or $20 a share, at which point its P/E ratio would be 6.7, having dropped 33% from P/E = 10.

On the second and third buy rounds the percent drop from P/E = 10 would have been 50% and 67%, respectively. At those declines in P/E ratio for the general market we would certainly expect to find a second and third buy round. Therefore, *check off L and N*.

Column 9

We've based the data in Table XII-6 on P/E ratios of general market declines. Consequently, a general market decline of 45% from high to low represents an average that will include individual declines of 50% to 80%, as note Table VIII-4, p. 215.

Therefore we expect that a 51 to 60% general market decline from P/E = 10 will produce 70% plus declines in individual securities that will meet our criteria for a third buy round (M). And that a 31 to 40% general market decline will produce enough 50% plus declines in individual securities that will meet our criteria for a second buy round (K). Therefore, *check off K and M*.

Column 10

What we have left, H, I, and J, is a squeeze between market drops that should produce a first buy round or a second buy round. A market decline, from a P/E of 10, of 1% to 30%, we expect will produce a first buy round. Therefore, check off *H, I, and J*.

We've shown in this exercise that we could have made at least one buy round for 19 of the 25 market declines that occurred in the past century. Next, we ascertained, through a listing of P/E ratios for the high price of each year, that stock prices rose enough for a sale before the subsequent buy-sell cycle; in other words, we assured ourselves, reasonably, that there was a minimal likelihood of overlapping of buy-sell cycles.

Then, going over the data (not shown here) for P/E ratios for the lows for the year and, in another column, the

P/E ratios for the highs for the year, we spotted at least 5 more likely buy-sell cycles, between some of the 25 market declines, thus raising the possible total of buy-sell cycles in this 108-year period from 19 to 24, according to our system.

6. As a further guide in choosing a funds distribution system, we computed the potential gains using our security evaluation system for a $1,000 initial investment for each of the 5 plans. We used the gains listed in the last column of Table XII-3. So, those long-lived investors who used any one of the 5 plans of funds distribution would have recorded the following results over the past 108 years. We assumed that for the 25 market declines that occurred in this 108-year period that we would have experienced no gain for 6 of these as per Table XII-6, column 4.

TABLE XII–7

APPROXIMATE RESULTS OF $1000 INVESTED FOR 19 SELECTED MARKET DECLINES, INCLUDING FOUR 2-BUY-ROUND CYCLES AND FOUR 3-BUY-ROUND CYCLES, 1870–1978, USING OUR SECURITY EVALUATION SYSTEM.

FUNDS DISTRIBUTION PLAN, TABLE XII–3	FUNDS DISTRIBUTION-INITIAL ROUND		RESULTS OF $1000 INVESTED AROUND 1870. THE COMMON STOCK PORTION COMPOUNDED AT 100% PER MARKET CYCLE FOR 19 MARKET CYCLES	BUY ROUNDS
	BONDS	COMMON		
A	0%	100%	$524,000,000	19 one buy rounds
B	25	75	266,000,000	11 one round, 4 two round, 4 three round
C	50	50	110,000,000	" " " " "
D	75	25	36,000,000	" " " " "
E	100	0	9,000,000	" " " " "
Buy-Hold 1870–1978	0%	100%	$41,700	

Example of Computation for Plan B:
Data From Last Column Of Table XII–3, Plan B:
$\$1000 \times (1.792)^{11} \times (2.021)^{4} \times (2.260)^{4} = \$266{,}000{,}000.$

* * *

Footnote for Table XII-7:

The investor may prefer to make his own computations for this table using 4% instead of 8% interest for "idle" money, including a quarter to half of a portfolio of stocks for the 6 periods for which we excluded interest gains and common stock gains, and using, say, an 85% gain for the common stock portfolio vs. the 100% we used for the first round (the 1973–1974 portfolio gained 102.6% while the Depression portfolio gained 73.5%), then finding a way to include interest on the "idle" money between portfolio sales and buys, and deducting brokerage costs, reinvesting dividends, and deducting taxes.

We expect that the relative values will be the same, however.

And in that connection note how Plan A would have worked out for the 19 stock market buy-sell periods if the rates of gain differed from the 100% per cycle:

IF THE GAIN FOR EACH BUY-SELL CYCLE IS	AFTER 19 CYCLES, COMPOUNDED, $1000. WILL GROW TO
100%	$524,000,000
75	41,500,000
50	2,220,000
25	69,400
21.7	41,700

While we're at it let's demonstrate that an extraordinary portfolio performance for 20 or so buy-sell cycles at 100% per cycle will be possible only for small portfolios.

Note that even for 10 cycles at a 100% gain per cycle a portfolio would have grown by 1024 times.

So, in 10 cycles, a fund a $1 billion would grow to a fund of $1 trillion on paper, an actual impossiblity since the total value of 3178 common stocks traded on the NYSE, the ASE, and the OTC was $1.160 trillion in March 1982.

* * *

A glance at Table XII-7 shows that the investor using any one of the 5 plans beginning in 1870, for which the predominant feature is to invest uniform amounts in common stocks of sound companies only at bargain-priced levels, and to sell these at investment value, outperformed a buy-hold policy by a considerable margin to 1978.

The investor will also conclude that the funds distribution plan designed to invest more in common stocks initially worked best over the past century.

So, with these data to help us, we are at the point of selecting a funds distribution plan for our use from here on.

Although the 0% Bonds—100% Common stock Plan A returned the most to the investor using our security evaluation system over the past century, we are wary of not having funds set aside for second and third round investments, from here on.

We opt for Plan B, which will permit us to have 25% of our portfolio funds set aside for use in more extensive market declines.

REFERENCES

Preface

On 10.3×10^9 tons:

U.S. Department of Energy, Energy Information Administration, *1979 International Energy Annual* (Washington, D.C.: U.S. Government Printing Office, August 1980).

Bureau of Mines, U.S. Department of the Interior, *Mineral Trends and Forecasts—1979* (Washington, D.C.: U.S. Government Printing Office).

More collect than produce:

Roy L. Ash, "Looking Beyond the Budget Deficit," *Wall Street Journal* (July 28, 1975).

By 2000 and 2017—Data from:

U.S. Bureau of the Census, *Statistical Abstract of the United States: 1977*, 98th ed. (Washington, D.C.: U.S. Government Printing Office, 1977).

Social Security:

A. F. Ehrbar, "How to Save Social Security," *Fortune* (Aug. 25, 1980), p. 34.

$4 trillion deficit on SS:

"$4,000,000,000,000, More or Less," *Wall Street Journal* (May 26, 1976).

HUD:

"Budget Landmines," *Wall Street Journal* (Feb. 26, 1980), p. 24. "HUD's Costly Subsidy Plan," *Business Week* June 5, 1978), p. 132. And data from HUD through Senator Paul E. Tsongas.

Deteriorating balance sheets:

Benjamin Graham, *The Intelligent Investor*, 4th ed. (New York: Harper & Row, 1973), p. 22.

CleveTrust Corporation, "Corporate Liquidity," *Business Bulletin* (July–Aug. 1977).

Increasing household debt:

"The Debt Economy," *Business Week* (Oct. 12, 1974), p. 45.

Import 90% of:

Bureau of Mines, United States Department of the Interior, *Mineral Commodity Summaries 1981* (Washington, D.C.: U.S. Government Printing Office), pp. 4–5.

Hostile news media:

Tom Bethell, "TV, Inflation and Government Handouts," *Wall Street Journal* (July 8, 1980), p. 26.

Introduction

On 85%:

A. W. Bigus, "Whatever Happened to Mutual Funds," *Esquire* (Dec. 1973), p. 50. There are 3 studies quoted here, one of them comprehensive, showing that, on the average, 85% of the investors who play the market lose.

Great fortunes:

Paul A. Samuelson, *Economics*, 10th ed. (New York: McGraw-Hill, 1976), p. 623.

Retrospective study:

A. W. Bigus, "Managing Portfolios with Graham & Dodd," *Journal of Portfolio Management* (Spring 1977), p. 58.

CHAPTER I

BUY-HOLD POLICY

Market performance data:

Alfred Cowles III and Associates, *Common Stock Indexes, 1871–1937*, Cowles Commission for Research in Economics (Bloomington, Ind.: Principia Press, 1938); and the Dow Jones industrial average.

ANOTHER 1929?

Paul Samuelson, *Economics*, 10th ed. (New York: McGraw-Hill, 1976), p. 267.

First National Citibank (now Citibank), "Monthly Economic Letter" (Sept. 1974), p. 6.

John K. Galbraith, *The Great Crash 1929* (Boston: Houghton Mifflin, 1961), p. 29, 182–191.

CHAPTER II

STOCK PRICES VS. INFLATION—LONG-TERM

Stock prices 1870–1980:

Cowles, *Common Stock Indexes 1871–1937;* and Dow Jones industrial averages.

Wholesale price index:

U.S. Bureau of the Census, *Historical Statistics of the United States, Colonial Times to 1970*, Bicentennial Edition, 2 parts (Washington, D.C.: U.S. Government Printing Office, 1975); and U.S. Bureau of the Census, *Statistical Abstract of the United States: 1977*, 98th ed. (Washington, D.C.: U.S. Government Printing Office, 1977); and Bureau of Economic Analysis, U.S. Dept. of Commerce, *Survey of Current Business* (Washington, D.C., Mar. 1978).

Stock prices and consumer prices:

Phillip Cagan, "Common Stock Values and Inflation—The Historical Record of Many Countries and Appendix," *National Bureau Report Supplement* (New York: National Bureau of Economic Research, Mar. 1974).

CHAPTER III

FORECASTING CORPORATE EARNINGS

Earnings and stock price correlation:

James H. Lorie and Mary T. Hamilton, *The Stock Market—Theories and Evidence* (Homewood, Ill.: Richard D. Irwin, 1973), p. 11.

Victor Niederhoffer and Patrick J. Regan, "Earnings Changes, Analysts' Forecasts, and Stock Prices," *Financial Analysts Journal* (May/June 1972), pp. 65–71.

Richard A. Brealey, *An Introduction to Risk and Return from Common Stocks* (Cambridge, Mass.: M.I.T. Press, 1969), p. 84.

Jack W. Cox:

Lorie and Hamilton, *The Stock Market*, p. 142.

Correlations low:

Richard A. Brealey, "The Character of Earnings Changes," in a paper for the Analysis of Prices seminar, University of Chicago (May 1967). (Quoted in Lorie and Hamilton, p. 161.)

Rates of change—earnings:

Lorie and Hamilton, *The Stock Market*, p. 163.

FORECASTING STOCK MARKET LEVEL

Benjamin F. King, "Market and Industry Factors in Stock Price Behavior," *Journal of Business, Security Prices: A Supplement* (Jan. 1966), pp. 139–90.

Dow Theory:

Alfred Cowles, III, "Can Stock Market Forecasters Forecast?" *Econometrica* (July 1933), pp. 309–324.

Short interest ratio:

H. A. Krow, *Stock Market Behavior* (New York: Random House, 1969), p. 130.

Money supply:

Beryl Sprinkel, *Money and Markets* (Homewood, Ill.: Richard D. Irwin, 1971), pp. 25–26, 111.

Michael S. Rozeff, "Money and Stock Prices," *Journal of Financial Economics* (Elsevier/North-Holland, Amsterdam, The Netherlands. Sept. 1974), p. 301.

A. F. Ehrbar, "How the Money Supply Drives the Stock Market," *Fortune* (Oct. 1975), pp. 108 and 109.

Price history:

Cowles, "Can Stock Market Forecasters Forecast?" and the DJIA.

Timing game:

Lorie & Hamilton, *The Stock market*, p. 25.

ECONOMIC FORECASTING AND THE STOCK MARKET

Ezra Solomon, "Economic Growth and Common Stock Value," *Journal of Business* (July 1955), pp. 213–21.

Susan R. Roesch, "The FOMC in 1974: Monetary Policy During Economic Uncertainty," Federal Research Bank of St. Louis *Review* (Apr. 1975), p. 13.

Commerce department:

James P. Gannon, "Studying the Slump," *Wall Street Journal* (Apr. 25, 1975), p. 1.

The 1980 recession:

"1980: The Year the Forecasters Really Blew It," *Business Week* (July 14, 1980), p. 88.

FORECASTING INTEREST RATES

From *A History of Interest Rates* by Sidney Homer. Copyright © 1963, 1977 by Rutgers, The State University. Reprinted by permission of Rutgers University Press, pp. 288 and 392.

Walter B. Wriston:

Lindley H. Clark, Jr., "Speaking of Business," *Wall Street Journal* (May 6, 1975, editorial page.

Benjamin Graham, *The Intelligent Investor*, 4th ed. (New York: Harper & Row, 1973), p. 113.

CHAPTER IV

High and close price:

Standard & Poor's Corporation, *Stock Guide* (New York: year-end 1976 issue).

Philip A. Fisher, *Common Stocks and Uncommon Profits* (New York: Harper, 1958).

CHAPTER V

TECHNICAL ANALYSIS

Robert Davis Edwards and John Magee, *Technical Analysis of Stock Trends*, 5th ed. (Springfield, Mass.: J. Magee, 1966), pp. 140, 55, 58, and 10.

Samuelson:

Paul A. Samuelson, *Economics*, 10th ed. (New York: McGraw-Hill, 1976), p. 78.

Chart reader:

Ralph G. Martin, *The Wizard of Wall Street* (New York: William Morrow & Co., 1965), p. 154.

TAPE WATCHING

Gerald M. Loeb, *The Battle for Investment Survival* (New York: Hurry House, 1956).

J. E. Granville, *Granville's New Key to Stock Market Profits* (Englewood Cliffs, N.J.: Prentice-Hall, 1963).

Nicolas Darvas, *How I Made $2,000,000 in The Stock Market* (New York: Lyle Stuart, 1971), pp. 187, 124, 59.

INSIDER TRADING

Richard A. Brealey, *Security Prices in a Competitive Market (Cambridge, Mass.: M.I.T. Press, 1971), pp. 116–128.*

Perry Wysong, How You Can Use the Wall Street Insiders (Fort Lauderdale, Fla.: Wilton House, 1971).

Carol J. Loomis, "A New Inside Track," *Fortune* (Dec. 1967), p. 216.

Lawrence A. Mayer, "The Inside Story (Con't)," *Fortune* (July 1968), pp. 127–128.

BROKERS' RECOMMENDATIONS

Michael J. Conner, "Wall Street Analysts Give Lots of Bad Advice Along with the Good," *Wall Street Journal* (May 25, 1973), p. 1

ADVISORY INVESTMENT SERVICES

Alfred Cowles III, "Can Stock Market Forecaster Forecast?" *Econometrica* (July 1933), p. 323.

Alfred Cowles, III "Stock Market Forecasting," *Econometrica*, (Jul.–Oct. 1944), p. 214.

W. X. Sheinman, *Why Most Investors Are Mostly Wrong Most of the Time* (New York: Weybright and Talley, 1970), pp. 16–17.

Robert W. Babson, *Business Barometer for Profits-Security-Income,* 9th ed. (New York: Harper, 1959), p. 165.

"Names":

Edward Angly, *Oh Yeah?* (New York: Viking Press, 1931), pp. 5, 10, 11, 12, 24, 27, 35, 39, 50, and 55. Angly, in this short, neatly put together book, compiled quotations from newspapers and magazines.

Gold:

John Brooks, *Once in Golconda—A True Drama of Wall Street 1920–1938* (New York: Harper & Row, 1969), p. 151.

Time:

Bill Adler and Catherine J. Greene, eds., *The Wall Street Reader* (New York: World Pub. Co., 1970), p. 250.

Sanford Rose, "Is This Any Way To Run Ten Banks?" *Fortune* (Dec. 1968), p. 146.

Pierre R. Bretey, "Railroad Prospects—Amber to Green," *Financial Analysts Journal* (Nov.–Dec. 1967), p. 64.

INDUSTRY ANALYSIS AND TECHNOLOGY ASSESSMENT

Ahlbrandt:

"The Smiles on the Faces of U.S. Steelmakers," *Business Week* (Sept. 14, 1974), p. 152.

Japan:

"Today Britain, Tomorrow the U.S.?" *Forbes* (Sept. 1, 1977), p. 56.

Japanese IQ:

Daniel Seligman, "Keeping Up—Brainpower Inc.," *Fortune* (July 12, 1982), p. 37.

Lithium and cesium:

"A Mine Full of Metals of the Future," *Business Week* (Aug. 26, 1972), p. 52D.

USGS:

James Dale Davidson, chairman, National Taxpayers Union, in a letter, Washington, D.C., July 1977.

Computers:

Peter F. Drucker, *An Introductory View of Management* (New York: Harper & Row, 1977), pp. 277–278.

BLUE CHIPS

Blue chips data:
Arnold Bernhard & Co., *Value Line Investment Survey* (New York: updated regularly)

PSYCHOLOGY AND THE STOCK MARKET

Securities Research co. (A division of United Business Service Co.), 208 Newbury St., Boston, Mass. 02116. *3-Trend CYCLI-GRAPHS*, quarterly.

THE FUTURES MARKET

Commodities Corp.:
Shawn Tully, "Princeton's Rich Commodity Scholars," *Fortune* (Feb. 9, 1981), pp. 94–98.

INVESTING IN FOREIGN COUNTRIES' STOCKS

British P/E ratio:
Gerald Krefetz and Ruth Marossi, *Investing Abroad—A Guide to Financial Europe* (New York: Harper & Row, 1965), p. 56.
Mexico:
"Mexico a Prospectus—$50,000,000 Mexico 9½% External Bonds Due March 1, 1981," courtesy of the First Boston Corporation and Bache Halsey Stuart Shields, dated Feb. 19, 1976.
Argentina:
"Devaluing in Advance," *Fortune* (Aug. 1970), p. 77.
Peru:
Everett G. Martin, "Peru's Cautious Revolutionaries," *Wall Street Journal* (Aug. 4, 1972).
Currency values:
RORENTO, a mutual fund, Rotterdam, Netherlands, a letter to shareholders dated Feb. 1975.
Investing in foreign countries:
A. W. Bigus, "Foreign Investment Potential—Mexico," *Financial Analysts Journal* (Nov.-Dec. 1964), p. 99.
U.S. Treasury, FRB, and Dean Taylor:
Lindley H. Clark, Jr., "Speaking of Business," *Wall Street Journal* (July 15, 1980), p. 26.

CHAPTER VI

INSTITUTIONAL FUND PERFORMANCE VERSUS MARKET AVERAGES

1927–1935:

Securities and Exchange Commission, *Investment Trusts and Investment Companies* (Washington, D.C.: U.S. Government Printing Office, 1939).

1953–Sept. 30, 1958:

Irwin Friend, Wharton School of Finance and Commerce, *A Study of Mutual Funds* (Washington, D.C.: U.S. Government Printing Office, 1962).

1960–June 1968:

Irwin Friend, Marshall Blume, and Jean Crockett, *Mutual Funds and Other Institutional Investors: A New Perspective*, a Twentieth Century Fund Study (New York: McGraw-Hill, 1970).

Zweig:

Jonathan R. Laing, "Bye-Bye, Go-Go? More Money Managers Now Aim Just to Match Popular Market Indexes," *Wall Street Journal* (June 7, 1973), p. 1.

Mutual fund data:

Wiesenberger Investment Companies Service (New York: Warren Gorham & Lamont, annual).

Pension funds:

Laing, "Bye-Bye, Go-Go?"

Bank trust departments:

Edwin W. Hanezaryk, *Bank Trusts: Investments and Performance* (Office of the Controller of the Currency, 1970).

Marshall E. Blume and Irwin Friend, *The Investment Performance of All Institutional Investors: An Initial Appraisal* (Philadelphia: The Wharton School of Finance and Commerce, early 1970s).

Colleges—J. Peter Williamson:

Performance Measurement and Investment Objectives for Educational Endowment Funds (New York: The Common Fund, 1972).

Trading skills:

Arthur M. Louis, "Those Go-Go Funds May Be Going Nowhere," *Fortune* (Nov. 1967), p. 143.

MUTUAL FUND PERFORMANCE

On 4.95%:
Boston 5 Cent Savings Bank average for the 10-year period.

On 5.7%:
Bernstein-Macauley, "Client Letter" (New York, Aug. 1, 1976).

On 7.13%:
Moody's Investors Service, *Moody's Industrial Manual* (New York: blue pages, annual).

CPI and WPI:
U.S. Dept. of Labor Statistics.

Fama:
Louis Engel, *How to Buy Stocks*, 6th ed. (Boston: Little, Brown, 1976), p. 285.

Janos Aranyi:
Dana L. Thomas, "Computerized Gun Slingers," *Barron's*, (Mar. 24, 1969), p. 3.

WHY INSTITUTIONAL FUNDS RECORD A POOR RELATIVE PERFORMANCE

Mutual fund managers:
James H. Lorie and Mary T. Hamilton, *The Stock Market: Theories and Evidence* (Homewood, Ill.: Richard D. Irwin, 1973), p. 95.

On 84%:
Nick Galluccio, "Mother, What's a Yield-Tilted Index Fund?" *Forbes* (Sept. 17, 1979), p. 202.

On 80%:
David Dreman, "Institutional Vulnerability," *Forbes* (May 26, 1980), p. 156.

Chapter VII

EVALUATING THE BALANCE SHEET

Data:
Moody's Investors Service, *Moody's Industrial Manual*, *Moody's Transportation Manual*, and *Moody's Utility Manual* (New York: annual).

Bond defaults:

W. Braddock Hickman, *Corporate Bond Quality and Investor Experience,* a study by the NBER (Princeton, N.J.: Princeton University Press, 1958), p. 413.

Discount data for leases:

Financial Publishing Company, *Financial Compound Interest and Annuity Tables,* 5th ed. (Boston: 1970).

OTHER BALANCE SHEET FACTORS

Ampex:

Thornton L. O'Glove and Robert A. Olstein, "No Small Issue—'Materiality' May Mean a Great Deal to Investors," *Barron's* (July 17, 1972), p. 5.

Pension deficiencies:

Touche Ross & Co., *1974 Pension Reform,* a pamphlet (Sept. 1974), p., 14.

Joint ventures:

Richard Greene, "How to Owe Money Without Seeming To," *Forbes* (May 26, 1980), pp. 54–56.

Chapter VIII

FURTHER STEPS IN SECURITY ANALYSIS

Standard & Poor's Corporation, "Stock Reports," published for 3700 stocks (New York: revised regularly).

Brunswick Corp.

"A Song of Wall Street," *Forbes* (May 1, 1972), p. 21.

Mattel, Inc.:

Alan Abelson, "Up and Down Wall Street," *Barron's,* (Mar. 19, 1973), p. 29.

T. W. Phelps, *100 to 1 in the Stock Market* (New York: McGraw-Hill, 1972), p. 181.

Chapter IX

Edward O. Thorp and Sheen T. Kassouf, *Beat the Market* (New York: Random House, 1967), pp. 127–139.

Chapter X

SHORT-TERM VS. LONG-TERM BONDS

Yields on Aaa bonds:
Moody's Investors Service, *Moody's Industrial Manual* (New York: annual).

BOND FEATURES

The agency rating:
Irwin Ross, "High Stakes in the Bond-Rating Game," *Fortune* (Apr. 1976), p. 132.

HIGH-GRADE VS. LOW-GRADE BONDS

Proportion of bonds in default:
W. Braddock Hickman, *Corporate Bond Quality and Investor Experience,* a study by the NEBR (Princeton, N.J.: Princeton University Press, 1958), p. 176.
Since World War II on defaults:
Ross, "Higher Stakes," p. 135.
Table on defaults:
Hickman, *Corporate Bond Quality,* p. 413.
Business cycles and agency rating:
Hickman, *Corporate Bond Quality,* pp. 140–141.
Errors in rating:
Hickman, *Corporate Bond Quality,* p. 27.

ANALYZING BONDS

Large Utility issues:
Hickman, *Corporate Bond Quality,* p. 176.
Debt to total capital:
Data from several issues of *Moody's Utility Manual.*
Economic unit—on debt and bond defaults:
George H. Hempel, *Measures of Municipal Bond Quality,* Michigan Business Reports no. 53 (Ann Arbor, Michigan: Bureau of Business Research, The University of Michigan, 1967), pp. 46–66. Copyright by The University of Michigan and reprinted by permission.

Aaa and Aa rated municipal bonds:
Hempel, *Measures of Municipal Bond Quality,* p. 107.
N.Y. City Notes default:
Ross, "Higher Stakes," p. 135.
Evergreen Valley:
"AAA-FFF," *Forbes* (Nov. 1, 1972), p. 26.
Overall quality of municipal bonds:
Hempel, *Measures of Municipal Bond Quality,* p. 132.
ACIR:
From *The Rating Game,* Report of the Twentieth Century Fund Task Force on Municipal Bond Credit Ratings, background paper by John E. Petersen. Copyright © 1974 by the Twentieth Century Fund, Inc., New York, pp. 130–131.
Four factors—credit worthiness:
Ibid., pp. 78–80.
120,000 issues:
Ibid., p. 32.
No central market:
"Investing in Tax Exempts," *Business Week* (July 25, 1977), p. 127.
Insurance on municipal bonds:
"A Boost for Municipals," *Business Week* (Mar. 24, 1975), p. 126.
Federal securities:
"Investing in Government Securities," *Business Week* (Aug. 17, 1974), p. 83; and
From *The Complete Bond Book* by David M. Darst. Copyright © 1975, McGraw-Hill, Inc. Used with the permission of McGraw-Hill Book Company; and
The First Boston Corporation, *Handbook of Securities of the United States Government and Federal Agencies* (1972, biennial); and
Moody's Investors Service, *Moody's Municipal & Government Manual* (New York: 1982), pp. 18–114.
Yields on defaulted bonds:
Hickman, *Corporate Bond Quality,* p. 20.
Secured issues:
Hickman, *Corporate Bond Quality,* p. 393.

SHORT-TERM MONEY MARKET INSTRUMENTS

Bankers' Acceptance—backing:
Darst, *The Complete Bond Book*, p. 170.
Bankers' Acceptance—66 years usage:
The First Boston Corporation, *Handbook* (1980), p. 192.
Maturity, 270 days:
Darst, *The Complete Bond Book*, p. 181.
Moody's Investors Service, *Moody's Bond Record* (New York: issued monthly).

CHAPTER XI

Portfolio and general market:
Lawrence Fisher and James H. Lorie, "Some Studies of Variability of Returns on Investments in Common Stocks," *Journal of Business* (Apr. 1970), pp. 99–134.
50% price fluctuation and general market:
Benjamin F. King, "Market and Industry Factors in Stock Price Behavior," *Journal of Business, Security Prices: A Supplement* (Jan. 1966), pp. 139–90.

CHAPTER XIII

Media General, *M/G Financial Weekly* (Richmond, Va).
Securities Research Co. (A division of United Business Service Co.), 208 Newbury St., Boston, Mass. 02116, *3-Trend CYCLI-GRAPHS*, quarterly.
Dow Jones & Company, *Wall Street Journal* (New York), 5 days a week.
Standard & Poor's Corporation, *Stock Guide* (New York), monthly.
Arnold Bernhard & Co., *Value Line Investment Survey* (New York), revised every 13 weeks.
Dow Jones & Company, *Barron's National Business and Financial Weekly* (New York).
Standard & Poor's Corporation, "Stock Reports" (New York), revised regularly.

CHAPTER XIV

STOCKS SELLING BELOW BOOK VALUE

Marine Midland Banks:
David L. Markstein, *Investing in the 70's* (New York: Thomas Y. Crowell, 1972), p. 28.

SECURITIES SELLING BELOW QUICK LIQUIDATING VALUE (QLV)

Bill Paul, "Publicker Industries' Losses on Operations Irk Critics," *Wall Street Journal* (Apr. 24, 1972), p. 30.

STOCKS WITH LOW PRICE-EARNINGS RATIOS

Drexel & Company:
Bill Adler and Catherine J. Greene, *The Wall Street Reader* (New York: World Pub. Co., 1970), p. 64.

Cleveland Trust:
Charles J. Rollo and George J. Nelson, *The Anatomy of Wall Street* (Philadelphia: Lippincott, 1968), p. 224.

B. Graham:
Benjamin Graham, *The Intelligent Investor*, 4th ed. (New York: Harper & Row, 1973), p. 81.

D. N. Dreman:
David N. Dreman, *Psychology and the Stock Market* (New York: AMACOM, 1977), p. 291.

COMPANIES REPORTING DEFICITS

Janos Aranyi:
D. L. Thomas, "Computerized Gun Slingers," *Barron's* (Mar. 24, 1969), p. 32.

Marine Midland Banks on deficits:
John Ellis, *Self-Reliant Investing* (Chicago: Henry Regnery Co., 1971), p. 66.

APPENDIX I

A. Heilbroner:

Robert L. Heilbroner, *Business Civilization in Decline* (New York: W. W. Norton & Co., 1976), pp. 101–108.

The Limits To Growth: A report for The Club of Rome's Project on the Predicament of Mankind, by Donella H. Meadows, Dennis L. Meadows, Jørgen Randers, William W. Behrens III. A Potomac Associates book published by Universe Books, N.Y., 1972. Graphics by Potomac Associates, pp. 54, 56–59, 66.

B. Toynbee:

John Carson-Parker, "The Options Ahead for the Debt Economy," *Business Week* (Oct. 12, 1974), p. 120.

C. Gimpel:

Jean Gimpel, *The Medieval Machine* (New York: Holt, Rinehart and Winston, 1976), pp. 240–46.

Data on population:

Bureau of the Census, *Historical Statistics of the United States, Colonial Times to 1970,* Bicentennial Edition, 2 parts (Washington, D.C.: U.S. Government Printing Office, 1975).

Bureau of the Census, *Statistical Abstract of the United States* (Washington, D.C.: U.S. Government Printing Office, annual).

Data on wholesale price index (WPI):

Bureau of the Census, *Historical Statistics* and *Statistical Abstract;* and Bureau of Economic Analysis, U.S. Dept. of Commerce, *Survey of Current Business* (Washington, D.C.: monthly).

Greenland:

John J. Putman, "Greenland Feels the Winds of Change," *National Geographic* (Sept. 1975), p. 366.

Micronesia:

Fox Butterfield, "The Improbable Welfare State," *New York Times Magazine* (Nov. 27, 1977), p. 55.

New York City:

Irving Kristol, "The Poverty of Equality," *Wall Street Journal* (July 12, 1976).

Patents:

"Why Science Can't Save Us," *Forbes* (Feb. 15, 1974).

Basic research:
Mitchell C. Lynch, "Backing off Basics," *Wall Street Journal* (Oct. 18, 1977), p. 1.
Sharia Law:
Ray Vicker, "Moslem Justice," *Wall Street Journal* (May 11, 1979), p. 1.
Dalai Lama and the Pope:
"The Dalai Lama's Verdict," *Wall Street Journal* (Oct. 24, 1979), p. 22.
D. Roman Empire:
Paul Johnson, *Enemies of Society* (New York: Atheneum, 1977), pp. 20, 78.
Government employees:
Bureau of the Census, *Statistical Abstract*.
Debased currency:
Rainer Esslen, *How to Buy Foreign Stocks* (Frenchtown, N.J.: Columbia Publishing Co., 1974), p. 56.
John Maynard Keynes:
Johnson, *Enemies of Society*, p. 86.
Edward Gibbon:
Dero E. Saunders, ed., *The Portable Gibbon: The Decline and Fall of the Roman Empire* (New York: Viking Press, 1952), pp. 361, 380, 601, 609.
E. Interest rates:
From *A History of Interest Rates* by Sidney Homer. Copyright © 1963, 1977 by Rutgers, The State University. Reprinted by permission of Rutgers University Press, pp. 64, 63, 274–288, and 91–555.
International Monetary Fund, *International Financial Statistics* (Washington, D.C.: monthly).
Moody's Investors Service, *Moody's Municipal & Government Manual* (New York: annual).

APPENDIX II. CHAPTER VIII

1. W. B. Hickman, *Corporate Bond Quality and Investor Experience,* National Bureau of Economic Research (Princeton, N.J.: Princeton University Press, 1958), p. 495.
2. Standard & Poor's Corporation *Stock Guide* (New York: 1974).

3. Benjamin Graham, *The Intelligent Investor*, 3rd ed. (New York: Harper & Row, 1965), p. 144.
4. Alfred Cowles III and Associates, *Common Stock Indexes, 1871–1937* (Bloomington, Ind.: Principia Press, 1938).
5. Maurice L. Farrell, ed., *The Dow Jones Investor's Handbook* (Princeton, N.J.: Dow Jones Books, annual).
6. Benjamin Graham, et al., *Security Analysis*, 4th ed. (New York: McGraw-Hill, 1962), p. 590.
7. Anatol W. Bigus, "Managing Portfolios with Graham and Dodd," *The Journal of Portfolio Management* (Spring 1977), p. 58.

INDEX

G

N

O

P

Q–R